Allen J. Fromherz is Associate P [illegible] Mediterranean History at Georgia [illegible] in History from St Andrews University and is the author of *Qatar: A Modern History* (I.B.Tauris) and *Ibn Khaldun, Life and Times.*

THE ALMOHADS

THE RISE OF AN ISLAMIC EMPIRE

ALLEN J. FROMHERZ

I.B. TAURIS
LONDON · NEW YORK

New paperback edition published in 2013 by I.B.Tauris & Co Ltd
6 Salem Road, London W2 4BU
175 Fifth Avenue, New York NY 10010
www.ibtauris.com

Distributed in the United States and Canada Exclusively by Palgrave Macmillan,
175 Fifth Avenue, New York NY 10010

First published in hardback in 2010 by I.B.Tauris & Co Ltd

ISBN: 978 1 78076 405 4

A full CIP record for this book is available from the British Library
A full CIP record is available from the Library of Congress

Library of Congress Catalog Card Number: available

Printed and bound by CPI Group (UK) Ltd, Croydon, CR0 4YY

from camera-ready copy edited and supplied by Oxford Publishing Services, Oxford

MIX
Paper from responsible sources
FSC® C013604

Contents

Maps, Figures and Tables

Maps

Figures

Tables

Acknowledgements and Preface

I could not have even begun thinking about this book without the support of Professor Gene Garthwaite who first introduced me to Islamic history at Dartmouth College. Professors Dale Eickelman, Kevin Reinhart and Marlene Heck, also at Dartmouth, have all continuously encouraged my interest in Islamic and North African history.

The Fulbright Scholarship program and the Moroccan American Commission on Educational and Cultural Exchange (MACECE), especially the executive director Daoud Casewit, made the initial stages of my research possible. It was through the connections provided by a Fulbright research scholarship that I have been fortunate enough to work with Moroccan Professors Abdessalam Cheddadi and Abderrahman Lakhsassi, both gifted mentors and scholars.

The Overseas Research Students Award Scheme (ORSAS), specifically under the sponsorship of the Royal Historical Society, funded my Ph.D. research at St Andrews University. The Royal Historical Society and the Royal Asiatic Society also provided small research travel grants while I was completing my Ph.D. Although funding for ORSAS is now under review, I want to make clear that I could not have completed my research as effectively without their support. I also received support from St Andrews University through a matching grant and travel grants.

I am grateful to Professor Hugh Kennedy (now at SOAS) who provided expert and thoughtful advice and encouragement well beyond the call of duty. Professors Robert Hoyland, Richard Bartlett, Ali al Ansari, all a part of the very active Middle East Studies community at St Andrews, also contributed to my research. Eduardo Manzano in Madrid similarly provided exceptional feedback.

My postdoctoral studies, essential for transforming my Ph.D. research into a book, were funded through a long-term grant by the American Institute for Maghrib Studies (AIMS). My AIMS grant in Marrakech from 2006 to 2007 allowed me to pursue research and questions of geography and history that could not be pursued as easily in a traditional postdoctoral setting. Fortunately, my research (and my life) was not cut short after my encounter with a vegetable truck and a *grand taxi* on my way to Aghmat. It was through AIMS and AIMS annual conferences that I gained from the expertise and advice of Professors Ron Messier, Kevin Perkins, Laurence Michalak and Jim Miller, all exceptional scholars of North Africa. Kerry Adams and the administrative team at AIMS, provided rapid and professional support.

Professor Amira Sonbol, the chair of my department while I was at Qatar University, and Sheikha Misnad, President of Qatar University, both encouraged and helped me develop this book.

Most recently, my colleagues at Georgia State University, including Professors Denise Davidson, Isa Blumi, Michelle Brattain, Hugh Hudson, Dona Stewart, Mary Rolinson and Jared Poley, as well as others, have all provided advice, reviews and encouragement as I have developed the final stages of my book.

Dr Lester Crook, my editor at I.B.Tauris, must be commended for his patience and perseverance.

Finally, my mother Dr Robin Fromherz and father Allen Fromherz, my two sisters Amy and Becky, my grandmother Lois Wright and family friends Bonnie Young and Bonnie Staebler, have supported me from the beginning.

All I wish to say in terms of a Preface is that although all the primary sources for this book used the lunar hijri calendar, I have converted almost all dates into Gregorian calendar dates. For the sake of specialized readers I have included long vowels in my Arabic transliteration. Berber transliteration to English is still being developed. I generally use the system established in the *Encyclopaedia of Islam* with one main exception: j, not dj.

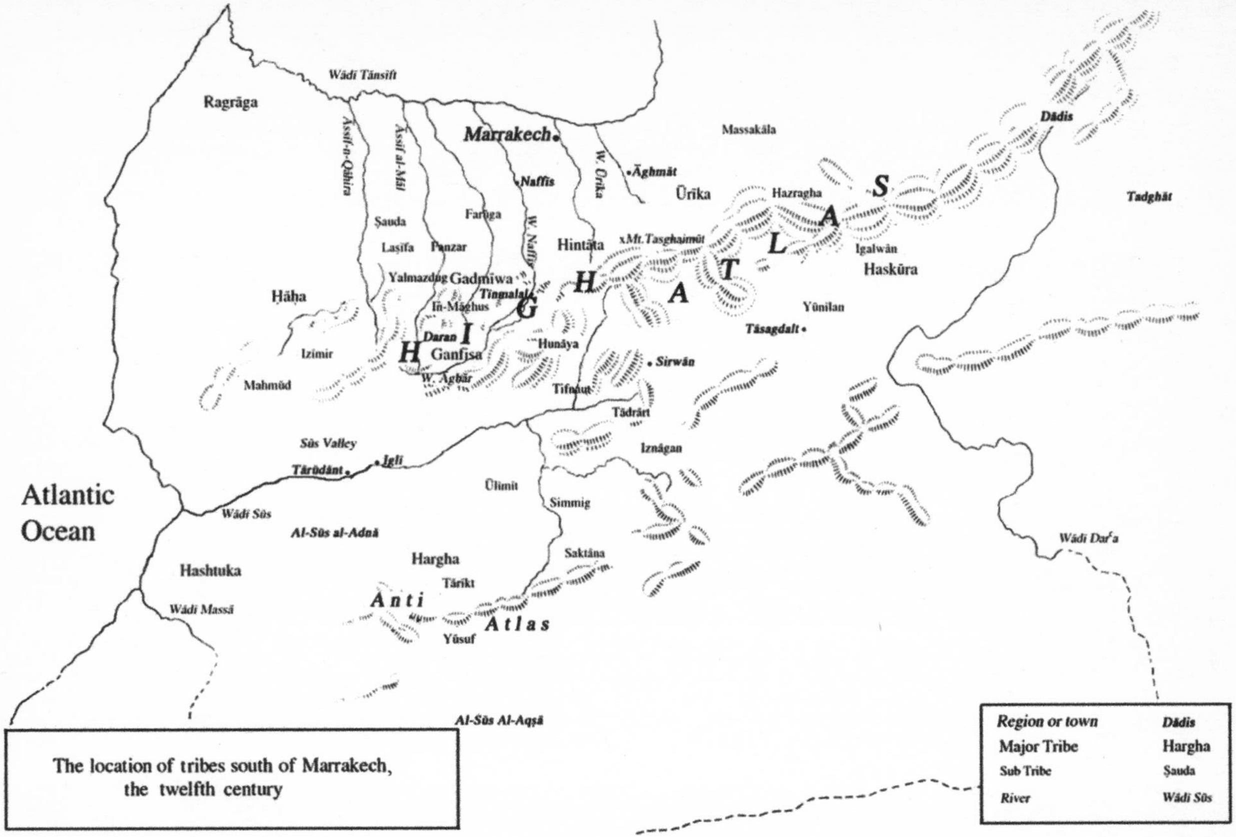

The location of tribes south of Marrakech, the twelfth century

The return of Ibn Tūmart from the East

Al-Mahdiya to Tīnmalal

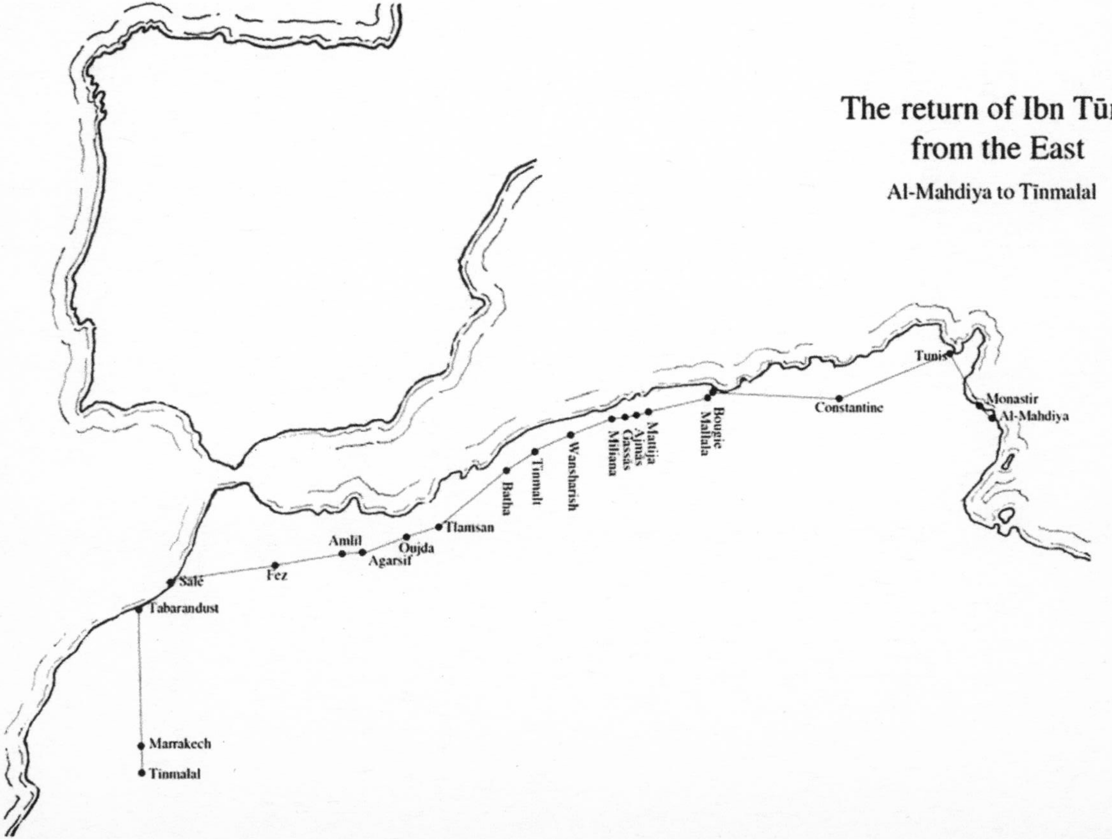

Introduction

The Almohads: A General Overview

Almohad history began with a journey, a journey from a place called the 'farthest west', the *Maghrib al-Aqṣā*. 'Maghrib' in Arabic means not only the 'west' but 'land of the setting sun'. It was a journey from the land of the setting sun, from the fringes to the heart of Islam and back again. Around 1100 Muḥammad Ibn Tūmart, the son of a minor Berber chief from the Atlas Mountains south of Marrakech in what is now Morocco, travelled to Baghdad, Cairo and Damascus, centres of knowledge in the Middle East. The Islamic world was under attack. The crusaders had captured Jerusalem in 1099. The ʿAbbāsid caliphs of Baghdad, symbolic spiritual leaders of all Muslims and inheritors of Muḥammad's leadership and call, were weak puppets.

Far from being the source of spiritual life, conquest and godly rule, the institution of the caliph, literally the 'successor' of the prophet, had become an empty shell, hollowed out by political expediency. Yet not all was lost. Reacting to this political crisis in Islam, a Sunni intellectual fortress was being built by thinkers like al-Ghazālī (d. 1111) whose work *On the Revival of the Religious Sciences* hailed a new era for Islam. Rather than the typical quietist approach to political oppression that official, state scholars and religious clerics so often expressed, al-Ghazālī authorized 'commanding right and forbidding wrong', a duty enshrined in the Qur'ān, not only against the local butcher or wine seller but also against rulers, states and whole societies. Ibn Tūmart claimed to have met al-Ghazālī. He told the great scholar about how his works were being destroyed in Andalusia, southern Spain. According to an Almohad legend that will be analysed later, al-Ghazālī gave Ibn Tūmart his blessing and predicted that the young scholar would soon lead a movement that would transform the Islamic world, restore the true vision of the prophet Muḥammad and herald a new era.

As Ibn Tūmart returned home to North Africa, he became more and more certain of his mission to command right and forbid wrong, to transform his world and inspire a new era of promise: Islam. After a few years of evading the wary and envious rulers of North Africa, Ibn Tūmart gained an unprecedented following of rough, rowdy and hitherto undisciplined mountain tribes of his homeland, tribes that were used to fending for their own or raiding their neighbours and the local village. Transfixed by his charisma and his divine message, he transformed these tribes into a disciplined army. They soon proclaimed him Mahdī – the one who would herald the end of time and the beginning of a new era in Islam. He delivered a message of absolute, uncompromising monotheism. The unifying ideal of the Almohad Empire was this absolute monotheism, the belief that there is one God without any physical attributes. The word 'Almohad' derives from the Arabic *al-Muwaḥḥidūn*, a word that means 'followers of the doctrine of divine unity'. Ibn Tūmart declared that the fundamentals, the roots, of Islam should be followed, as opposed to the branches, the interpretations of jurists, who, according to Ibn Tūmart's fiery statements, had corrupted the words of the prophet. He wrote a book that declared his purified vision of Islam. He proclaimed the necessity of armed *jihād*, holy war.

Ibn Tūmart would not live long enough to see the fulfilment of his dream. He died around 1130. His closest followers kept his death secret for three years for fear that the tribes would abandon their beloved Mahdī. Soon, however, Ibn Tūmart's capable 'successor' or caliph, ʿAbd al-Muʾmin, was able to consolidate the tribes and conquer Marrakech, the door to the Saharan gold trade, and the greatest city of trade and commerce in North Africa, in

1147. Tired of heavy taxes and inspired by the message of Almohad doctrine, tribes after tribe soon fell under the Almohad yoke and the spell of ideal egalitarianism preached originally by Ibn Tūmart. The Almohads would dominate the entire western Mediterranean to Tripoli.

By the late twelfth century the great Almohad caliph Yūsuf Yaʾqūb al-Manṣūr, 'the victorious', ruled over a vast, diverse and improbable empire of deserts, mountains, tribes and cities: the Almohad Empire, an interlocking system of enforced tribal loyalties and carefully cultivated bureaucracy, was at its zenith. Its domains stretched across the Mediterranean from Tunis to Andalusia and south, deep into Africa to the Sous valley in today's Morocco. Marrakech, the capital, with its famous deep-red walls and Seville, the golden centre of Andalusia, were home to the caliph and elite Almohad tribal leaders. Both were brilliant garden cities bustling with learning and trade from distant lands, supplied with plentiful water channelled from the hills in complex pipes and aqueducts, and adorned with stark, monumental architecture.

The Almohads were the first and only effective system of government in history to control the entire wild and treacherous chain of the Atlas Mountains in North Africa. When the Romans had ruled, centuries before they did not venture far into the Atlas range. The entire region from Tunisia to southern Morocco and Andalusia was united; almost every piece of useful land was divided and sorted for tax and revenue collection. The Almohads also ruled the rich coastal plains of Morocco and the cosmopolitan, luxurious cities of southern Spain, one the most culturally and intellectually advanced regions in medieval Europe at the time. The Almohad army, a hotchpotch of tribes and tongues, often numbering up to 100,000 for major expeditions, was paid through a complex government bureaucracy. The Almohads were the major power in the Mediterranean throughout most of the twelfth-century Renaissance. Some of the most famous scholars in Europe at the time, including the physicians and philosophers Abubacer and Averroes, were Almohads. Scores of scholars, thinkers, mystics, saints, poets and philosophers swelled the biographical dictionaries of the time.

The decline of the Almohads, according to the medieval North African sources, only really began with the disintegration of relations between the Berber tribal sheikhs, portrayed as defenders of the 'authentic' movement, and the refined caliphs or successors of the Mahdī. By 1229, these caliphs, especially the negatively portrayed al-Maʾmūn, began to reject the doctrine of the Mahdī Ibn Tūmart and even began massacring the tribal leaders. The sources generally see the later Almohad caliphs in a negative light. Al-Maʾmūn, a late Almohad caliph, rejected Ibn Tūmart as Mahdī and declared, 'there is no other Mahdī than Jesus, son of Mary, who alone has a right to the title of Mahdī.'[1] Unlike his predecessors, ʿAbd al-Maʾmūn could not depend on a disciplined cohort of Berber tribal fighters so praised in early sources. Replacing Ibn Tūmart with Jesus seemed popular with those who destroyed the tribal forces of Yaḥyā, the favourite of the original Almohad Berber tribes, and put al-Maʾmūn in power, namely Christian mercenaries purchased from King Ferdinand III, who specified the stringent conditions under which he would allow ʿAbd al-Maʾmūn to borrow his troops.

> I will give you the army only under the condition that you give me ten fortresses on the frontier of my reign, selected by me. If God favours you and you enter Marrakech, you must build a church in the middle of the city for those Christians who go with you, where they ... [are able to] practise their religion and ring their bells at the time of prayer.

In other words, the whole character of Marrakech as an exclusive, Muslim city at the heart of a Muslim empire would be threatened.[2] The king, perhaps fearful that some of his mercenaries would try to curry favour through conversion, even required 'Abd al-Ma'mūn to refuse to allow any Christian to convert to Islam. 'If a Christian attempts to convert himself to Islam, he shall not be received as a Muslim and will be returned to his brothers so that he may be judged in accordance with his laws and if a Muslim converts to Christianity, none shall do a thing to him.'[3] After conquering Marrakech back from the Berber tribal elders in 1227, he immediately made his pact with Ferdinand, the Spanish king. Instead of gaining loyalty from the Berbers, he would have to purchase it. He would rely on Ferdinand's European mercenaries, who were disciplined troops under his direct control.

By 1269, the Marinids, a Berber dynasty from Figuig, an oasis south of Oujda and east of the Atlas Mountains, had almost completely extinguished the Almohads sheltered in the High Atlas Mountains. Although the decline of the Almohads is not the focus of the book, it confirms how the sources saw the relationship between the Berbers and their rulers. The loyalty and tribal solidarity of Berber tribal sheikhs was essential to the Almohads' success. In this historical narrative, the extinguishing of the power of the mountain Berber hierarchy led to the extinguishing of Almohad power in general, except for the small community of Berber sheikhs who heroically continued Almohad traditions in the valleys of the High Atlas Mountains.

Surprisingly, there is only the slightest understanding of the Almohads and their role in history, especially the role of the Berber tribes in the foundation of Almohad power. The few brief books on the Almohads in English are translated from French and, at best, they are too short.[4] Most scholarship on medieval Islam has focused almost exclusively on either the 'Abbāsids in the east, or Córdoba and the Umayyads in Andalusia. Even though they controlled more territory than the Spanish Umayyads and arguably had just as much influence on the course of Mediterranean history, scholars writing in English have almost completely overlooked the Almohads. Scholars working in Spain,

France and Morocco have recently made vigorous efforts to rectify this yawning gap of historical literature.[5] Nevertheless, a great deal of work still needs to be done, especially on the rise of the Almohads in the non-Andalusi context.

The Almohad movement only really started when Ibn Tūmart embarked on his journey back to North Africa and began to attract a large number of followers as he preached among the Maṣmūda Berber tribes of the Atlas Mountains. Obedient to the Mahdī, the rightly guided Ibn Tūmart and his Berber followers would lead all Muslims at the end of time. The Berber tribes burst out of the Atlas Mountains. Within decades the remote Atlas Berber tribes, at one time seemingly lost to history, became rulers of the western Mediterranean and altered the course of world history. In this book I shall demonstrate how North African sources explain the way this remarkable transformation occurred. I shall argue that the structure of Berber tribal society, as portrayed in many of the sources, was not an impediment to the establishment of an Almohad government but its main source. Ibn Tūmart and his successors did not have to destroy tribal society and create the structures of a governing movement from scratch. Rather, he and his successors used and adapted existing tribal customs and ways rooted deeply in Berber experience. According to several sources that will be discussed, including al-Baydhaq, al-Qaṭṭān and Ibn Khaldūn, the cooperation and incorporation of the Berber tribes was the main reason the Almohad Empire ever came into being.

Despite the importance of the Almohads in African, Near Eastern and European history, very little is currently known about who exactly the Almohads were and why they were so successful. In this book, which is the first systematic study and analysis in English of the foundational myths about the rise of the Almohads as portrayed from within the Almohad tradition, I shall attempt to fill this gap. Rather than taking a simple narrative approach, I interpret the rise of the Almohads as a model for understanding revolution, tribalism, identity and change on the western edge of the Islamic world. A good place from which to begin this discussion of revolution, tribalism and change in Islamic history is with the work of Ibn Khaldūn (d. 1406), the philosopher and historian who worked for the descendants of the Almohads and whose insight into the tribal, Berber origins of the Almohad movement profoundly influenced his philosophical understanding of history.

On Founding Myths

Writing towards the end of the fourteenth century, more than 100 years after the fall of the Almohad Empire, Ibn Khaldūn described how Berbers in the remote High Atlas outpost of Tīnmallal continued the practices of their Almohad forefathers.

> The tomb of the Mahdī [Ibn Tūmart] still exists among them, as honoured, as revered as ever. The Qur'ān is recited day and night; men still come there. There is a corps of guardians, conserving the same organization and following the same ceremony as that followed during the time of the Almohad Empire, receiving pilgrims and devotees from afar who are introduced into the sanctuary with an order and solemnity that inspires profound respect.[6]

It would be difficult to verify Ibn Khaldūn's report. He may have written this glorified account of a lost remnant of the defeated Almohads to please his patron, the Ḥafṣid ruler of Tunis, who, though hundreds of miles away, maintained a semblance of an Almohad tradition in his realm. Nevertheless, what Ibn Khaldūn's writing indicates is the pull of a certain powerful myth, a myth about the rise of Almohad doctrine and Almohad ambitions to reform the Islamic world as a reflection of claimed, innate Atlas Mountain Berber virtues, and the power of the mountain Berbers when united under a common cause. In fact, according to some sources, Ibn Tūmart's body was actually removed from its tomb in

Tīnmallal and taken to a secret location where Berber tribesmen have venerated it ever since by remembering the period when Almohad and Tashelhit-speaking Berber power was at its height.[7]

My purpose in this preliminary section of the book is to address and challenge prevailing views of how primary sources of Almohad history were manipulated at the time they were produced. In later sections I provide an overview of the content of the Berber historical myths. I argue that although Andalusis may have manipulated some Almohad history and doctrine far from the Atlas Mountains, most of the first sources of Almohad history were written by Berber Almohads (the first converts to Almohadism) within the Berber social hierarchy established in the High and Anti-Atlas under the leadership of the Mahdī Ibn Tūmart and his successor, the first Caliph ʿAbd al-Muʾmin. The myth about Almohad origins was primarily constructed in a way that confirmed the power and standing of the early Almohad elite, the Berbers of the High Atlas and Anti-Atlas Mountains.

Scholars of medieval North African dynasties have noted that even basic facts about the life of Ibn Tūmart (d. *circa* 1130), the founder of the Almohad doctrine, which formed the basis of the Almohad Empire, are conjectural.[8] Yet the facts were not conjured arbitrarily. The history of Ibn Tūmart and of Almohad doctrine was influenced and shaped to fit a certain mystical narrative, a narrative that reinforced not simply the infallibility of Ibn Tūmart but also the ideology and social structure of the Berber Almohad elite.[9] Sources allegedly written during the life of the Mahdī, Ibn Tūmart, the messianic founder of the Almohad movement, described the foundational mythical narrative of the Almohads in a way that reinforced the prestige of the Berber tribes. Such sources included the biography written by Ibn Tūmart's personal scribe al-Baydhaq, chroniclers writing after the deaths of many of the first Almohads, such as the son of an Almohad enforcer of values and ranks Ibn al-Qaṭṭān, and even later historians including Ibn Khaldūn (d. 1406) whose philosophy of history was influenced by the Almohad example. Most writers from North Africa generally accepted or glorified Ibn Tūmart's biography and many of the claims attributed to him. By contrast, scholars from the east who wrote accounts of Ibn Tūmart, such as Ibn al Qalānisī (d. 1160), approached him and the rise of the Almohads from a detached, disdainful distance, claiming that he 'perpetuated the failure of Islamic law and encouraged bloodshed'.[10] In the North African context, however, almost all the chroniclers, even some enemies of the Almohads who had reason to be at least ambiguous towards Ibn Tūmart, portrayed him in a generally positive light as a reformer who tapped into the latent energies and virtues of the Berber mountain tribes. These sources created historical myths about Almohad origins.

The creation of the founding myth is the subject of several historical studies in European and American history. Patrick Geary's *The myth of nations*, for example, deconstructs modern attempts to write medieval 'ethnic' histories of nations and groups.[11] In Islamic and Middle Eastern history the founding of Islam has been the subject of often extremely contentious debate, usually centred on modern challenges to the validity and usefulness of early Islamic history, history tied to the life and example of the Prophet Muḥammad and the first, rightly guided caliphs. The subject of foundational narratives and myths in North African medieval history, however, has been somewhat neglected. A great deal of work is still being done on what exactly the historical myths and narratives of medieval North Africa were, let alone who constructed them and how they were constructed.

In the course of examining and analysing historical sources on the origins of the Almohads and the life of their Mahdī Ibn Tūmart, I shall try to come up with an accurate description of their founding myth. Thus, in portions of this book I provide overviews, translations and narratives based on the accounts of Almohad writers within the tradition, especially the account by al-Baydhaq. The analysis takes place when I compare different historical sources and accounts of Ibn Tūmart's encounter with the rival Berber dynasty, the desert born Almoravids. As part of my analysis, especially in the second chapter, I describe the basic outlines of the High Atlas Berbers' social and political system in the twelfth century. For, as much as Ibn Tūmart and his personal charisma was an essential factor in the rise of the Almohads, the mountain Berbers' social tribal structures supported Ibn Tūmart and led to the successful spread of his doctrine.

Studying the Almohad founding myth is not a completely new approach to the sources. Many scholars have already undertaken serious work on how the Andalusis influenced the Almohads. Madeleine Fletcher and Maribel Fierro have emphasized some of the influence of the post-conquest (after *circa* AD 1150) Andalusi Iberian milieu on the Almohads' doctrine and founding myths. According to these scholars, the Almohad conquest of al-Andalus was among the most important factors in explaining the construction of the Almohad foundation myth. Fletcher, for example, described how, as Almohad power spread and as intellectuals possibly antagonistic to Berber messianism adopted the Almohad doctrine, the idea of the Mahdī may have been minimized or cut out of official doctrine.[12] In this sense, some scholars claimed that the sources went through a process of 'de-Almohadization' in order to be more acceptable to the Andalusi context.[13] Fletcher even attributed the Almohads' central doctrine, the profession of faith found in the *Aʿazz mā Yuṭlab*, a book of Ibn Tūmart's doctrine that I shall discuss here, mainly to the pen of Andalusi philosophers like Ibn Rushd.[14] Other scholars such as Dominique Urvoy, however, have emphasized the original nature of Ibn Tūmart's thought.[15] Following Urvoy, who puts the Almohads in the context of their own myth making, I similarly argue, but much more extensively, that the development of Ibn Tūmart's Almohad doctrine should be seen in the context of High Atlas Berber society, and not only of the Andalusi milieu.

Maribel Fierro also viewed the historical sources of the

Almohads in a primarily Andalusi context and identified many instances of possible myth making. According to Fierro, the Mahdī tradition and Mahdī Ibn Tūmart's biography were constructed as a way of justifying the conquest of al-Andalus and of a rival Andalusi – Mahdī, Ibn Qasī, who had recently emerged on the scene in what is now Portugal. According to this view, the Almohads developed their doctrine not only because of their interest in maintaining Berber solidarity, but also to legitimize their conquest of al-Andalus. The Almohads claimed to be against the lawyers, judges and scholars of the Maliki legal school in power before the Andalusi Mahdī, Ibn Qasī, and against Ibn Qasī himself. Thus, a main reason for the Mahdīsm and doctrine of Ibn Tūmart was to counter the claims of Ibn Qasī.[16] The Almohad doctrine was created and subsequently manipulated, according to this theory, largely as a reaction to events and intellectual currents in Andalus. In this sense, both Fletcher and Fierro have analysed the founding historical myths and doctrines of the Almohads in the light of al-Andalus and not from the North African context in which the Almohads originally emerged. The conquest of al-Andalus was seen as the turning point, even though Almohad ambitions went far beyond Islamic Spain. This Andalusi method is enlightening and useful in many ways because it points to the possible manipulation of some Almohad sources. However, the sources from within the Almohad tradition, that is within the Berber tradition, need also to be considered. It should also be remembered that the Almohads did not see the conquest of al-Andalus as the be all and end all of their movement. As Jamil Abun-Nasr indicated in his *A history of the Maghrib in the Islamic period*, the conquest of al-Andalus was really only a sideshow; the unification of the Maghrib was the first objective of the first Almohads.[17]

Although clearly many Almohad sources would have been manipulated in the Andalusi context, this shaping of the Almohad narrative in al-Andalus did not fully account for those sources that seem to confirm, and not diminish, the original Berber tribes (the first 'Almohads') and their claims on power. Not enough allowance has been given to sources that seem to come from 'within' the Almohad tradition.[18] In fact, at least four of the earliest and most extensive accounts seem to come from within, or be primarily influenced by, the Berber, not strictly Andalusi, Almohad tradition. These sources claim to have been written by Almohads and Berbers who, from what little we know of them, adhered to founding Almohad principles, the Almohad hierarchy and the Almohad, Berber myth of origins. These 'inside' accounts are, in order of importance and chronology, first al-Baydhaq's biography of Ibn Tūmart, found in an unedited collection of manuscripts at the Escorial; second, the anonymous *Kitāb al-Ansāb*; third, the chronicle of al-Marrākushī, an Almohad; and fourth, the chronicle and a treatise on Almohad hierarchy by the writer Abū Muḥammad Ḥasan ibn al-Qaṭṭān (d. *circa* 1266).

Al-Baydhaq was Ibn Tūmart's personal scribe and biographer and his account, the lengthiest and most detailed of all sources, certainly confirmed the important role of the original Almohads of North Africa.[19] There is the anonymous *Kitāb al-Ansāb*, also in the collection of manuscripts at the Escorial near Madrid. Being anonymous, it is not absolutely certain that an Almohad wrote this text. Certainly, the manuscript would have been manipulated for certain political purposes but without clear knowledge of who did the manipulation, it is important to look primarily at the content. As I shall show in this book, the content supported Berber power structures, not simply Andalusis. The description of the Almohad hierarchy and the illustrious Berber ancestry of Ibn Tūmart and his followers, including Ibn Tūmart's successor ʿAbd al-Muʾmin, whose ancestry was even associated with Kahina, the Berber priestess who resisted the original Islamic conquests, seemed very favourable to a specifically Berber, North African understanding of the rise of Almohad power.

Also, there is *al-Muʿjib*, the account of ʿAbd al-Wāḥid

al-Marrākushī (d. 1224), 'from Marrakech', who, although he wrote during the waning of Almohad power, was not unfavourable towards the Almohad Berber sheikhs and, in many respects, seemed to portray attempts to maintain Almohad orthodoxy as heroic.[20] Then too, there is the fascinating account of Ibn al-Qaṭṭān who probably died around 1266 or the end of Almohad power but whose father Abu al-Ḥasan ʿAlī bin al-Qaṭṭān (d. 1231) was an enforcer of the Almohad Berber ranks. He was known to whip those who did not fall into line or who did not properly memorize and adhere to the Almohad doctrine and system![21] Ibn al-Qaṭṭān, especially in his elaborate description of the early Almohad hierarchy and the discipline of the tribes loyal to Ibn Tūmart, seemed clearly interested in preserving an account of the golden legacy of Almohad origins at the end of the empire.

Although written primarily in Arabic, generally the written language of the time, these sources on Ibn Tūmart's life include, especially in al-Baydhaq's account, significant quotes and anecdotes in the Berber tongue transliterated with Arabic letters.[22] Even some later sources written during the reign of the Marinids, the Almohads' successors and enemies, such as the account of Ibn ʿAbī Zarʿ are by no means unfavourable towards Ibn Tūmart and his claims to being the Mahdī.[23] This Marinid – the Marinids were Berbers from the oasis of Figuig on the edge of the Sahara desert – saw him as a powerful, inspired Berber leader. As just one example, he described Ibn Tūmart as having facial features similar to the Prophet Muḥammad.[24] In fact, as Ibn Khaldūn mentioned, remnants of the Almohads in the Atlas Mountains were allowed to visit Ibn Tūmart's tomb even after the Marinid conquest.[25] Thus, even the elite Andalusi, Arab Ibn Khaldūn (d. 1406) was part of the Berber myth making. Ibn Khaldūn lavished praise on the founding Berber tribes of the Almohad movement who conveniently happened to be the ancestors of his Ḥafṣid patron in Tunis.[26] The Ḥafṣids famously preserved Almohad doctrine in their realm despite the Marinid defeat of the Almohads at Marrakech.

If anything, some of the Almohad history that historians like Ibn Khaldūn presented was as much a re-Almohadization as a de-Almohadization of history. Accounts of preserving the Mahdī's ideal original doctrines could only serve to uphold the power of Ibn Khaldūn's Berber patron.[27] Indeed, Ibn Khaldūn's highly favourable depiction of the Almohad Berber tribes of the Atlas Mountains and the way they were arranged in the Almohad hierarchy, which al-Qaṭṭān also described, is a significant part of this book. All these sources, from al-Baydhaq to Ibn Khaldūn confirmed and glorified the biography of Ibn Tūmart. Certainly, there were likely to have been some important Andalusi modifications of Almohad history, but these main sources from North Africa are, to say the least, hagiographical towards Ibn Tūmart and, in the case of al-Qaṭṭān, Ibn Khaldūn, and al-Baydhaq, clear about the importance of the Berber tribes in the foundation of the Almohad movement.

Although the Andalusi context would to some extent have influenced the doctrine and history of the Almohads, the Andalusis were not the only myth makers in the medieval western Mediterranean. The writings of al-Baydhaq and the *Kitāb al-Ansāb* were too full of Berber writing and too praising of Berber traditions and practices to have been written or extensively rewritten solely by an elite Andalusi Arab. As I shall show, these sources, even if Andalusis manipulated them later, seem generally pro-Berber and supportive of a mythology about an ideal Almohad hierarchical structure. They do not completely minimize the Berber tribes' role in founding the Almohad movement. Perhaps, elite Andalusis who were sympathetic to the Berber sheikhs rewrote the Almohad myths, but, apart from Ibn Khaldūn who was as much North African as Andalusi, that seems even less probable. If this were proven to be the case, and Andalusis did, indeed, heavily manipulate or write Almohad sources, it would alter current assumptions about the Andalusis' hostile reaction to the Almohad presence.

By directly examining the medieval sources and focusing on a narrative that follows the Berber sources mentioned above, I shall in this book explain the creation of the myth of Almohad origins within the specifically Berber social framework in which the empire arose. I shall demonstrate how Ibn Tūmart and the most powerful Berber tribes of the High Atlas Mountains organized and inspired the tribes and rearranged the pre-existing Berber institutions of the Atlas region. According to the earliest sources within the Almohad tradition, Berber tribes and an Almohad Berber hierarchy not only prepared for battle and conquest, but also came to dominate al-Andalus. Those in power made and shaped historical myths. As I shall demonstrate, Berbers and Berber tribes were in positions of power during the formative period of the Almohad movement. The writing of Almohad history in a Berber context, and not just in al-Andalus, fundamentally shaped the creation of the Almohad myth of origins. The evidence does not necessarily suggest that the Berber myth about the Almohad foundations was any more historically factual or accurate than any other, especially Andalusi myths, but rather that the historical presence of the Berber myth has not been fully examined or analysed. To orient the reader, I will first provide a brief summary of the foundations of the Almohad Empire as first portrayed by Almohad sources.

The Almohads and Ibn Khaldūn

> In the beginning of this century a man by the name of al-ʿAbbās appeared among the Ghumārah. ... He marched on Bādis, one of the [Ghumārah] cities and entered it by force. He was then killed, forty days after the start of his mission. He perished like those before him. There are many similar cases.
>
> (Ibn Khaldūn, *The Muqaddimah*)[28]

Not only is Ibn Khaldūn one of the most important sources on

Almohad history, but his ideas about the cyclical rise of dynasties in North Africa also help to introduce important insights into how a group of formally disorganized Berber tribes managed to rule so much of the Mediterranean world. Ibn Khaldūn's writings are essential to understanding the Almohads' Berber historical myth. According to his understanding of history, Berber, specifically Maṣmūda, tribal solidarity with Ibn Tūmart was the reason for the rise of the Almohads.[29] As Ibn Khaldūn explained, Near Eastern history from the Maghrib to Persia was full of figures like al-ʿAbbās mentioned in the quote above. The potential for tribal revolution and revolt was constant. There was a basic, inevitable geographic reason for tribal revolutions in North African history.

In much of premodern (and modern) North Africa, even the strongest dynasties and governments only nominally controlled the fringes between the cultivated plains and inaccessible deserts; the mountain tribes ruled themselves without a formal government or written laws and, being well away from any administrative controls, tribal armies were easily assembled around common causes and leaders. Potential revolutions and potential revolutionaries were bound to appear in the wild regions, the borderlands between dynasties and the most inaccessible lands. Inspired by religious doctrines, disgruntled by attempts to tax them or their trade, compelled to unite and to give up their petty differences, tribes on the fringes of rule formed armies of the faithful and threatened the urban centre of power.[30] These tribes were led by men claiming to be agents of God, saints, prophets, saviours or Mahdīs.

In most cases, the lives of such movements were cut short. Sometimes, however, they lasted longer. A tribal movement could harass the edges of urban power and even take some important towns away from the ruling dynasty. The tribes might even set up their own petty government and army, but these would then quickly dissolve. In exceptional cases, a united tribal coalition led by a gifted leader or inspired prophet would arise during a time of dynastic succession and division in the ruling dynasty. United in a perfect storm of economic advantage, tribal cohesiveness, doctrinal novelty and charismatic leadership, these tribal movements succeeded in shaping history. They established powerful dynasties and empires. They would rule for decades, even centuries, until yet another inspired group of tribes, often also led by a religious leader, appeared. Then they themselves were subject to the threat of a new tribal coalition. It was in such exceptional circumstances of successful tribal revolution that the Almohads, the *al-Muwaḥḥidūn*, the followers of the Mahdī Ibn Tūmart, entered the stage of history.

Once isolated in independent fortress villages surrounded by the towering heights of the Atlas Mountains, the Berber tribes of the High Atlas forgot their grievances and inherited divisions to unite around the charisma and doctrine of the Mahdī Ibn Tūmart (d. 1130). His was a leadership that demanded absolute obedience. His was a doctrine that demanded total belief in the supreme unity of God. His was a doctrine and a message suited and crafted specifically to the Berber context. According to the sources, far from destroying all Berber tribal traditions at their foundation, the Almohads created a government, a system of rule that incorporated the tribes and their customs into a large and remarkable hierarchy, a hierarchy of scholars, sheikhs and tribal leaders that was maintained even at the height of dynastic rule.

At their apex the Almohads controlled, taxed and governed North Africa from the Sūs valley to Tripoli. They ruled the rich cities of al-Andalus and were the dominant power in the western Mediterranean. While the tribal revolt of al-ʿAbbās and the Ghumārah achieved no more than pools of blood on the dusty streets of Badīs, the Almohads created a civilization.[31] This, according to Ibn Khaldūn and the Almohad chronicles, which he mainly used, was through the charisma of the Mahdī and the solidarity, support and obedience of the Berber tribes.

1

The Life of Ibn Tūmart and the Birth of the Almohad Movement

The available sources disagree about the precise date of Ibn Tūmart's birth. In fact, much of the chronology of his life varies from source to source.[1] Huici Miranda, the Spanish historian, claimed that he was born between the years AD 1078 and 1081 (AH 471–474).[2] It is clear, however, that the early sources portray his birth and his Berber name 'Tūmart', which means 'happiness' or 'earth', as sanctified in terms recognized by Berber society.[3] During these years the desert Berbers' powerful Almoravid Empire, the future enemy of Ibn Tūmart and the Almohads, was at the peak of its power and influence.

The story of the rise of the Almoravids, who were in control when Ibn Tūmart was born, would in some ways be similar to that of the Almohads. The Almoravids raided from the desert, whereas the Almohads would rain down from the mountains. The Almoravid capital was Marrakech, a city founded by desert people who were unused to urban life. The desire to create an earthly paradise by conforming man's will to God's drove the Almohads and Almoravids alike and Marrakech was to be a symbol of this paradise achieved.[4] Soon the powerful and fiercely religious Almoravids, with their trading empire stretching from Ghana to

Córdoba, would meet a dangerous rival whose own message of religious fervour preached to the tribes was in many ways like their own.[5] This rival was Ibn Tūmart and his movement would eventually breach the high, red walls of this city of palaces, fountains and gardens.

The Berber village life of his birth shaped Ibn Tūmart's character.[6] He was born near the Wādī Sūs in the Anti-Atlas, south of the High Atlas[7] in what was most likely the small village of Igīlīz on the edge of the Sūs valley.[8]

The Hargha, or more precisely the Aīt Argan (*Aīt* in Berber means 'people of'), were Ibn Tūmart's ethnic and tribal group, which remains in the area today.[9] They were a part of the loosely knit Maṣmūda confederation of tribes that would occasionally come together in the face of common threats or for a common cause.[10] Like many mountain tribes, the Hargha had a reputation for strength and survival. Ibn Tūmart lived his early childhood in these bare and hardy conditions. He would have attended school near Igīlīz, where, according to later sources, he established a reputation as 'the light' for his ability to acquire and memorize religious knowledge, possibly either under the lamp of the mosque or at home.[11]

It is important to remember that Ibn Tūmart was born into a Berber tribe and an Atlas Mountain Berber social context. As he grew into manhood, he soon learnt that survival depended on all members sharing their wealth and labour for the benefit of the community as a whole. Intrinsic, tribal social unity and solidarity, *ʿaṣabiyya* in Arabic, was a matter of life and death. In fact, as the sources portray his message and its reception by Berber tribes, Ibn Tūmart used the latent power of tribes to form larger groups, larger circles of loyalty, to unite not simply one tribe, but whole confederations of tribes.

Ibn Tūmart knew that if tribal *ʿaṣabiyya* failed, the demanding climate and frequent drought could wipe out a community or even an entire small tribe.[12] There were usually no larger institutions outside the tribe on which to depend.[13] The Atlas Mountains are still dotted with small, close-knit villages sustained by labour-intensive terrace agriculture. In an endless battle against erosion, small plots of wheat or grain would have been terraced snug against the hillsides. The effort behind some of these terraces, often built on the most improbable of slopes and stacked in all variety of ways to accommodate yet another small plot of grain, was, like today, a remarkable feat of rural Berber engineering. Members of the tribe would be expected to help their neighbour; they may have then divided food in the community.[14] This shared communal labour scheme is preserved in many parts of the Atlas and Anti-Atlas.[15] Ibn Tūmart's community of Igīlīz, or Iglī n Wargan, probably held a market every week to exchange goods and news, settle disputes, negotiate marriage and generally maintain contact with the larger tribal confederation, both those in and outside an immediate kin group. Green olive oil, the highly prized oil of the Argan tree with its smoky taste, oranges, citrus fruits, vegetables, grains, sheep and goats are still the rich products of the region, supplied by the waters of the Wādī Sūs. There was frequently a set day of the week for market, often Friday to correspond with the main Friday sermon; some towns had markets two or more times a week and larger cities were often able to have markets open every day.[16]

Market day was, and remains, a day of particular economic and social importance for the Atlas tribes. Those who shared a market would often also share loyalties if a dispute with an outside group arose.[17] Ibn Tūmart, who was probably aware of the many disputes that would come before the elected tribal council, would have discussed these matters with his family. Methods of dealing with murder, robbery and other violations varied between tribe and region. There were no prisons and no formal enforcement institutions outside the largest towns. The main purpose of these tribal councils was to prevent disputes from dividing the tribe internally, which could be very dangerous for everybody. It was a matter of survival for the community, not simply individual justice. As the son of an *amghar*, or chief, Ibn Tūmart was exposed to the ways of tribal justice and community cohesion. He would make use of tribal traditions later in life as he consolidated them and created a government out of tribes and tribal traditions.[18]

One of the more important notions of tribal life in the Atlas was the meaning of the name, or names, of individuals. Each name or sets of names indicated loyalty in the complex web of balancing blood interests. Ibn Tūmart's own name revealed much about the many ways he wished to identify himself. In twelfth-century Berber society the name was a type of concise and summarized autobiography of its user. The name revealed not only claimed ancestors, but also claims to the glories of the past.

Ibn Tūmart's Name: The Myths and Uses of Ancestry

Ibn Tūmart's name revealed how he wished to portray himself. It also revealed his position in a long line of distinguished ancestors, a type of apostolic succession of blood that tied him to the prophet himself.[19] One version of his name was Muḥammad son of ʿAbd Allah, son of Ūgallīd, son of Yāmṣal, son of Ḥamza, son of ʿIsā, son of ʿUbaid Allāh, son of Idrīs, son of ʿAbd Allāh, son of al-Ḥasan, son of Fāṭima, daughter of the Prophet Muḥammad: this was one version of Muḥammad Ibn Tūmart's name and genealogy.[20] Another longer and more Arab version of his name also traces his lineage to the daughter of the Prophet: Muḥammad, son of ʿAbd Allāh, son of ʿAbd al-Raḥmān, son of Hūd, son of Khālid, son of Tammām, son of ʿAdnān, son of Ṣafwān, son of Jābir, son of Yaḥyā, son of Rabāḥ, son of ʿAtā', son of Yasār, son of al-ʿAbbās, son of Muḥammad, son of al-Ḥasan, son of Fāṭima, daughter of the Prophet Muḥammad.

There was a reason why Ibn Tūmart had these different sets of names. Names, especially those of holy men and leaders, were never completely static or unchangeable in this period and region. There was a difference between Ibn Tūmart's Berber and Arab ancestry. Many of his names could have been acquired later in his life out of fame and associations, and the need to have his legitimacy bestowed by a lineage that stretched back to the prophet. Although he was born into a respected Berber family, it was doubtful that Ibn Tūmart had so many distinguished ancestors. The first version of his genealogy put him in the line of the first sharifian rulers of the Maghrib, the Idrīsīds.[21] A *sharif* was a descendant of the Prophet Muḥammad.[22] Other Berber names, like the Berber *Ūgallīd* or 'king', appealed to Berber loyalties. Yet, even his Arab name was meant in a way to secure his status as a descendant of the prophet who could rise above local Berber loyalties.

In an effort to amplify the myths of Berber tribal origins and to shore up the support of his Ḥafṣid sponsor al-ʿAbbās, who maintained Almohad doctrine in fourteenth-century Tunisia where Ibn Khaldūn first wrote the *Muqaddimah*, Ibn Khaldūn defended not only the Mahdī Ibn Tūmart's possibly mythical descent from the Prophet Muḥammad but also the distinctness and importance of Ibn Tūmart's Berber, Hargha heritage. In his intellectual efforts at re-Almohadization, or legitimization of Ibn Tūmart's claims, he described those who doubted Ibn Tūmart's ancestry as the product of 'weak-minded jurists'.[23] According to Ibn Khaldūn, it was only 'jealousy', not any legitimate reason, that led the Almoravid jurists, enemies of the Almohads, to call Ibn Tūmart a liar. Ibn Khaldūn described the Mahdī's character in highly positive terms, 'always frugal, retiring, patient in tribulation, and very little concerned with the world to the last; he died without fortune or worldly possessions. He did not even have children ... if his intention had not been good, he would have not been successful'.[24] Ibn Khaldūn naturally denounced the Almoravids' disavowal of the Mahdī's claimed descent from the Prophet Muḥammad. Getting around the difficult matter of proving Ibn Tūmart's claim, Ibn Khaldūn put the burden of proof in the hands of the opponents of the Almohads, saying cleverly, 'Were it established that he himself claimed such descent, his claim could not be disproved, because people are to be believed regarding the descent they claim for themselves.' Yet, as Ibn Khaldūn stressed throughout his writing on the Almohads, it was not on the basis of his descent from the prophet that Ibn Tūmart gained a following; rather, it was very much a Berber-centric movement. The Almohads were not simply renewed followers of earlier, Fatimid doctrine of the Mahdī. 'They followed him because of their Hargha-Maṣmūda group feeling, which was firmly rooted in them.'[25]

Further confirming the centrality of his Berber identity, the name 'Tūmart' itself is Berber and does not hold the classic Arabic meaning of so many eastern names associated with Arab qualities and virtues, such as *Amīn* (trustworthy). Ibn Tūmart was the Berber son of a minor Berber chief and his first name was merely ʿAbd Allah. When he became older his name changed to Tūmart ibn Ūgallīd, Tūmart son of Ūgallīd. His mother, full of satisfaction with her son, once said in Berber *ātūmart īnū īssak āyīwī*: 'Oh my joy for you my little infant.'[26]

Several French colonial historians, but most notably Georges Marçais, have viewed the Arab ethnic invasions into the Maghrib, especially the famous Hilālian invasion, as the great disaster of the era that pitted Arab against Berber.[27] In Ibn Tūmart, however, it seemed that the most important aspects of Arab and Berber culture, their ancestry, had combined. As the twelfth century Almohad *Kitāb al-Ansāb* (*Book of Ancestry*) demonstrated, the use of names to identify a simultaneous Berber and Arab ancestry was widespread among the Almohad tribes.[28]

The *Book of Ancestry* shows names were more than simply identities; a name secured power and legitimacy. Names reflected the complex network of ties that prevented disorder in tribal societies. Ernest Gellner, the anthropologist, undertook a detailed study of the names and ancestral relationships of modern-day central Atlas Berbers. Though many tribal affiliations and even land-use patterns have changed since the twelfth century, Gellner's analysis of naming practices provided a useful tool for dissecting the complexities, counter claims and contradictions of Ibn Tūmart's contested ancestry. Most Berber ancestries were what Gellner called occamist. In an occamist name ancestors were not multiplied beyond necessity. A member of a tribe would only quote ancestors who were useful in securing alliances and protection. 'The individual knows the name of his father and grandfather: after that, he will name or know of only those ancestors who perform the useful task of defining an effective social group.'[29] Sedentary tribes may have defined individuals according to place names and geography. Saints and holy men, however, indulged in what Gellner called a 'conspicuous display of genealogical wealth'. A holy man will have a long list of names. Many of the names define several different agnatic or blood-based groups. Ibn Tūmart and the most prestigious Almohad rulers certainly fit into this long naming scheme.

Before his journey to the east and his spiritual awakening, he may have had only a short 'occamist' name, reflecting his local tribal origins. This explained Ibn Tūmart's first, more Berber-sounding genealogy. His sharifian genealogy connecting him to the prophet's blood and family may have been invented, as Ibn Khaldūn seemed to suggest. It is also possible that Ibn Tūmart was related to the many Arab tribes that flooded into the region after the Hilālian Arab invasions before his birth.[30] His family could also possibly have had some form of relationship with the original Idrīsīds who founded the first independent Muslim Moroccan state at Fes, and who dispersed widely into the Sūs valley. In any case, the attempt in the *Kitāb al-Ansāb* to highlight both his prestigious Berber and Arab ancestries had a specific purpose: to make him qualified and esteemed inside and outside Maṣmūda tribal society. He was a prestigious Berber whose grandfather was regarded as a 'king' among Berbers, but he was also fully connected in blood to the Arabs and the Prophet

Muḥammad. In his multiple names and identities Ibn Tūmart seemed to blend two worlds in his person: the world of the Berber tribes he would try to convert to his doctrine, and the sophisticated but declining world of the east where Islam began. As the sources suggest, he legitimized the Berber institutions of *ugāllīd* and *amghar* as much as that of the Arab sharif.[31] Neither is considered superior to the other. In this sense, Ibn Tūmart's elite Berber background confirmed Berber institutions, even if he also claimed the mantle of Arab authority.

The Journey East

Ibn Tūmart began his journey to the east at the beginning of the sixth century after the hijra of Muḥammad (*circa* AD 1106). He returned from his journey around the year 514 after the hijra (*circa* AD 1119).[32] He travelled possibly to Córdoba[33] and then to Babylon, Syria and Egypt. He returned by land and sea through Tunisia and Algeria.

According to al-Baydhaq's portrayal of his journey, there were several possible reasons for Ibn Tūmart's trip to the east. Since his youth he had longed for knowledge and spiritual certainty. He set out as a young Berber tribesman from his obscure place of birth in the Sūs valley in search of knowledge in the east. He left the unique customs of his mountain tribe, the Hargha, broke from his family and travelled into an uncertain world, searching for himself and his destiny. Wandering from teacher to teacher, doctrine to doctrine, he slowly discovered his version of Islam, which would restore righteousness and Islam.[34] It did not happen suddenly; it was a gradual process, a product of his journey and his encounters. It was also a product of the times and the profound challenges facing the Islamic community, the *umma*, in the twelfth century. Along the way he socialized, studied, lectured, preached and exhorted, and rulers and jealous jurists denounced and exiled him. He survived raids, pestilence and countless other close encounters with death.

At first, his journey would have seemed neither unusual nor special. Similar stories of physical hardship, travel and discovery were told over and over again by the thousands of people from the farthest reaches of Islamic influence who sought to fulfil their duties as pilgrims and to perform sacred rituals at the *Kaʿba* in Mecca. Others sought enlightenment and education from the great cities at the heart of Islam in Arabia, Syria and Iraq.[35] When, or if, they returned to their homes, these travellers would bring back fantastic tales and accounts of bravery, survival and spiritual fulfilment. The pilgrim would become a highly respected member of the community.

Although pilgrimage is a pillar of Islam, it is required only for those with means.[36] Sometimes pilgrims were sent out as representatives of whole villages or towns, which would pool their money to pay for the person in question's journey. The traveller would often perform the holy pilgrimage for an entire community. If travelling scholars did achieve letters of reference (the *ijāza*) by the great masters of law and scripture in Cairo, Damascus and Arabia, there were still further benefits for a person's social and often political standing.[37]

Ibn Tūmart met many of these travellers and students on his journeys. Like him they were from faraway places, often on quests for answers they could not find in their own communities. Indeed, it has often been argued that this journeying, this propensity to travel in search of knowledge, to see the holy places, in which so many people from such different backgrounds in Islam engaged, maintained the vitality and at least theoretical unity of the Islamic *umma*, the Islamic community as a whole.[38] Kings, rulers and princes both valued and feared experienced traveller-scholars like Ibn Tūmart, Ibn Baṭṭūṭa and Ibn Khaldūn because of their uniquely articulate and free-minded spiritual and political views. Although travelling did not automatically make them revolutionaries, it did open their minds to new, varied and sometimes radical views on interpreting Islam.[39]

Unlike most of his fellow travellers, the North African sources describe Ibn Tūmart as having unique physical and personal traits of comprehension, concentration, eloquence and, perhaps more importantly, the ability to convince himself and others of absolute truths. The political establishment saw him as one of the more potentially dangerous wandering itinerant preachers and scholars. His life was often saved from danger in ways that might only be considered miraculous.

Even his physical features were said to resemble those of the Prophet Muḥammad.[40] Regardless of whether or not this was the case, his alleged physical resemblance to the prophet served to legitimize Berbers in the eyes of the Arab world that the Almohads were intending to conquer. Even according to one later source that was critical of the Almohads, Ibn Tūmart had an upright stature, light complexion, aquiline nose, luminous eyes, a black mole and a full beard.[41] The Prophet Muḥammad was likewise reported to have an aquiline nose, white sun-tanned skin, a full beard and a light in his eyes.[42] In addition to his alleged physical resemblance to the prophet, many aspects of the Mahdī's life would come to mimic that of the Prophet Muḥammad.[43] By constantly referring both indirectly and directly to the Prophet Muḥammad, he identified his mission with the original and, in his mind, true spirit of Islam.

Ibn Tūmart travelled to an Islamic east in the midst of political fragmentation. In 1099 (AH 492), only nine years before his journey, Jerusalem fell to the crusaders who massacred approximately 40,000 of the holy city's inhabitants.[44] The shocking news of Jerusalem's fall, the place of the Dome of the Rock and one of the three holiest sites in Islam, spread quickly from Damascus to Baghdad to Cairo. With the Muslim world politically fractured and divided, there was no unified response to the crusader invasions. The Seljuk Turks controlled Baghdad and the Fatimids were in power in Cairo. The ʿAbbāsid caliphate was losing its power to nomadic invaders and schismatic groups. While the office of the caliph existed until 1258 as the symbolic vice-regent of God on Earth, the Turks held effective power.[45] The caliph was no more than the puppet of Turkish rulers, holding spiritual authority but having no more power than a twenty-first-century British monarch.[46] As the Christian armies advanced, the Muslim east seemed to be in a state of impotence and confusion. Islam became more and more internally divided; ideologically, politically and militarily the Muslim world adopted a defensive posture and out of its defensiveness grew new stirrings of thought, new attempts to create a unified vision of Islam that would withstand even the most divisive political circumstances. If the political citadel of Islam had been penetrated, the ideological keep would need special reinforcement and consolidation in the face of external attack. The Islamic west was aware of these developments. Thus, as the Almohad chronicles allege, Ibn Tūmart travelled east at a turning point in Islamic history. The sources in fact indicate that this period, which was 500 years in the Muslim calendar since the hijra from Mecca, was especially ripe for revolution. In this hectic political and intellectual milieu, it would have been almost impossible for a character like Ibn Tūmart not to think of revival and revolution.

Perhaps not unexpectedly, since Ibn Tūmart was portrayed as a hero fashioned in the North African Berber context but legitimized by the few 'true' Muslims of the east, there were no detailed descriptions of his travels in Iraq, Syria and the heart of the Muslim east apart from a mention of his interactions with a few key Muslim thinkers who had not fallen from the truth. The account of his biographer, al-Baydhaq, starts on his way home from Tunisia. The Almohad chronicler ʿAbd al-Wāḥid al-Marrākushī wrote that Ibn Tūmart set out for the east in the year 1107–08 (AH 501) 'to seek knowledge'.[47] He ended up in Baghdad where he studied the fundamentals of Islamic law with renowned scholars like Abī Bakr al-Shāshī. He listened to the famed sermons of ʿAbd al-Jabbār.[48]

AL-GHAZĀLĪ AND IBN TŪMART

Ibn Tūmart's most important encounter in the east, if the encounter ever really happened, was with the famed scholar al-Ghazālī (1058–1111) in Damascus.[49] Al-Ghazālī was so important to the development of Islamic thought that many people in the Islamic world considered him the greatest Muslim after Muḥammad.[50] There was no way, however, to prove that Ibn Tūmart met al-Ghazālī as the Almohad chronicles claimed. Most likely he did not physically meet him.[51] Apparently, the dates of Ibn Tūmart's voyage and al-Ghazālī's time in Damascus simply did not match.[52] Vincent Cornell, a specialist of medieval North Africa, suggested that although al-Ghazālī claimed to have met Ibn Tūmart, he may have confused him with a different Ibn Tūmart, namely with Muḥammad ibn Tūmart al Andalusī, a fairly unknown sufi figure whose work was discovered in Baghdad.[53]

The sources on Ibn Tūmart's early life leave many questions unanswered about the meeting between Ibn Tūmart and al-Ghazālī. Yet, they all agree that in the end, even if they never met face to face, al-Ghazālī's doctrine clearly influenced Ibn Tūmart, who sought his legitimacy. Legendary meetings with esteemed scholars when sanctified by foundational myth are sometimes more important than actual encounters. In fact, had Ibn Tūmart met al-Ghazālī, he would almost certainly have been aware of the master's animosity towards the Fatimid doctrine of the imam and Mahdī. He did not see the institution of the imam or Mahdī as sufficient to assure the community's adherence to God's will. Had he lived long enough to witness its rise in the West, al-Ghazālī may have abhorred the Almohads' Mahdī doctrine as much as he did the Fatimids'.[54] This was made clear in his work *The Revival of the Religious Sciences.*

The chronicler al-Marrākushī, an Almohad, probably influenced by propaganda, even described a short conversation between al-Ghazālī and Ibn Tūmart. Ibn Tūmart told al-Ghazālī that the Almoravids were burning al-Ghazālī's books as heresy. Outraged, al-Ghazālī foretold Ibn Tūmart's rise to power against the Almoravids, investing Ibn Tūmart with the duty to overthrow the Almoravids and establish a new government, presumably based on al-Ghazālī's doctrine.[55] Confirming and legitimizing Almohad doctrine, al-Marrākushī, the Almohad chronicler from Marrakech, writing long after the rise of Almohad power, claimed that al-Ghazālī was outraged at the Almoravids for burning his books. [ʿAlī bin Yūsuf, ruler of the Almoravids] will be removed from his few possessions and his son will surely be killed. I consider the one charged with this [task] to be none other than one presently attending our meeting.'[56] The Almohads were so successful in portraying this legend of Ibn Tūmart's meeting with al-Ghazālī that even their future antagonists seemed to believe it. The *Rawḍ al-Qirṭās* of Ibn ʿAbī Zarʿ, a chronicler from the dynasty that came after the Almohads, the Marinids, and who was not always sympathetic to the Almohads, still provided a slightly different account of the meeting. According to this source, the imām Abū Hāmid al-Ghazālī, when presented with the young Ibn Tūmart, examined him and asked him about things both 'internal and external'. When Ibn Tūmart had left, al-Ghazālī said to his assistants, 'this Berber will found an empire. He will revolt and gain control of the entire Maghrib. This is evident from personal signs and is apparent from his qualities.' These various signs predicted the establishment of the Almohad Empire.[57] Even though it is almost certain that the dialogue with al-Ghazālī was apocryphal, the aim of the scene was to show that Ibn Tūmart and the Almohad Empire were somehow the true fulfilment of al-Ghazālī's thought, the manifestation of an ideal caliphate that would restore unity to the lands of Islam. Not merely fighting for reform in the west, the Berbers could see themselves as saviours of the Islamic east. The Almohads' Marinid Berber successors, including their chronicler Ibn ʿAbī Zarʿ, were only interested in portraying the legitimacy of movements and rebellions starting in North Africa.

Despite these attempts to mythologize the meeting between

al-Ghazālī and Ibn Tūmart, his admonition against the Shia notion of the imamate, many of al-Ghazālī's ideas would have been directly useful to the early Almohad community. Al-Ghazālī, almost unique among jurists of the time, authorized the Islamic community to take up arms against wrongful rulers, to collect armed helpers and even to train troops. Although he has become a symbol of supposed orthodoxy for some scholars, al-Ghazālī was somewhat extreme in his justification of revolt against unjust government.[58] If al-Ghazālī directly influenced Ibn Tūmart, it would almost certainly have been on this point. Ibn Tūmart not only wanted to command right and forbid wrong, to perform the moral duties that God had set down, but he also ended up commanding an army of Berber tribesmen against those whom he considered wrongdoers.[59]

The wazīr in Baghdad, Niẓām al-Mulk, who attempted unsuccessfully to reunify the caliphate politically, appointed al-Ghazālī to one of the most important academic positions in the caliphate. Yet, after living comfortably as a tenured academic he experienced a profound spiritual crisis. A rhetorician and lecturer, he was suddenly unable to speak. Like the world surrounding him, al-Ghazālī was in turmoil. He retreated to the life of a mystic, gaining insight into the practices of Sufīs and their deep spiritual knowledge, a knowledge that human words could not grasp. After about a decade, al-Ghazālī returned to scholarship, determined to integrate Sufīsm with classical philosophy and Islamic theology. The result of this massive and ambitious undertaking was the *Iḥyaʾ ʿUlūm al-Dīn*, or *The Revival of the Religious Sciences.*[60] The importance and impact of this work cannot be underestimated. Even as the caliphate, the political foundations of Islamic unity, was crumbling, al-Ghazālī created an intellectual fortress of words. In an attempt to deflect a variety of dangerous arguments that both mystics and jurists used in the medieval period and that threatened to split Islam asunder, al-Ghazālī combined popular mystical experience with standard theology and sharia law. In other words, he revived, renewed and even defined the original sources of Islam as the basis of Muslim identity. Yet, even his efforts to create a unified belief system could not stop the decay of the caliphate and Muslim political unity. Ibn Tūmart, however, came to believe that he could restore or revive Islam from the outside inwards, beginning in the Maghribi west and moving to the east and the heart of the Islamic world. Ibn Khaldūn (d. 1406), again confirming a now well-established myth, described al-Ghazālī's alleged realization of Ibn Tūmart's potential to change the world in his *Kitāb al-ʿIbār*, or *Book of Forms.*

> [He saw] the weakness of the Muslim Empire in the East, knowing that the columns of power that had united the people and sustained the religion had severely deteriorated. He encouraged the hope [of a new Caliphate from the West], after being asked by his friends about the power of the tribes and peoples and if they would be powerful enough to accomplish the good cause and will of God. The Imām Muḥammad [Ibn Tūmart], having become an ocean of science and a flame of faith, returned to the Maghrib.[61]

Disappointed high expectations douse religious fervour and create an urbanized sophisticated coolness, after which an almost Machiavellian realism ensues.[62] Among special figures like prophets, reformers and Mahdīs, however, disappointment in the status quo enflames the reforming spirit, even in the most intensely conservative minds. According to the way Berber sources portray his visit to the east, Ibn Tūmart would have witnessed the slow dissolution of the caliphate, the flouting of Islamic ideals for the sake of mere political expediency. A journey originally intended as a means of gaining knowledge and guidance from the east quickly turned into a mission to reform the entire *Dār al-Islām*, the abode of Islam. Whereas the Almoravids merely sent an envoy to the ʿAbbāsids in Iraq to gain their seal of legitimacy as nominal clients of the caliph,[63] Ibn Tūmart would return to the Maghrib with an ambition to reconstruct the entire Islamic caliphate, to reform the core of Islam from the outside.

Sources indicate that Ibn Tūmart remained in the east with great scholars like al-Ghazālī for several years. Ironically, and perhaps an indication of the lack of knowledge that North African chroniclers and myth makers had about eastern scholarly debates, he also met extensively with scholars such as the Egyptian Abī Bakr al-Ṭurṭushī (d. 1126) who rejected many elements of al-Ghazālī's work.[64] Having allegedly received the seal of approval, the *ijāza*,[65] from these eminent scholars and thinkers, even scholars who disagreed with each other, Ibn Tūmart began, according to the Almohad chroniclers al-Marrākushī and al-Baydhaq, to attract a great following, speaking in mosques to enraptured audiences.[66] According to this portrayal, Ibn Tūmart was wildly successful in the east and chose to come back to North Africa to confirm and fulfil al-Ghazālī's call. He was ready to return to the Maghrib and begin his reformation of Islam from the fringes of the Islamic world. There were too many conflicting ideas and interests in the east, too many pre-established doctrines and tribes. In the remote parts of the Maghrib Ibn Tūmart would have an almost unchallenged reputation and a ready audience of kinsmen. In the Atlas Mountains Ibn Tūmart would not need constantly to deal with claims that his doctrine did not conform to al-Ghazālī,[67] that he was engaging in heretical activity or that he was following some Shīʿite principles. In the Atlas, Ibn Tūmart would have a much cleaner slate.[68]

According to the sources, however, it was the journey back into North Africa, into the soils of North Africa and into the support of North African Berber tribes that really established Ibn Tūmart's claims. For it was mainly in North Africa, not in the East, that Ibn Tūmart actively commanded right and forbade wrong. It was in North Africa, according to the North African sources, that Ibn Tūmart really became a reformer. As he approached his home in the Maghrib, at the very edge of the Muslim world, he became more radical, more certain and more confident about confronting all that stood in the way of his absolute message.[69] He had reached the point of almost reckless courage. He was, in a sense, confronting his former self. He was reborn as he attempted to reshape, revolutionize and even reject the world of his childhood and outward journey. It was not in leaving home, but in coming back that he realized who he was and for what he lived. Perhaps this is the true power of pilgrimage: the homecoming. It so happened that a set of historical, social and economic conditions along with his special traits, made his message, gained from the east, an incredible new force in the western Islamic world.[70]

The Journey Home

As the Almohad sources suggest, Ibn Tūmart's mission in North Africa was to reform and fulfil the law in the decadent cities, to transform the souls and morals of the people, and to punish the decadent, mainly urban, leaders who had led North Africans astray. He became a vehicle for salvation. The life of the Mahdī Ibn Tūmart, especially according to al-Baydhaq's sanctified biography, was the life of a holy man determined to shape human life according to a strict moral code. Ibn Tūmart did not appeal to a temporal authority to make these moral claims. He did not appeal to an official to ask permission to enforce morality. Instead, it was in North Africa that Ibn Tūmart began to appeal not to the rulers of this world, but to God himself.[71]

The duty to command fundamental morals and forbid sin, the duty to fulfil God's true intentions, dominated Ibn Tūmart's journey from the East to his establishment of Almohads in the Atlas, which his close companion al-Baydhaq chronicled in detail. From the beginning of his journey, when he had only four followers until his death in a mountain enclave where he had built a nation of thousands, Ibn Tūmart subverted, integrated and then transformed the tribal Berber society around him.

Although Abū al-Baydhaq and other Almohad chroniclers edited and embellished Ibn Tūmart's biography, the story they told provided a compelling account of a man whose life would become an inspiration for an empire, the life of a man who could legitimately claim the title of Mahdī. Those embellishments, which are often impossible to extract completely from more 'legitimate' text, reveal the intentions behind the construction of the *sunna*, the life and example of the infallible Mahdī Ibn Tūmart by the Almohad chroniclers.[72] This example of his life was intended not exclusively for an elite Andalusi but primarily for the Berber tribes that formed the core of the Almohad movement.

Ibn Tūmart's biography, as much as his doctrine, was the confirmation of his holiness and his right to lead an Islamic revolution. Al-Baydhaq's life story of Ibn Tūmart was written as a series of chronologically ordered scenes in which each scene, or anecdote, provided a parable and example of Ibn Tūmart's holiness and authority. The scenes can be divided into three basic types. The first was those in which Ibn Tūmart forbade wrong, enforcing 'true Islam' over paganism or ignorance. The second proved the divinely inspired, intellectual power of Ibn Tūmart, his alleged ability to quieten all dissenting scholars in a mosque. These scenes demonstrated his ability to attract students and followers who sought to gain his blessing or *baraka*. Finally, there were the miracle scenes, where it seemed that Allāh had intervened for the sake of Ibn Tūmart's mission.

There was a pattern to Ibn Tūmart's interventions in the local enforcement of Islam. First, an incident would occur. Next, unskilled scholars would judge the incident unfairly. Then, Ibn Tūmart would declare the truth and all would be brought to right. The people and judges either vehemently protested against his intervention or accepted his wisdom with contrition and awe. In almost every instance, Ibn Tūmart inspired an extreme reaction. Disinterest, quiet embarrassment, or silent marginalization was never used against him, only fear, disgust, awe and praise. This ability to inspire extreme reactions that upset the normal course of life was perhaps the central characteristic of a holy man. It was natural for a Mahdī to inspire extreme reactions – the worthy praise of the righteous and the fearful spite of the ignorant. Extreme reactions were reserved only for those with extreme ambitions. The sources never spoke of truly ambiguous reactions to Ibn Tūmart.

Ibn Tūmart believed he had direct authority from God and the Prophet to command right and forbid wrong.[73] As the Qur'ān declared, 'Let there be one community of you, calling to good and commanding right and forbidding wrong, those are the prosperous.'[74] The prophetic tradition written by Abū Sa'īd summarized the idea behind commanding right and forbidding wrong, 'Whoever sees a wrong, says the Prophet, and is able to put it right with his hand, let him do so; if he can't, then with his tongue; if he can't then with his heart.'[75] Ibn Tūmart commanded right and forbade wrong with his right hand and his tongue. He almost never simply used his heart or stayed quiet.

The fragmentary al-Baydhaq biography of Ibn Tūmart began with a parable about commanding right and forbidding wrong. The students of the city had been gathering around Ibn Tūmart to learn from him. One Friday, he was in the mosque for the main, afternoon prayer. After the prayer, another was made for the dead. Ibn Tūmart saw a cadaver sitting behind the rest. He asked, 'Why don't you pray over this cadaver?'

'He was a Jew, but he prayed like a Muslim,' they responded.

'Is there among you anybody who can attest that he performed the canonical prayers?'

'Yes,' they said on all sides.

Hearing this, Ibn Tūmart declared, 'You have shown that he was a believer! Thus you are obligated to put him among the row of believers.'[76]

The great scholars of the mosque checked the law books and confirmed that Ibn Tūmart was correct in this matter. They confessed meekly, 'We are in ignorance, oh master.'[77]

This was Ibn Tūmart's opportunity to teach the people the proper ways of the law and there were several other instances in which he overturned incorrect enforcement of the law. When he travelled to Constantine, in modern Algeria, with his three close companions he discovered a man who had been whipped for armed robbery. The proper punishment for a thief would have been amputation of the hand, but since they had already punished him with the whip and 'it is not permissible to apply two punishments to the same crime' the one punishment was deemed sufficient. Having undermined the authority of the judge, Ibn Tūmart asked the criminal to repent.[78]

The most numerous anecdotes about Ibn Tūmart were those in which he corrected the actions of those who practised what he considered pagan or ignorant customs, with his words and even with his staff if needed. In Bougie (in modern Algeria), a particularly indulgent place, Ibn Tūmart forbade the turbans of the pre-Islamic period that supposedly made men look like women. While the scholars of Bougie surrounded him and were awed at his knowledge and counsel, Bougie's general pleasure-loving population was less pleased by his presence.

One day after Ramadan, men and women were mixing freely on the streets of Bougie. Seeing this spectacle, al-Baydhaq wrote, 'the Imām placed himself among them, and struck them with his staff on the right and the left and they dispersed.'[79] The Hammadid[80] ruler in Bougie, al-Azīz, warned Ibn Tūmart against actions that might cause the people to turn against him. In fact, as al-Azīz predicted, the immoral were unwilling to follow Ibn Tūmart's commandments. Entering the gates of Bougie, Ibn Tūmart saw a group of Muslim slaves drinking wine.[81] When he forbade wrong the sinners spoke back to Ibn Tūmart asking, 'Who made you morality police?' Ibn Tūmart's response was simple, but revealing, 'Allah and his Prophet!'[82] His authority was not ordained by simple human rules, but by God.

In fact, Ibn Tūmart's claim of divine authority to command right and forbid wrong contradicted common legal practice in North Africa. This probably explained the reaction of the slaves in Bougie when a stranger reprimanded them. Instead of allowing just anybody to enforce morality, there was a special office, the *muḥtasib*, entrusted by a town or village to enforce moral behaviour in the markets. Several guides from eleventh-century Andalusia like the *Kitāb fī ādāb al-ḥisba* by al-Saqatī, provided specific legal roles for the *muḥtasib*, the morality police.[83] There was also the Almoravid tract on urban life and morals written by Ibn ʿAbdun of Seville. His description of the Almoravid *muḥtasib* revealed a rigorous enforcement of Islamic morals. According to Ibn ʿAbdun, 'the *qāḍī* cannot designate a *muḥtasib* without authorization from the prince ... the *muḥtasib* must be a man of good morals, honest, pious, knowledgeable.'[84]

Ibn Tūmart did not think the Almoravid system went far enough or that it was based sufficiently on the true sources of Islam, *al-uṣūl* – the sayings of the Prophet and the Qur'ān. The *muḥtasib* often used only law books that made little reference to the original Islamic texts; he was beholden to political forces, not moral ideals. Ibn Tūmart also rejected the idea that the *muḥtasib* should be appointed by what he considered an unqualified or politically motivated *qāḍī* or prince.[85] Ibn Tūmart knew he had a duty to enforce moral standards when the government failed. There was every reason to believe that Bougie, along with most of the communities Ibn Tūmart visited, had its own *muḥtasib*, even if he was not doing a good job by Ibn Tūmart's standards. Ibn Tūmart took on the role of *muḥtasib* himself, usurping the role of the prince who was supposed to appoint the morality police. Ibn Tūmart thus claimed to be above political authority. He combined political and religious authority in his own person.[86]

Although Ibn Tūmart was born and raised among Berbers and would incorporate many Berber tribal traditions into the Almohad government, he often had little respect for particular local 'pagan' customs that violated his universal view of Islam.[87] This was especially evident in the town of Tlemsan where Ibn Tūmart encountered a traditional wedding party.[88] As is still the custom today, the bride was bedecked with splendid clothes and held up in a seat of honour. Preceding her was a troupe of musicians making loud celebrations and proclaiming the new marriage to the town. Declaring the spectacle immoral, he made the bride descend from her wedding seat. He interrupted the bridal procession and broke its drums and musical instruments.[89]

Musical merriment and the drunken revelry it inspired disgusted Ibn Tūmart. After entering Fes and assembling an entourage of students, he told his small group of followers to gather dried sticks from the olive trees growing near the river. As they entered the market and approached the musical quarter, Ibn Tūmart and his band took out their sticks and began to smash everything in sight.[90] Despite reprimands from the civil authorities and protests from various sectors of the population, his caravan of followers, who were commanding right and forbidding wrong without official permission, steadily increased as he made his way across the Maghrib.

When Ibn Tūmart walked into markets he crushed or demolished objects of sin with his hand or staff. He railed against 'feminized'[91] and ignorant people who were so enraptured by music and song that they only superficially upheld Islam. He did not respect local cultures that strayed from the straight path. He upset daily life and did not follow worldly, local custom. He revolted against the world and attacked it with his stick. By overthrowing the rules of this world, Ibn Tūmart believed that he would be able to create the conditions for a new, ideal society based on rules from God and his infallible example.

After some months of living in a city, he was thrown out into the hills – in effect, out of civilization. He went back to his birthplace where he started to preach the beginning of a new world to the basic unit of society in North Africa, the tribe. Thus, the message from his encounters in the city and village streets was clear. Whereas he could not change the ways of decadent city dwellers, he could inspire the tribes. They might have been ignorant of basic Islamic conventions, have practised pagan customs and even pledged allegiance to the Almoravids, but they were not irredeemable.[92]

Ibn Tūmart was portrayed as a man of miracles, which protected him from the wrath of those who grew tired of his constant moralizing. These miraculous incidents only strengthened his claim to be speaking the will of God. The chronicles describe a miraculous incident on the boat Ibn Tūmart used to travel from Alexandria to Bougie.[93] While he was on the boat, the renegade cleric's refusal to stop pointing out people's violations so frustrated and annoyed the sailors and passengers that they threw him overboard. Ibn Tūmart followed in the rapid wake of the boat for half a day and eventually, the sailors pulled him back onto the vessel. Amazed at his miraculous survival, they did not cease to honour him until they reached Bougie. It was unclear what exactly Ibn Tūmart was preaching in the boat that made the sailors so annoyed. Perhaps there was alcohol or music on board.[94] In any case, this incident, and incidents like it, seemed to confirm that Ibn Tūmart's mission was divinely guided. Although treated as an outcast, he was the chosen one of God.

According to several *ḥadīth*, Muḥammad the Prophet said, 'Islam began as a stranger and shall return to being a stranger just as it began. Thus blessed are the strangers!' Simply put, this *ḥadīth* refers to the situation at the beginning of Islam when several believers were outcasts from Meccan society. The outcast or stranger was the true Muslim, the minority who kept the true word of God in the face of innovations, *bida*ʿ, and the creeping influence of paganism. Even if he was mocked and shunned from society, the real Muslim would still stand up for the true faith. This seemed to describe Ibn Tūmart. He was a *gharīb*, a stranger to a fallen urban society. He commanded right and forbade wrong often in the face of mockery. However, there was a much more subtle process involved.

Yet Ibn Tūmart did not only engage in sometimes unpopular moralizing, but his activities also necessitated God's miraculous intervention to protect him from harm. He was not simply a *gharīb*, a 'stranger' or outcast whom a sinful majority community ostracized for preaching the truth.[95] He was a populist. It was through his deft use of popular support, especially in preaching against non-Islamic taxes, that Ibn Tūmart gained so much support. Even his religiosity and moralizing could appeal to the crowd. In fact, he used the *gharīb* tradition of the outcast from authority to legitimize himself. Being an 'outcast' was a positive trait if it meant being outcast by a sinful ruler. Indeed, his image as a simple man on a donkey commanding right may have been used specifically to appeal to the general populous, especially tribes, who often most vehemently opposed taxation. People would have asked, what type of man, well versed in scholarship and steeped in the power of experience rides around on a donkey wearing simple clothes and preaching radical sermons against the ruling authorities?[96] Jesus entered Jerusalem on his humble donkey; he smashed the tables of the money changers. Ibn Tūmart was a man who used the image of humility, of simple, moral Islam, to galvanize popular support. He smashed pots, broke instruments and so annoyed the sailors that they threw him overboard. Yet he was also a consistent and powerful critique of the political status quo that made him popular at the time. Thus, his experience as an 'outcast', a *gharīb*, in the name of true Islam was a means of solidifying his legitimacy, not only as a moral but also as a political reformer. He was also keenly aware of the importance of appealing to popular sentiment. As he continued on his journey west, he became an increasingly deft master of persuasion.

An especially colourful example of Ibn Tūmart's popular appeal involved an ostrich owned by the Wazīr of Āgarsīf.[97] When the people of Āgarsīf saw the 'infallible Imām'[98] commanding right with authority and calling on their women to cover themselves, they cried out to him to judge the case of the ostrich that a citizen of the town had killed. The wazīr was so angry about the killing of his precious ostrich that he imposed a fine of 1000 mitqāls on the entire community. On hearing about this, Ibn Tūmart informed the man's overlord, the prince Yaḥyā ibn Fānnū, who ordered the wazīr to return the money to the population. The prince wanted to put the wazīr to death but Ibn Tūmart prevented him, saying the action did not merit death. So, in a stroke Ibn Tūmart did two things: he reformed the ways of the governor and reproached the prince for his overreaction.

When the population heard that Ibn Tūmart had gone to the prince, they rejoiced saying 'None will have to pay anything for the ostrich, neither in this life nor the next!'[99] The ridiculous levy on the population for the death of the wazīr's ostrich was symptomatic of what Ibn Tūmart saw as a much broader problem, namely that of rulers imposing non-Islamic taxes. By smashing instruments and turning over wine pots Ibn Tūmart provoked popular protest, but promoting just 'Islamic' taxes instead of unjust excessive taxation endeared him to the very traders and merchants whose markets he ransacked. Ibn Tūmart may have been an upright Muslim, but he was not ignorant of either politics or the necessities of Maghribi economics. As I shall discuss later, he became especially adept at accusing the Almoravids of major violations of proper Muslim principles of taxation. Moreover, the governor, by putting the welfare of his ostrich over the welfare of his people, was a powerful symbol of decline and decadence. The governor had become so unaccountable to Islam that he cared more about a bird than about his duties as an Islamic ruler.

The governor and his ostrich was only one of many instances in which Ibn Tūmart commanded right towards others, regardless of their rank and status. Al-Ghazālī, his alleged teacher held similar views about the duty of a man to command right and forbid wrong, even when it meant disobeying rulers and bad governments.[100] Ibn Tūmart's commanding right and forbidding wrong in this way was a useful political strategy. The one who commanded right justly was also a person of higher moral standing. Higher moral standing in a context in which religion was never thought of as separate from governance meant higher political legitimacy. Some of those who commanded right to power had no political ambitions whatsoever. In that sense they were useful to the ruler in the same way as a joker was useful to King Lear, they would show where the ruler had gone wrong in a non-threatening way. Ibn Tūmart, by contrast, did not want to be a mere critic of the dynasty; he wanted to overthrow it.[101]

Another example of popular appeal was Ibn Tūmart's constant involvement in a mosque restoration scheme throughout North Africa. In addition to enforcing the moral edifice of Islam, and taking on the role of God's elected *muḥtasib*, Ibn Tūmart was a builder and restorer of mosques and *zāwiyas*,[102] yet another indication of his future restoration of Islam in the Maghrib. Since the mosque formed the centre of an Islamic community, building or restoring them had a significant appeal to the communities that prayed in the mosques that Ibn Tūmart's teachings inspired. Everywhere he turned, a new mosque or lodge would sprout up, sometimes filling a spiritual vacuum.[103] Building or rebuilding mosques linked the people to Ibn Tūmart and his teachings.

Symbolic of the moral decline Ibn Tūmart saw throughout North Africa, several mosques and prayer halls were in a state of ruin or decay. By consecrating and restoring mosques and *zāwiyas* as he travelled west, Ibn Tūmart left behind him not only a trail of whitewashed prayer halls but also groups of organized followers and students who would prepare for his expected, triumphant return. The residents of Mallala built a *zāwiya* in his honour in which his new students and followers from the town would gather.[104] He restored small mosques throughout North Africa in even the most remote locations and ordered a renewal of daily prayer. In al-Baydhaq's glorified version of these events, mosques sprung up everywhere Ibn Tūmart went. Despite the Almoravids' previous efforts and reforms, many rural tribes would not have had access to established religious institutions. Establishing a mosque meant establishing structured places of prayer. Ibn Tūmart built houses of worship where once tribesmen had only fields or a roadside shrine at which to pray. It was likely that different tribes shared the same mosque, which would have been an important method for developing cohesion between different blood groups.

In this way, he brought his own form of religious practice into the countryside. By building mosques, he both physically and morally repaired Islam, even in the most minor, rural villages. He also reconstructed structurally sound mosques that did not follow his interpretation of proper Islamic practice. In Oujda, when Ibn Tūmart saw a group of women at a fountain where men were performing their ablutions for prayer, he declared, 'Is this not a most blamable spectacle of men and women mixing? Construct a canal system and a basin for the mosque.'[105] Here, Ibn Tūmart ordered an improvement in public works for the benefit of spiritual and moral purity. As he tore down the immoral and the licentious, he built up mosques and prayer houses in the name of God.

Ibn Tūmart enforced a pure and strict notion of Islam on supposedly degraded, cosmopolitan and worldly communities. At the same time he prevented abuses of the legal system and encouraged the reconstruction of a religious ethic.[106] Ibn Tūmart was upsetting a stratified order, an order that, at least in his mind, had fallen to corruption, decadence and most importantly had distanced itself from God. Also, Ibn Tūmart's strict interpretation of the law was tailored to have some popular appeal. This was most evident over the issue of taxes. While he ordered women to cover themselves and music not be played, he also railed against superfluous laws and taxes enforced by 'decadent' rulers.[107]

A common pattern in most of these cases of Ibn Tūmart commanding right and forbidding wrong, especially as portrayed by al-Baydhaq and even al-Marrākushī, was that they almost always occurred in urban environments, or were directed towards urban luxuries and wrongdoings. If urbanized and elite Andalusi writers altered Ibn Tūmart's biography later, it is difficult to understand why they failed to edit out his clear antagonism towards certain urban practices. If anything, Ibn Tūmart's journey seemed to reinforce the Berbers' anti-city sentiments and attempts to control outlying tribes. Ibn Tūmart's campaign against urban luxuries justified the conquest and purification of urban excesses both in Marrakech and al-Andalus, the place where al-Gazālī's books were burned.

ENCOUNTER WITH ʿABD AL-MUʾMIN

In addition to gaining public support by criticizing luxurious urban rulers and building religious sanctuaries, during his journey Ibn Tūmart also set about acquiring allies and close followers or disciples. These disciples, drawn from a population far away from the Sūs valley where the Almohad movement would begin, would be potentially less biased than the tribal chiefs and clan leaders towards their own people. Ibn Tūmart needed a unifying figure, a second in command who would be absolutely loyal to the Mahdī. A miracle of fate brought him and ʿAbd al-Muʾmin together near Mallala where Ibn Tūmart was so impressed by his new follower that he built a hall of worship to commemorate the meeting. This meeting between the Mahdī and future caliph was depicted as a fated, astrological event. Ibn Tūmart predicted the encounter through his skills in sand divination, *ʿilm al khaṭṭ*.[108] From lines in the sand and alignments of stars Ibn Tūmart foresaw the young ʿAbd al-Muʾmin of the Kūmya tribe's future fortunate rule.[109]

The genealogy of his deputy was one of Ibn Tūmart's first concerns. Clearly, Ibn Tūmart wanted somebody who could lead an uprising in the Atlas Mountains without an automatic bias towards his own tribe.[110] He also wanted somebody in search of a new understanding of Islam. Ibn Tūmart asked, 'Where are you going young man?' ʿAbd al-Muʾmin responded, 'To the East in search of knowledge (*'ilm*).'[111] Confident that the East had fallen into disunity and that his own understanding of Islam lay in the future, Ibn Tūmart responded, 'This knowledge you want to acquire in the East, you will come to find in the West!' 'Abd al-Mu'min became the most gifted among Ibn Tūmart's group of *ṭullāb*, the growing convoy of students who followed the Mahdī's every word and action. Al-Baydhaq related an incident in which the future caliph grew tired after months of study without sleep. The Mahdī said to him, 'How can one sleep, for whom the entire world awaits?'[112] After this encounter, both Ibn Tūmart and 'Abd al-Mu'min could turn confidently towards Marrakech, the heart of Almoravid world.

Setting out to Marrakech, he left Fes, passed through Meknes and Salé, and then crossed the Umm Rabi' river between Salé and Rabat. As the imām and his followers were being taken across the Umm Rabi', the boatman asked them to pay for the crossing. The imām responded in Berber, saying: 'The road has appeared to the Muslims but you are blockers of the route! Your pretension is illegal according to religious law!' This scene contained two important meanings. First, it indicated that Ibn Tūmart was beginning to enter his own land, the land of his birth where he could speak in his own tongue. This was one of the first times that the imām spoke to his followers in his local Berber dialect.[113] Second, at another, more symbolic, level his response made clear that Ibn Tūmart believed that the road from Baghdad to Marrakech was, figuratively and literally, the straight path of Islam restored.[114] The Almohad warriors would return on this very path as they conquered the region. As the Almohad chronicles warned, anybody who blocked his path, like the petulant boatman, blocked the future of Islam. In this sense the chronicles foreshadowed the future victories of the Almohads, placing events in a mythical, predictive context.

Ibn Tūmart's ambition was much larger than the duty of commanding right, or enforcing morals. He was not simply an isolated, vigilante moralist. Ibn Tūmart's ambition was to revive the original intent of Islam as the basis of governance, the basis of what he thought was a true Islamic community. He sought to transform the Islamic world. Overturning pots and upsetting wedding parties was only a symbol of a much larger purpose, namely to renew the entire Islamic community, both morally and politically.

Ibn Tūmart in Marrakech[115]

On Friday 2 April 1120 [AH 514] Abū ʿAbd Allah Ibn Tūmart entered the grand mosque of Marrakech and signalled the beginning of a new order in North Africa and Islam.[116] He passed through the lines of notables, chieftains, powerful wazīrs, learned *qaḍā*ʾ and counsellors assembled to hear the Friday sermon and to affirm the holy and legitimate rule of the prince of believers, ʿAlī bin Yūsuf. Ibn Tūmart sat down squarely in the first line of prayer, close to the *Minbar*. To the astonishment and shock of all, this stranger calmly performed his prayer and genuflections. The guardians of the mosque interrupted saying: 'This place is reserved for the prince of the Muslims [ʿAlī bin Yūsuf].' Ibn Tūmart replied, 'places of worship [mosques] are for God [alone].' He continued reading verses of the Qurʾān, probably finishing with this same verse, 'And the places of worship are for God [alone]: so invoke not any one along with God. Yet when the servant of God [literally, *ʿabd Allahi*, conveniently the name of ʿAbd Allah Ibn Tūmart] stands forth to invoke Him, they just make round him a dense crowd.'[117]

When the amir ʿAlī bin Yūsuf entered the mosque with pomp to find his seat, everybody rose to their feet to honour him, all except Ibn Tūmart. He remained seated and continued to read verses in the place reserved for the amir, seemingly not distracted by the amir's presence. Ibn Tūmart finally finished his recitation and calmly saluted the amir who was standing before him with 'may peace be with you'. Then Ibn Tūmart proclaimed, 'Change the abominations of your country: you are responsible for [the ways of] your flock.'[118] Ibn Tūmart's humiliating and even irreverent treatment of ʿAlī bin Yūsuf reflected a common tactic among religious reformers and preachers of many types. When Pilate asked Jesus a question, Jesus remained silent. When powerful Quraysh confronted the Prophet Muḥammad, a poor orphan, he did not lower himself to their level. Even the Old Testament writers were aware of this classic pauper-to-prince irony, 'Folly is set in great dignity, and the rich sit in a low place. I have seen servants upon horse, and princes walking as servants upon the earth.'[119] When a decadent, illegitimate ruler confronted Ibn Tūmart with questions, he similarly responded with measured contempt, calling upon the ruler to change the abominations of his country. In the portrayal of this encounter Ibn Tūmart appeared to be the simple, humble man speaking truth to the power wielded by a slightly bewildered and bemused ruler, a ruler who was so steeped in his own self-satisfied power that he was blind to the imminent danger to his rule. Thus, the importance of this story to the mythical history of the Almohads was that it linked Ibn Tūmart's life to the life of the prophets before him. The message was clear: the eternal richness of spirit and truth will always prevail over the vanity of temporal wealth and power. The encounter between Ibn Tūmart and ʿAlī bin Yūsuf, indeed the entire ensuing struggle between the Almohads and Almoravids, was a struggle of eternal truth over temporal power, spiritual illumination[120] over temporal authority.

The story continues: ʿAlī bin Yūsuf did not respond to this stranger in the mosque but waited until he had returned to his castle and called him into his court. The amir said hospitably, 'If you need anything, I will provide it.' However, Ibn Tūmart responded bitingly, 'I need nothing nor desire anything but to change what is reprehensible.' The meaning of his words was clear. Here was a clear threat to the rule of the 'reprehensible' Almoravids.

The *qaḍāʾ* and the amir's advisers were divided over what to do with the man who insulted their amir. Several said he was a dangerous threat who gathered the people around him, separating them from their loyalty to the Almoravids and the amir. The respected Mālik bin Wuhayb of Andalusia, said 'Put this man in a house of iron, for if you do not, he will fight against you with a house full of gold.' Others said, 'Put this man into chains, for if you do not ... you will hear the drums of war.' One, however, suggested that Ibn Tūmart was but a weak man compared with the strength of the Almoravid prince.[121]

Ibn Tūmart was either released, or somehow found his way out of prison in Marrakech. After spending time in the cemetery of Marrakech, he ventured deep into the Atlas Mountains around Ūrīka, Āghmāt and Tīnmallal, the land of the Maṣmūda Berbers with whom he would unite against the Almoravids and their prince. Five years later, the Almoravid prince spent 71,000 gold dirhams in the construction of a massive wall to protect Marrakech from the onslaught of Ibn Tūmart and his followers, the Almohads.[122]

Initially, Ibn Tūmart's encounter with ʿAlī bin Yūsuf may seem a classic example of the former, a Muslim, performing his duty to command right and forbid wrong. The chronicler ʿAbd al-Wāhid al-Marrākushī, claimed that none other than the Alexandrian Abī Bakr al-Ṭarṭūshī had instructed Ibn Tūmart in the proper ways of commanding right and forbidding wrong.[123] Commanding right and forbidding wrong was also, however, a way of making specific political and religious claims about right and wrong. In the case of Ibn Tūmart, these claims were made against a society that had very different moral, political and cultural systems, and in which concepts like 'right' and 'wrong', 'pure' and 'impure' had very different meanings. The main problem with any unified theory of commanding right and forbidding wrong in Islam was its inconsistency in application, even to the point of irrelevance, between diverse cultures within the Islamic world.

Despite the disintegration of the caliphate into several regional powers during the eleventh and twelfth centuries, Islam was also expanding (and continues to expand), into remote regions on the far borders of the classical Islamic empire. In these regions it encountered and absorbed local customs and practices that were quite different from those in the largely Arab regions that formed the basis for the early schools of Islamic law. With the slow breakup of the caliphate, an essential reference had disappeared, not only in politics and law, but also in standards of morality and practice.

The fundamental issue in this period of Islamic history was not how to command right or forbid wrong. Rather, faced with the double disintegration of the ʿAbbāsid caliphate in the Middle East and the caliphate in Spain, the real issue was what *was* right and what *was* wrong, and even more importantly, what was Islam? What does it mean to command right and wrong if those whom you command have a very different idea of what is right and wrong, or even a very different idea of what is true Islam? Michael Cook suggests that the problem was alleviated legally by an agreement between the main schools of law. They agreed that when it came to questionable practices you should not forbid wrong against those not in your specific school or philosophy. Chess, for example, was forbidden by some schools of thought, but accepted by others.[124] Also, some sects would not allow their practitioners to forbid wrong outside their school or community. But Ibn Tūmart's was more than a modest legal challenge. The tacitly tolerant agreement between different legal schools did not apply to Ibn Tūmart's moral revivalist mission.[125]

Although the study of the details of Islamic law was very useful for describing the gradual development of ideas, it sometimes failed adequately to describe dramatic rifts in Islamic history. The dispute between Ibn Tūmart and ʿAlī bin Yūsuf was neither simply a matter of law or legal differences over minor concerns with the Maliki school dominant at the time[126] nor a matter of calling a single person or small group of people wrong. It was a matter of social, cultural and ethnic difference and the creation of a new eschatological ideology.[127] Ibn Tūmart was not simply forbidding wrong against an amir, a person on the street or a group of drunken revellers. Ibn Tūmart, who represented the interests of the Berber mountain tribes, was proclaiming wrong the culture, beliefs and ways of the prince, government and society of Marrakech.

As the Almohad chronicles explained, Ibn Tūmart's daring, perhaps even foolhardy, performance in the mosque at Marrakech was more than the humbling of an amir by a deluded stranger; it was challenging the very legitimacy of the Almoravid rule. It was a challenge that took place in the symbolic core of Almoravid Islam, the great mosque at Marrakech. It created a personal legend, a narrative of piety, and a dichotomy of the pure and impure.[128] When he said, 'mosques belong to God', Ibn Tūmart was expressing his desire to return the Muslim community to God. Like incidents of dramatic piety in the life of Muḥammad, the story of Ibn Tūmart in Marrakech incited the loyalty and respect of restless mountain followers. Those around him elevated him to the same level as amir ʿAlī bin Yūsuf. While everybody stood up for the prince, Ibn Tūmart did not. He remained praying to God. It was not simply prayer. It was a political challenge. This was not just personal piety. This was not simply commanding right and forbidding wrong for its own sake. This was the politics of piety. He appealed to and depended on the support of the mountain Berber tribes, not on wealthy urban merchants or settled peoples satisfied with the status quo.[129]

Into the Mountains

Ibn Tūmart may have wanted to remain longer in the cemetery outskirts of Marrakech. There, he was not 'in the territory of ʿAlī bin Yūsuf', but in the territory 'of the dead'.[130] Even the spirits of the dead knew to follow him. It would have been risky for the Almoravids to spill the blood of a holy man and upright Muslim in the city's cemetery. However, ʿAlī bin Yūsuf had grown more determined to dispatch this new and peculiar foe who claimed moral and political authority over his reign. Ibn Tūmart continued to preach from his tent. Then, one of his companions received word of Almoravid intentions.[131] Just as a council of Egyptians had determined to kill the Prophet Moses, the council of the Almoravids was determined to kill the Mahdī of God.[132] Having escaped the Almoravid ruler in Marrakech, Ibn Tūmart made his way to the two Āghmāts, Āghmāt Wailān and Āghmāt Ūrīka. These were the great trading centres near the Atlas Mountains before the establishment of Marrakech.[133]

Ibn Tūmart and his followers stayed for several days with 'Uthmān al-Mu'allim, the teacher at the *madrasah* of Āghmāt Wailān. During that time, al-Baydhaq discovered some Yo-Yos. This led to an episode in which Ibn Tūmart reprimanded the boy's mother for giving him toys that were a sign of heresy. The woman had nine Yo-Yos; three were for the moment of his birth, three for his circumcision and three for his marriage. It is difficult to decipher these cryptic passages or to know why Ibn Tūmart should have prohibited the use of children's toys. Perhaps they were not toys, but amulets given to boys in Āghmāt when they passed important stages in their life like birth, circumcision and marriage. As such, they may have been tied to pagan, Berber rituals.[134]

On leaving Wailān, Ibn Tūmart went to Āghmāt Ūrīka. According to al-Baydhaq, Ūrīka was divided into two camps – believers and infidels.[135] A certain imām, 'Abd al-Ḥaq ibn Ibrāhīm, who was also closely affiliated with the Almoravids and had a large group of followers and students, was envious of Ibn Tūmart's science and learning. By referring to his learning in the East, Ibn Tūmart quickly reduced 'Abd al-Ḥaq's followers to silence and was able to leave Āghmāt Ūrīka, the Almoravids' original capital before the founding of Marrakech, without serious challenge. In al-Baydhaq's version of events, the Mahdī's impressive knowledge alone secured his safety, even among enemies. The people respected his knowledge and he reduced his enemies to silence.[136]

Ibn Tūmart's preaching was so convincing and his background so esteemed that he easily secured the loyalty of tribes and chiefs subjected to the Almoravids. Having left Āghmāt, Ibn Tūmart stayed in the land of the Igalwān where Ismāʿīl Igīg was leader. The governor of Āghmāt had sent a man to ask the amir to stop the Mahdī from preaching in the area and an order to capture him arrived in Igalwān. However, instead of obeying the ruler's order the Igīg encouraged Ibn Tūmart to flee before the amir's mercenaries arrived. Ismāʿīl Igīg was later rewarded for having so bravely protecting the Mahdī by being made a member of the council of ten that Ibn Tūmart set up to help govern the Almohad hierarchy.

Ibn Tūmart quickly gained a following in the High Atlas Mountains. Unlike the Almoravid ruler who simply sent in mercenaries to extract taxes and enforce his control, the Mahdī Ibn Tūmart built mosques and schools in the villages. He built a mosque at Tīynītīan where he passed the winter. In Tāmādghūst he built an assembly hall for tribal councils, councils that would play a major role in the Almohad hierarchy. He also built a granary and a garden. Here he convened a *jamāʿa*, a meeting of tribal notables who circled around him. He preached a new message in an accent and language familiar to his Maṣmūda brethren.[137] Eventually, he went back to the place of his birth in Igīlīz: the place that would become the 'Mecca' of the Almohads. It was near here, in a *ribāṭ* built in the foothills, where he could consolidate his powerful following and plan an attack on the decadent enemies of Islam.

Ibn Tūmart in Igīlīz

Proclaim! In the name of the Lord and Cherisher who created ...
(Sūra, XCVI: 1)

The history of Islam began when Muḥammad the Prophet received the divine revelation from Allah in the Cave of Ḥirāʾ near Mecca. The basic components of this revelation, most importantly the belief in one God, would be repeated in various cultural and ethnic manifestations as the Muslim faith spread to North Africa and Central Asia. Muslims throughout the world consider the revelation to Muḥammad in the Cave of Ḥirā' as one of the most important events in their faith: being a place where God had spoken, the Cave of Ḥirā' (*Ghar al-Ḥirā'*) became a sacred space that Muslim, or pilgrims, have visited throughout the centuries.

Considering what a central role the Cave of Ḥirā' played in Islam, it was hardly surprising that Ibn Tūmart, the Mahdī of the Almohads, should also proclaim the beginning of Almohad Islam in a simple cave near the place of his birth. Muḥammad Ibn Tūmart attempted to mirror, even exceed, the life and example of Muḥammad the Prophet.[138] If Muḥammad the Prophet proclaimed the word of God to the Arabs, Muḥammad Ibn Tūmart, who proclaimed the beginning of a new era, was the Mahdī of the Berbers in the Atlas and Anti-Atlas Mountains of Morocco.

Ibn Tūmart spent many days inside the cave near Igīlīz. He spread out his burnous (a long, rough, usually white woollen cloak) like a carpet.[139] One day Ismā'īl Igīg saw it and asked, 'Oh my brother, is it only but a burnous that you make like a carpet that inspires the light of knowledge? Light is nothing if not worn by light!' Ibn Tūmart later wore this 'sacred' burnous of Yaliltan, as it was called in the text, during various battles against the Almoravids. Ismā'īl took off his cloak and put it on the floor declaring, 'Sit here, you are more dignified than me for this, and God has ordered us to treat you with honour.' After sitting down at the entrance of the cave, the imām looked to the left and right and said, 'Make a great enclosure for the horsemen.' Then he ordered the construction of mangers saying, 'Those who have one horse will construct one, those who have two will construct two, and those who would judge my word about the mangers, may God castigate them!' A communal meal (the Berber *āsmās*) was prepared. Ibn Tūmart put salt in his hand and said, 'Here is a pact of God, a pact of the Prophet, between us and them, to conform to the Book [the Qur'ān] and the *sunna*!' When the food was ready the people said, 'The Imām neither drinks nor eats!' He turned towards them, detached a portion of meat from a lamb shoulder and brought it to his mouth. He said, 'I eat as people eat, I drink as people drink. I am from the offspring of Adam, I must do as they do. ... Eat as all the Prophets have eaten!'[140]

The first purpose of the scene in the cave with the burnous was to confirm the status of Ibn Tūmart as a Mahdī with special access to God. Alone in the cave, he was somehow transformed. The cave became a liminal space between the sacred and the earthly, a channel to the light of prophecy, a passage only the Mahdī Ibn Tūmart could follow.

Ibn Tūmart's followers were astounded that a sacred man should eat simple earthly food, and to them it confirmed the fact that Ibn Tūmart's experience in the cave had transformed him. He was no longer a mere preacher and moral reformer but the leader of a new promise, ushering in a new era fired by the light of prophecy. In his followers' minds he was so transformed that he had to remind them, 'I am the offspring of Adam!' The meal was another instance of Ibn Tūmart mirroring his life after the Prophet Muḥammad. His meal probably recalled the Prophet Muḥammad's meal with his closest followers before any summons to Islam had been made in public.[141] A revelation had come from God saying, 'Warn thy family who are your nearest of kin.'[142] Muḥammad assembled his family and closest followers and shared a miraculous meal. Miraculously, the mutton never ran out.

Another purpose behind these scenes was to enforce the absolute loyalty and just participation of his followers. Or, as Ibn Khaldūn might have put it, to solidify their *ʿaṣabiyya*, their group feeling against a common enemy – the ruling Almoravids. Although the practice is slowly fading, Berbers in the Sūs valley still give their labour communally and share the rewards of their joint work.[143] A whole community will be involved in the cultivation of each family's field. When Ibn Tūmart called on his followers to 'build the mangers' for the horses, he said, 'those who have one horse shall construct one, those with two will need to construct two.' In effect, he was saying, 'give up your horses (the most prized asset of any male Berber) to the cause.' Not only should they provide their horses, but they must also build a manger for the horse in Ibn Tūmart's *ribāṭ* near Igīlīz. Those who have one shall give their one; those who have more will give more. The purpose of this was to solidify his followers' loyalty, to sanctify the tribal tradition of communal sharing, to become, as it were, one tribe, one messianic community following the Mahdī's commands. Those who did not follow his words were to be punished.

After the death of Ibn Tūmart, the *Kitāb al Ansāb* or *Book of Ancestry*, described the Cave of Igīlīz as a centre of pilgrimage and devotion.[144] Abū Marwān ibn Yaḥyā, for example, remained at the *ribāṭ* of Igīlīz as a hermit until the end of his life. The *Book of Ancestry* made clear the reasons for the constant devotion to the cave, both during and after Ibn Tūmart's life. The cave was the place where the rituals of allegiance took place, where a new brotherhood was formed.

> All these great men ['the men of 50', the ruling cadre of the Almohads] passed in review [a tribal display of force, usually on horses, still practised today] with the Hargha tribe. ... When the Imām went inside the cave to go on a [spiritual] retreat in Igīlīz, at the *ribāṭ* of the Hargha, the people of the Hargha came to the entrance of the cave early in the morning and saluted the Imām who spoke to them: 'What is it that you need?' he would ask. They responded, 'We have come to obtain your *baraka* [blessing or holiness] so that you may invoke Allah in our favour!'[145]

Having said this, they inclined toward him and saluted him. Then he passed his hand over their heads and invoked God in their favour. This ceremony was performed several times. Ibn Tūmart blessed what seemed to be a throng of followers from his cave, transferring the *baraka*, the blessing and grace of God, onto them. The Hargha and 'adopted' Hargha sheikhs remained at Iglī-n-Warghan (Igīlīz) until the imām decided to move to Tīnmallal (much like Muḥammad's hijra to Medina). They accompanied him until he had fixed his residence there.

The display of loyalty at the cave in the *Kitāb al-Ansāb* showed how Ibn Tūmart confirmed his spiritual legitimacy and solidified his support around the Cave of Igīlīz.[146] He publicly blessed his followers and invoked the name of God in their favour. He was constantly surrounded by a great procession of horsemen as warriors and sheikhs abandoned their former tribes and proclaimed themselves Harghan (members of Ibn Tūmart's Hargha tribe). Like the *anṣar* of the Prophet Muḥammad, the 'adopted' Hargha gave up their former deep-seated loyalties of blood, tradition and honour to follow the Mahdī. Ibn Tūmart's cave was the ceremonial centre of the process of transforming their blood and redefining their ancestry and identity. From this select band of followers, the Almohads would sweep across the mountains of North Africa and Andalusia, transforming loyalties, demanding conformation to Almohad Islam, 'submission' and *tawḥīd*, and strict unity of belief from all.

This practice of manipulating and adopting identities was not limited to the Berber context. The social anthropologist Paul Dresch described a similar practice of changing tribal identities and loyalties in his description of Yemeni tribal factions on the border between North Yemen and South Yemen during a recent civil war. Members of a tribe would often change their tribal identity and name in order to favour the North Yemen government in Ṣan'ā' or the South Yemen government in Aden. Paul Dresch observed 'the effect of broader politics on the details of tribal classification'.[147] Similarly, tribal identities were realigned under the influence of Ibn Tūmart's revolution. The rapid and fluid reformation of tribal identities in Islam requires a reassessment of classical models of tribal anthropology.[148]

According to basic principles of social anthropology, tribal societies existed around blood loyalties and were regulated by circles of relations. Boundaries and rules to defend those loyalties ensure the propagation of one's blood and maintain a certain level of informal order between tribes. This 'segmentary' theory was used widely by anthropologists including Gellner and Evans-Pritchard, to explain the supposedly static nature of tribal societies.[149] However, as this scene of 'adopted' Hargha sheikhs showed, ancestral loyalties were never really static. Although blood was important, history was even more important. The 'adopted' Hargha sheikhs were a perfect example. In fact, Ibn Tūmart's mission was to disrupt the status quo of blood relations and reconstruct a powerful movement where old loyalties did not disappear, but were redirected towards a spiritual purpose: oneness with God and the Mahdī, the sheikh of sheikhs.

Mahdī Proclamation

After gathering supporters, building his *ribāṭ* and securing the protection of the mountain tribes, Ibn Tūmart knew it was necessary to state his intentions formally and to harness tribal traditions to build the rudimentary institutions of resistance that would eventually evolve to form the Almohad state. In a speech near Igīlīz, Ibn Tūmart proclaimed his purpose and destiny as a Mahdī.[150] Before this sermon, there was no distinct point of time when Ibn Tūmart was transformed into a Mahdī. For him, this sermon, held under a tree, proclaimed the culmination of his fate as the one chosen to save Islam from internal and external enemies. Most of the speech has been lost and the chroniclers seem to have recorded only a shortened version of what was a much longer statement of purpose. What survives of it summarizes the ambitious strategy that Ibn Tūmart would use to unify the Atlas tribes. First, he legitimized his claim as Mahdī and described how God and his messenger had chosen him to wipe the world of sin. The Mahdī was necessary for ultimate salvation; he was the will of God. No one could contradict the will and word of God and his messenger Muḥammad. At a turning point in his development as a revolutionary Islamic leader, Ibn Tūmart made his speech during Ramadan in AH 515 (AD 1121).

> Glory be to God, who does what he desires and realizes what he wishes; there is none who can resist his mandate nor contradict his judgement. The word of God, revealed to our master Muḥammad, messenger of God, he who has announced the Imām al-Mahdī the one who will fill the earth with justice and equality, just as he shall empty it of injustice and oppression. [This Mahdī] has been sent by God to extinguish falsehood with truth and to sustain equality in the face of injustice. The remote West will be his homeland and his time the end of time and his name is the name, his ancestry the ancestry, his doing the doing.[151]

The last sentence of the speech was the most revolutionary to the assembled tribes. Essentially, with one bold statement, Ibn Tūmart challenged centuries of ancestral loyalties and tradition. Ibn Tūmart's name was the name, his time the time, his ancestors the ancestors, any other names, other ancestors, other loyalties, other times could simply be washed away. This did not mean that tribal loyalties disappeared. Nor did it mean that suddenly Ibn Tūmart had overcome ancient blood ties by declaring them nonexistent. Rather, Ibn Tūmart used this opportunity to integrate tribal traditions into his revolutionary vision, creating an organized resistance out of a disorganized multitude of ill feeling against the Almoravid overlords. Even the method used to deliver his declaration would support Ibn Tūmart's newly established, tribal hierarchy of loyalty.

Just as Muḥammad the Prophet carefully told of the revelations he received from Gabriel to his closest family and followers, so too did Ibn Tūmart slowly reveal himself as God's Mahdī. The first to receive the message was ʿAbd al-Muʾmin, the future caliph of the Almohads. Next were members of the ten, the close body of advisers and tribal chiefs. Those who heard his message first were destined to lead. The final declaration was delivered before his entire assembly of followers.

Abū Bakr was among the first of Prophet Muḥammad's companions to convert to Islam. He was the first of the caliphs after Muḥammad. Similarly, ʿAbd al-Muʾmin was the first to convert to the Mahdī's Almohad doctrine. In this way, Ibn Tūmart set out to create a 'spiritual lineage', with levels of loyalty corresponding to levels of power and commitment to the Almohad cause. Ibn Tūmart had no children and ʿAbd al-Muʾmin was not a direct blood relative. Nevertheless, he became the spiritual heir of the Almohads.

The tribal council was one of the more important tribal concepts that Ibn Tūmart adopted. As I shall discuss in more depth in the chapter on tribal affiliations, Ibn Tūmart and his immediate followers created a multi-tiered structure of councils – the ten, the fifty and the seventy. Each of these councils of prominent sheikhs or valiant warriors would be convened to discuss important matters. The council of ten would be consulted most often and the council of seventy least often. Ibn Tūmart was careful to ensure that these groups included representatives from all the major tribes and clans.[152]

Shortly after making his famous proclamation as Mahdī and organizing the tribes, Ibn Tūmart began his hijra. In 1121 (AH 518), he left Igīlīz, his place of birth, and went to Tīnmallal, a place of greater security deeper in the High Atlats mountains. Like Muḥammad the Prophet, he left with some hesitation as the band of followers headed into the almost impenetrable mountain valleys to the north of Tarūdant and south of Marrakech. The roads were treacherous and too often blocked by snow and falling rocks.

Having formally had his status proclaimed as the Mahdī of Islam, having established the beginning of a coherent, obedient group of followers, and having established a secure base of operations in Tīnmallal, Ibn Tūmart was ready to start his campaign against infidels who resisted him. Many of these 'infidels' were not, in fact, directly attached to the Almoravids. They may have been sections of tribes loyal to the Almoravids, or they simply did not want to give up their independence.[153] It is difficult to know since al-Baydhaq's account is usually so resoundingly favourable to the Almohads. Yet they still had to be persuaded to give up their freedom and local authority to the new Mahdī, whose very existence as a Mahdī severely threatened elements of the established order.[154]

According to al-Baydhaq, nine major battles were fought under Ibn Tūmart's leadership. Each battle was divinely guided, a *jihād* against those who resisted the will and doctrine of the Mahdī.[155] In the Qur'ān, *jihād* is only to be used under circumstances of defence. 'Permission to fight is given unto those who fight because they have been wronged; and God is able to give them victory. Those who have been driven from their homes unjustly, for no cause other than for their saying: Our Lord is God.'[156] Ibn Tūmart was defending the right of his followers to believe in the one true God. He was also in a defensive struggle against the Almoravid ruler who wanted to eradicate him and his uprising. Yet he was also engaged in active conversion by force. Where preaching and enjoining were not effective, success in battle convinced recalcitrant tribes of the truth of the Mahdī's claims. Sheikhs and clan chiefs who supported the Almoravids for practical, economic reasons, such as the benefits of trade and commerce, or because of special contracts that gave certain tribes the right to collect taxes for the regime, would have to be shown the material as well as spiritual advantages of following the Almohad cause.

One of these chiefs, Yīntān ibn 'Umar, was the leader of the Ḥasham, the first tribal group to resist the growing Almohad movement in an organized fashion. Ibn Tūmart and the Almohads met the chief in battle at Tāudust. The battle was significant not only because it represented the beginning of the armed struggle but also because it displayed the confidence of Ibn Tūmart and his followers. They believed they were on a divine mission against all those who did not follow the Mahdī's doctrine, infidels who only recently were members of a neighbouring tribe. The 'infidels' may even have shared close blood relations with many of the Almohad followers, yet the Mahdī had convinced them of the right path, the path of unity over dissonance and of faith over freedom. It was that almost complete freedom and independence that so many tribes did not want to sacrifice. As the Almohads were arranged in battle they fixed their eyes on the Mahdī who said, 'Do not fear. The enemy will be routed!'[157]

The Almohads triumphed in their first battle against those who resisted the divinely guided ones and the surviving Ḥasham were integrated into the Almohad system. In a second battle, the Almohads confronted the Almoravid army directly. The Almohads were confident enough to expand their hold on parts of the Sūs valley and they faced the Almoravid contingent led by the *qāḍī* of the Sūs. By this time the Almoravids had lost the fervour of religion and many of the skills of war. Their army was a hotchpotch of Christian mercenaries brought from Andalusia and various tributary tribes. They had superior equipment and technology, but not superior will. This was a classic illustration of Ibn Khaldūn's theory about the life span of empires and their armies. After a succession of generations, the original fervour and involvement of the founding tribe, driven by religious conviction, had receded. They began to hire mercenaries as the leader tribes became settled in merchant trades or government positions, or returned to the desert and mountains with their loot. A new group of religious adherents arose with their newly found *ʿaṣabiyya*. Ibn Tūmart was skilled at whipping up religious fervour on the battlefield. As the 'anthropomorphist' Almoravids advanced with their semi-pagan beliefs and Christian mercenary troops, Ibn Tūmart declared 'Do not be afraid. You will receive presents from them!' The followers asked, 'How will we receive presents from them?' The Mahdī did not respond, saying only, 'God will throw out the fear in your hearts and inflame them!' The Mahdī then ordered his followers to repeat the name of God and say, 'There is no force or power but in God the highest, the magnificent!' As the two armies finally clashed their weapons together the Mahdī said '*Allahu Akhbar!* God is Great!'[158] As the enemy retreated, Ibn Tūmart took a clot of dirt and launched it in their direction. The Almoravids were in such rapid flight from the energized tribal fighters that they abandoned their horses, mules, arms and provisions.

According to al-Baydhaq's version of events, after this spectacular defeat, the Almoravids knew Ibn Tūmart was more than merely a radical preacher. He was a serious threat. They tried to hire people to assassinate the Mahdī, but failed. Highly skilled Almoravid generals, under the command of Yānnū and Ākūdī ibn Mūsā were dispatched to quash firmly the Almohad uprising. Ibn Tūmart also gathered his generals and warriors and organized the different tribes into an army. Instead of mixing the tribes together into a homogenous fighting force, each Almohad confederation of tribes had a commander with a specifically coloured cloak. In this way different tribes could compete for victory and compare honour and valour in the cause. Ibn Tūmart gave a white cloak to the future caliph, ʿAbd al-Muʾmin to lead the Gadmīwa tribes. To Abū Ibrāhīm, commander of the Hargha, he gave a yellow cloak. To ʿAbd Allah Ibn Mawīya, commander of the Ganfīsa, he gave a red cloak. The fourth cloak he gave to Yaliltan who met him in the cave at Igīlīz; he was placed in charge of the people of Tīnmallal. ʿUmar Intī was put in charge of the Hintāta.[159]

As long as the Almohads remained in the mountains waiting to ambush the Almoravid troops, who were unused to mountain combat, they were successful. In mountain battles the Almohads followed the simple tactical advice of Ibn Tūmart, 'Do not go down towards the plain, but let the enemy climb up and meet you!'[160] The Almohad tribes, with their knowledge of the difficult terrain, had a distinct advantage. The desert nomads were used to battle in fairly open spaces. Being far from home their Christian and Turkish mercenaries knew little of the local geography. Planned ambushes made the Almoravids look more and more like the invader, not the defender: the Qur'ānic justification of defensive *jihād* would thus apply. It was simple for the Almohads to block approaches, to cut off supply routes and to subvert even the most organized Almoravid offences into the mountains. The Almohads failed, however, when, full of early confidence, they ventured onto the plains seeking to strike the Almoravids a mortal blow at Marrakech, their capital. The overconfident Almohads, led by the vicious and energetic general al-Bashīr, attempted to capture Marrakech, but were eventually pushed back from the city in the infamous battle of al-Buḥaīra.[161] The Almohads retreated to their mountain fortresses and returned to the high walls of Marrakech only after they had conquered most of North Africa.

Before his death on the plains of al-Buḥaīra, al-Bashīr had been Ibn Tūmart's main enforcer. He had been responsible for maintaining the discipline and unity of the Almohad tribes, and did so with an iron fist if necessary. Ibn Tūmart was fighting battles not only against the Almoravids, but also against reluctant Maṣmūda tribes like the strong and naturally rebellious Haskūra tribes who did not, at first, willingly join his venture. Even among the loyal tribes there were many supposed 'traitors' to the cause, many of whom were unhappy about the loss of their freedom as independent tribes. When preaching and accommodating tribal culture did not work, Ibn Tūmart would call upon al-Bashīr to terrorize those who questioned the will of the Mahdī.

Al-Bashīr led the *tamyīz* (the separation or dividing out) of the Almohads. He divided the good and loyal from the 'dissidents, hypocrites and deceivers'. According to al-Baydhaq, the unjust were cleansed from the just and the people 'redoubled their faith'.[162] Al-Baydhaq recorded that entire clans were gathered up and massacred at places called Īgar-an-ūsannān and Īgar-an-Aīt

Kūriyīt. The Īmattazgā of the Hintāta were executed, as were the Gadmīwa living in Tākūsht and the In Māghūs, along with several other clans and individuals. After the killings and before his spectacular defeat at Marrakech, al-Bashīr lined up the Mahdī's followers and passed them in review.[163] The savagery of his discipline may have contributed to that defeat.

Although Ibn Tūmart wished to temper tribal independence, he knew the importance of respecting, even encouraging, the pride of various tribes and he directed that pride and competitiveness to the service of the Almohad cause. The tribes that were best in battle received higher honours. There was an incident at Tīnmallal when Ibn Tūmart called all his warriors together to pass before them and review them in tandem. He passed before the Hargha, the Ganfīsa and the rest riding bareback on his mule. Having omitted to call forth one of the chiefs, 'Umar Āṣnāg, he called for the entire ceremony to be repeated so that he could display the absolute solidarity of all the chiefs and honour the tribe of 'Umar. Ibn Tūmart was aware of the importance of tribal honour, despite the brutal means he used to maintain collective discipline.[164]

After the battle of al-Buḥaīra the surviving Almohad warriors returned to Tīnmallal. The Almoravids had built the fortress of al-Tasghimūt in the pass into the Tīnmallal valley.[165] In fact, the Almoravids built an entire line of 20 fortresses in a vain attempt to control the Atlas tribes.[166] The situation grew worse for the Almohads with the illness of the 'infallible' imām; the Mahdī was growing weaker every day. Sensing that the time for him to travel 'on a voyage where none other may accompany [me]'[167] was growing near, the Mahdī assembled his followers for a last sermon to the believers, just as Muḥammad the Prophet spoke his famous last sermon before a company of his followers. It was not a sermon of defeat, but of victory, a sermon that would set out the high ambitions of the movement.[168] He said they would conquer 'Persia and the Christian lands'. This was often predicted for the end of time. He was preparing his followers for the end days.

Although most sources say that the Mahdī died on 13 or 14 August 1130 (AH 524),[169] his body was hidden from most of the Almohads for three years, giving time for ʿAbd al-Muʾmin to establish his authority as the successor to the great Mahdī. Several legends survive concerning Ibn Tūmart at the threshold of death and a new life. Many of these stories may have been elaborated upon as the Almohad Empire expanded rapidly under the caliph and his powerful successors. Al-Baydhaq tells us that at the end of three months in Tīnmallal, the Mahdī began to feel ill. He and his companions went to the Faddān Āmadyūs for some fresh air. On the road back to Tīnmallal, Ibn Tūmart told a parable about the pea plant. He said, 'Those over there! Take those.' Everybody went and collected the peas. Ibn Tūmart then said, 'In the same fashion you will pick the good things of this world after us!' Ibn Tūmart began to predict his own passage to another world.[170]

As he grew weaker, his followers took the reins of his iconic sturdy donkey, the symbol of his simplicity and humility, and led him to his house. There he addressed the Almohads who had assembled, anxious to hear from their leader. He said, 'Look at me well and fix my traits in your memories, for I will leave you for a long voyage.' The people cried uncontrollably and said to him, 'If you must go again to the East, we will accompany you!' He responded saying, 'On the journey I will take, none will accompany me. It is for me alone!' Al-Baydhaq never explicitly mentions death. Rather, he described the Mahdī as going on a journey from which he may ultimately return. This seemed to mirror certain aspects of the Shīʿite tradition of occultation, of the ever-present imām and Mahdī going into hiding.

Five people accompanied Ibn Tūmart into his humble house; the future caliph ʿAbd al-Muʾmin, his close friends, Abū Ibrāhīm, ʿUmar Āṣnāg and Wasnār, and his sister Zainab. Every once in a while, Wasnār would emerge from the house of the deceased or nearly deceased Mahdī and say, 'The Imām orders you to do such and such a thing' and the people obeyed. This continued even after the

Mahdī's death. According to al-Baydhaq, the Almohads were led this way for three years. The Almohads were even able to continue their wars against the Almoravids in this intermediary period.[171]

There is a gloss on the manuscript of uncertain date and mysterious origin about the last days of the Mahdī. It is a citation from the *Kitāb al-Majmūʿ* written on the side of the original al-Baydhaq manuscript.[172] An almost identical text is also found in the body of the *Rawḍ al-Qirṭās* of Ibn ʿAbī Zarʿ, written a significant time after al-Baydhaq.[173] According to this passage, the imām and Mahdī heard a soft voice inside his house shortly before his death. The voice seemed to come from the other side of the wall. The voice told the Mahdī that he would have to prepare for a voyage. He would have to know what he would say at death. The Mahdī responded saying, 'I will say that God is true and I have been a witness to this.' The mysterious voice said, 'So prepare yourself for death, for you will soon pass away.' This mysterious voice from heaven, this angel, prepared Ibn Tūmart for his entry into paradise.

Six days later, Ibn Tūmart's closest followers gathered around him to hear his last words. He said, 'Question me as you wish about your religious and material concerns.'[174] The future caliph, ʿAbd al-Mu'min, and the Mahdī's companions questioned him about their daily life, about maintaining the straight path. They also asked when was the best time to mount attacks on the Almoravids. To these questions the imām said to follow the laws of God. Reflecting the words of the Prophet Muḥammad, the Mahdī said with his last breaths, 'Do not hate one another, do not envy one another, do not break away from one another, and do not oppose one another. Be servants of God and brothers. Truly, I have transmitted you the truth! I have transmitted you the truth! I transmitted to you the truth!'[175] He died in the month of Ramadan AH 524 or September 1130.[176]

Just as Muḥammad the Prophet was buried in Medina, Ibn Tūmart was buried in the Almohad Medina, in a simple grave at

Tīnmallal. Just as the mosque at Tīnmallal, with its austere and dominating beauty would become the model for Almohad architecture throughout North Africa and al-Andalus, so would the story and message of the great Mahdī be repeated throughout the conquered lands of the new empire.[177] It was Ibn Tūmart's successor, the stranger from outside the Maṣmūda, ʿAbd al-Muʾmin, who would finally lead the Almohads to Marrakech after systematically conquering the Almoravid rulers' land, trade routes and mercenaries. The great and opulent cities of Bougie, Fes, Oran and Tlemsan, places where Ibn Tūmart had preached against sin a few decades before, had fallen to the Almohads. Marrakech and the Almoravids were utterly defeated in 1147 after a bloody siege that saw acts of great bravery and brutality by men, and even women, on both sides. The now rich and sumptuous capital that was being built at the birth of Ibn Tūmart was under the control of his successors.[178]

By 1183 (AH 578) the Almohad Empire was so strong that even the Egyptians feared an invasion by the Almohads. Describing the ruler's construction of new passageways across the Nile, the traveller Ibn Jubayr recorded a rumour that these bridges were an augury of the coming of the Almohads, who would storm across the Nile and into Syria and the Hijaz.[179] The rise of the Almohads was known throughout the Islamic world; their influence could not be escaped. Al-Baydhaq made clear that Ibn Tūmart had followers not only in North Africa but throughout the Islamic world. One unfortunate Almoravid *faqih* (jurist) fled to Egypt in a state of panic at the rise of Almohad power and left for Mecca. There, still in fear of rumours about the mighty Almohads, he ran all the way to India where he died in peace in 1156.[180] If it were not for the stagnation and eventual defeat of the Almohads at Las Navas de Tolosa in 1212, Ibn Tūmart's dream of a reunited Muslim caliphate stretching from the Maghrib to Persia may have been fulfilled.[181]

In the next chapter I explain how this powerful empire was originally constructed. I describe the specific methods Ibn Tūmart and the Almohads used to create an army and a hierarchy out of the disparate tribes of the Atlas Mountains. First, however, I shall wrestle with some of the methodological challenges of writing the history of the early Almohad period, describing and analysing the primary historical sources used in writing this history. Finally, I shall interpret how Ibn Tūmart and his followers used gender and ethnic generalizations to construct the Almoravids as an enemy, the 'other'.

The Writing of History in Medieval North Africa

There were several different primary sources for Ibn Tūmart's famous visit to Marrakech and his encounter with the Almoravid amir. It is necessary to demonstrate the differences between the sources on this particular scene, a central event in Almohad history. I shall describe how different sources presented the scene and then provide a critical analysis of each source. Finally, I shall discuss the methodological implications of these different interpretations of the mosque scene.

The Anonymous Chronicler was used earlier as the source for the short description of Ibn Tūmart's mosque appearance in Marrakech. The Anonymous Chronicler, writer of the *al-Ḥulal al-Mū shiyya*, was possibly sympathetic towards the Almoravid amir ʿAlī bin Yūsuf.[182] In his version of the encounter, ʿAlī bin Yūsuf was a hospitable, if confounded, amir and Ibn Tūmart seemed to be inexplicably petulant, if not insane. The chronicler said he finished writing his work in AH 783/AD 1381, 200 years after the meeting between Ibn Tūmart and the amir. By this time the Almohads had fractured. They suffered a fate similar to the Almoravids: the Almohads were denounced as impious tyrants by the next wave of 'pious' successors.[183] The Anonymous Chronicler wrote in this period of rapid Almohad decline. Even so, the mysterious chronicler, writing long after the event, was not wholly incredulous; he frequently quoted from other authors or witnesses; in this case he quoted a certain Ibn Bajir, who was closer to the encounter. Even this possibly anti-Almohad was not systematically de-Almohadizing history.[184]

In contrast, a primary source used to promote Ibn Tūmart's systematic politics of piety was the writing of Ibn Tūmart's close confidant Abū Bakr al-Baydhaq al-Ṣanhājī.[185] Al-Baydhaq's version of the encounter was much more dramatic and clearly considerably more favourable to Ibn Tūmart. It was also very direct. Al-Baydhaq was travelling with Ibn Tūmart and witnessed the event. According to Baydhaq, they were in Marrakech on Friday and entered ʿAlī bin Yūsuf's mosque for prayer where they found ʿAlī bin Yūsuf covered with a 'head veil'.[186] The viziers and counsellors sat surrounding the caliph. They said to Ibn Tūmart, 'Salute the amir with the title of Caliph!'

Ibn Tūmart responded, 'Where is the amir? For I see nothing but veiled women!'

Incredibly, in al-Baydhaq's version of events, the caliph simply said, 'You are right' and took off his veil without question.

Seeing him unveiled, Ibn Tūmart, 'the infallible', said to him, 'The Caliphate belongs to God and not to you oh ʿAlī bin Yūsuf!'

Ibn Tūmart went even further to mock the unclean ways of ʿAlī bin Yūsuf in the mosque, saying, 'Rise up from your tainted mat. If you want to be a leader of righteousness, do not sit on this indecent fabric!'

The Almoravid caliph got up off the mat asking him childishly, 'Why is it so indecent?'

This weak and humbled response left a perfect opening for Ibn Tūmart's climax, 'It is made of manure!' *(al-najāsa)*.[187]

Abū Bakr Ibn ʿAlī al-Ṣanhājī al-Baydhaq's memoirs possibly form the most important source for the life of Ibn Tūmart and the rise of the Almohads. Unfortunately, the only significant information we have about al-Baydhaq comes from his work. Also, the surviving manuscript of his work, found at the Escorial library in Spain, is incomplete.[188] As Lévi-Provençal noted, it had lost its beginning and no title was mentioned.[189] Thus, there was no indication of when al-Baydhaq was born. However, it was clear that he was alive during Ibn Tūmart's life and that he served him from the beginning as a loyal and steadfast follower.

For some curious reason, the French historian Le Tourneau did not have a very high opinion of al-Baydhaq. He saw him as some sort of simpleton. Instead of acknowledging the fact that the first part of al-Baydhaq's book was simply missing, he says:

> It is regrettable that some clarifying information on this [early] period of Ibn Tūmart's life is not available, but the first section of al-Baydhaq's book, which might have been helpful, was either lost or, more likely, the author, being a simple man, was unable to trace adequately the development of the thought of such a man as the Mahdī.[190]

Le Tourneau gave no credible reason for his low judgement of al-Baydhaq's intelligence. The book was, in fact, well written and original and at least on the same level as most standard chronicles of the time. Certainly, the many scholars and great teachers he met when travelling with Ibn Tūmart would have influenced him. Everywhere Ibn Tūmart went, al-Baydhaq followed. He was a close companion and an adviser to the Mahdī as well. Furthermore, as a Ṣanhāji he may have been instrumental in converting members of the Ṣanhāji tribal confederation who formed the basis of Almoravid power.

His work was an intimate window into the birth of a movement. Al-Baydhaq's writing was certainly not the work of a credulous, country bumpkin. It was a unique manuscript, a text with special features that placed it outside any easy category of Islamic historical writing from the period.[191] It was a memoir, a direct, first-hand account of events. Most historical writing occurred decades or even centuries after the event took place. In this case, however, al-Baydhaq provided an inner view into the development of the Almohad state. Yet, even as it provides a unique view, his text poses an important challenge. Al-Baydhaq was obviously intensely biased in favour of Ibn Tūmart, ʿAbd al-Muʾmin and the Almohad idea as a whole. It would have been easy for al-Baydhaq to ignore potentially damaging or discouraging information about the Almohads, even as he railed against the Almoravids. He was a panegyric or even a sycophant. Indeed, it was not inconceivable that Ibn Tūmart or his followers may have ordered and then edited al-Baydhaq's work as a way of preserving a narrative for posterity, a *sīra* of the Mahdī.

Thus, there are many reasons to trust this text, just as there are reasons to be sceptical in certain instances. Under the intense glow of ideological fervour even first-hand memories were not necessarily as they seemed. Al-Baydhaq could easily have edited the early sections of his book in the light of later events. For example, Ibn Tūmart was not proclaimed Mahdī until he appeared from the Cave of Igīlīz. Despite this, al-Baydhaq still described people calling Ibn Tūmart 'infallible' long before he was proclaimed. Also, he attributes miracles to Ibn Tūmart, such as the assistance of God when passengers threw him off a boat because of his pestering and preaching. Nevertheless, al-Baydhaq remains a unique, primary witness. In his chronicles he used not only his eyes, but also his own imagination and his beliefs as a follower and devotee of the Mahdī to write Ibn Tūmart's history.

In the *Rawḍ al-Qirṭās* by Ibn ʿAbī Zarʿ, the story of Ibn Tūmart's encounter with the amir is different yet again. Although it provides a wealth of unique information, the *Rawḍ al-Qirṭās* is replete with inconsistencies, legends and unlikely accounts.[192] Written in the first part of the fourteenth century, long after the encounter between Ibn Tūmart and ʿAlī bin Yūsuf, Ibn ʿAbī Zarʿ describes events and details that did not take place in other sources.[193] It is not clear if Ibn ʿAbī Zarʿ was consciously aware of creating these legends or if he was simply expressing the shifting oral memory of his sources. Either way this represents a transformation of the Ibn Tūmart narrative to suit changing political and social situations.

This story of Ibn Tūmart's encounter with the Almoravid ruler was subject to numerous accretions and colourful anecdotes that reflected as much the myth making and perspectives of historical sources as an account of what actually happened. For example, according to Ibn 'Abī Zar' Ibn Tūmart came into Marrakech commanding right and forbidding wrong, pouring out wine and breaking the instruments of pleasure. He forbade wrong 'without the permission of the Prince of the Muslims, or of any *qāḍī* or wazīr'.[194] One of the conditions of commanding right was that it must be done with legal sanction, unless the legal authority was not legitimate. The Ibn Tūmart of Ibn 'Abī Zar' felt above the law of the Almoravids. In some respects he was portrayed as more of a reckless troublemaker, less of a sanctified reformer. Nevertheless, the account of Ibn 'Abī Zar' was full of anecdotal details that, in many respects, put Ibn Tūmart in a favourable light.

According to Ibn 'Abī Zar', the news of Ibn Tūmart reached 'Alī bin Yūsuf who ordered that the trouble maker be brought to him. Thus, in this version, instead of confronting 'Alī ibn Yūsuf in the mosque, Ibn Tūmart was called to the amir.

> Ibn Tūmart said 'I am only a poor, humble man who searches for the eternal life; I have no other purpose than to command right and forbid wrong, and you are the one who should be doing this, but you have lost account. You must revive the *sunna* and destroy the reprehensible. Sinful things have appeared in your Empire and heresies have been spread. God commands you to uproot [the heresies] and revive the *sunna*. For you have power by God alone. ... For God reproves the people who should prohibit innovation (*bida'*) but do not.'[195]

When the prince heard this he 'inclined his head to the ground, thinking of [Ibn Tūmart] and his words'. He called all of his great judges and *faqīhs* for a conference with Ibn Tūmart. They wished to question him, but Ibn Tūmart only revealed their impotence. Ibn Tūmart was expelled from the city of Medina to the graveyard outside Marrakech where he could find some sanctuary from the ruler. He set up a tent, read the Qur'ān and preached. To the great irritation of the amir, he attracted many more followers to the cemetery. One man feared for the life of Ibn Tūmart asking, 'Did [the amir] not mandate that you leave the city?' Ibn Tūmart responded 'I have followed his orders and left the city for the cemetery, I have set up a tent between the dead [for] I am occupied with the next life: do not listen to the deceitful!'

With each of the amir's attempt's to suppress Ibn Tūmart and his message, Ibn Tūmart only attracted more followers. He did not simply leave Marrakech. Occupied with the life hereafter, he went to the cemetery and preached against the Almoravids. Although the amir was supposed to have power, he was described as remarkably powerless. He could not even prevent 1500 people from joining Ibn Tūmart in the nearby cemetery, a place of apocalyptic symbolism.

Another chronicler of the encounter born in AD 1185, the writer al-Marrākushī, could not have witnessed the encounter between Ibn Tūmart and the Almoravid amir. Although an Almohad, al-Marrākushī lived during the reign of the later, urbane caliphs, Yūsuf Ya'qūb and Ya'qūb Yūsuf. By this time, many of Ibn Tūmart's more radical concepts and claims were being toned down. However, unlike some later writers, he held Ibn Tūmart in the highest respect. Huici Miranda, the Spanish expert on the Almohads, believed that al-Marrākushī was one of the most reliable sources for the period.[196]

Unfortunately, al-Marrākushī provided only a cursory version of the encounter. He may have attempted to tone down some of Ibn Tūmart's more strident comments. This would have made them more digestible to the worldlier, ruling elite of the Almohad Empire at its height. There was no cemetery scene, no dramatic encounter in the mosque. Al-Marrākushī described the meeting between the amir, his advisers and Ibn Tūmart in staid, legalistic language, contrasting the position of Ibn Tūmart against the excessive judicial interpretation of the Almoravids.[197] This did not necessarily mean, however, that al-Marrākushī explicitly rejected al-Baydhaq's historical legends.

In the *Muqaddimah*, an analytical introduction to his *Kitāb al-'Ibār*, a history of the Almohads, Ibn Khaldūn set out a methodology for rejecting fanciful histories and the Mahdī's contradictory accounts. He compared and contrasted primary sources and oral accounts. He used the libraries of Tunis, al-Andalus, Fes and Cairo. He was sometimes the only source for important events in North African history. Yet, even Ibn Khaldūn, a historian whose method and sociological theory were remarkably rigorous, even 'modern', was immediately vulnerable to bias and political circumstance. For Ibn Khaldūn, the science of astrology held as many secrets about humanity's actions as his more interesting theories of economy, tribalism and state development. He was keen to show instances in history when astrology worked. For him, the rise of the Almohads was as much a confirmation of astrological theory as historical theory. Also, as his autobiography made clear, he was far from a neutral observer, very much in the midst of political struggles and machinations, and writing often in the court of the Ḥafṣids who maintained Almohad doctrine in Tunisia. Ibn Khaldūn was a researcher, not just a recorder of hearsay. His own complex, political context should not be forgotten.[198]

Ibn Khaldūn was the last of the medieval Maghribi chroniclers to write about the Almohads in any detail. According to his brief version, Ibn Tūmart did meet 'Alī bin Yūsuf in the mosque during Friday prayers where he addressed the amir with a vigorous remonstrance. He then went out and encountered Sura, the prince's sister, who was out in public uncovered. Ibn Tūmart reprimanded her with vigour. He was also brought before a council of *faqihs* and judges, presided over by the famous Mālik ibn Wuhayb who enjoyed a certain reputation as an astrologer and prognosticator. This was an opportunity for Ibn Khaldūn to prove his belief in the power of astrology through the use of hindsight. At the very least, it was a useful poetic expression of fate in historical events.[199] Mālik ibn Wuhayb said, 'Throw fire at his feet or one day he will have you listen to the drum [of death]. I believe that this is the man of the square dirham!'[200] While the Almoravids used a round *dirham* for their money, the Almohad coins were square.

It was the rise and fall of the Almoravid, Almohad, and Marinid empires, and, to a lesser extent, the earlier rise and fall of the Arab dynasties of the East that led Ibn Khaldūn to his most important theories on the development of states in pre-modern Islamic society. He had seen figures like Ibn Tūmart in previous histories, in other, long-lost empires, founded on hopes of reform and the return of true Islam. Ultimately, however, empires were corrupted from within. His account of Ibn Tūmart and the rise of the Almohads and the fall of the Almoravids fits neatly, perhaps too neatly, into his theory. Historical events in Ibn Khaldūn's major work, the *Kitāb al-ʿIbār*, did not just happen, they often seem fated, fated to fall into his pattern of history, a pattern determined as much by what was to come as by what was before.

The discrepancies between the sources of Almohad history open up important questions about the uses and meaning of history and the effectiveness of history in the medieval Islamic period. Several questions arise. Which account was most accurate? Where there was a contradiction in dates or location, which chronicler should be believed? What about unique information, such as the potentially biased accounts of Ibn ʿAbī Zarʿ that are not even mentioned in other sources? There are four main challenges in Almohad historiography – the limited number of sources, the lack of any exact parallels between any sources, the influence of political motive on contemporary chroniclers and the development of legendary, mythical stories over the course of time.

Each source had its particular bias and an interest in shaping history through their view of Ibn Tūmart and the Almohads. It is even conceivable, if unlikely, that the one direct source, al-Baydhaq, fabricated the meeting entirely. The purpose of this fabrication would have been to improve Ibn Tūmart's image by making him the one who single-handedly confronted the amir. Al-Marrākushī was less directly biased, but was not a direct witness. He may have come across the invented story after it developed into a legendary account of a bold encounter with the Almoravid prince. It was in his interest as a later Almohad chronicler to confirm the heroism of Ibn Tūmart. The Anonymous Chronicler, Ibn 'Abī Zar', Ibn Khaldūn and others may simply have further developed al-Baydhaq's version. If this were true, then even history was made to follow Ibn Tūmart's programme of political piety, creating events that may have never happened except in symbolic terms. Whether imagined or real, the encounter between 'Alī bin Yūsuf and Ibn Tūmart was certainly a significant historical myth in North African history.

Muslim historians in North Africa and the Middle East dutifully wrote down events, supporting with sources and citations. They gave rich descriptions of personalities and people. Yet, only in a few instances did medieval Muslim historians explicitly interpret events.[201] Only rarely did they systematically attempt to understand the meaning behind events. One brilliant exception to this was the *Kitāb al-'Ibār* of Ibn Khaldūn (d. 1406), a significant, if late, source of the Almohad Empire. It is worth quoting the beginning of Ibn Khaldūn's *Muqaddimah*, not only for what he revealed about the state of historical writing at the time, but for his analysis of problems still widely debated by historians and philosophers of history, problems at the very heart of historical methodology.[202]

> History is a discipline widely cultivated among nations and races. It is eagerly sought after. The men in the street, the ordinary people, aspire to know it. Kings and leaders vie for it. Both the learned and the ignorant are able to understand it. For on the surface history is no more than information about political events, dynasties and occurrences of the

> remote past, elegantly presented and spiced with proverbs. ... The inner meaning of history,[203] on the other hand, involves speculation and an attempt to get at the truth, the subtle explanation of the causes and origins of existing things, and deep knowledge of the how and why of events. [History] therefore, is firmly rooted in philosophy. It deserves to be counted as a branch of it.[204]

As Ibn Khaldūn stated, few Islamic histories provided information about the meaning and patterns behind events. Rather, the focus was on appearing to portray the events accurately and persuasively in a narrative form. With the exception of the famous Ibn Khaldūn, the typical medieval, Muslim historian was much more a craftsman than a thinker. As Ibn Khaldūn said, 'They [historians] did not look for, or pay attention to, the causes of events and conditions.'[205] The craftsman must produce his product for consumption and will shape the product according to the consumer's tastes and preferences. Most often, the consumer was a political figure, an amir, ruler, or king who had his own interest in forming history. These consumers wanted custom-built products. The basic structure of events was difficult to alter, but the details, the filigree, features, legends, names, associates and players could all be crafted, added, chipped, polished and inlayed into the final product. There are several standard historical narratives of the Almohad period available. Each one, including the narrative work of Ibn Khaldūn, has often slight, but occasionally major, variations with other works regarding dates, events and personalities. If we imagine each history to be a cabinet for a specific customer, they all look similar from a distance. As one moves closer, however, the details, the filigree and idiosyncrasies of each craftsman begin to appear, even as the basic structure might seem quite similar. Sometimes almost all similarity is lost between the details. Ibn Khaldūn criticized the typical medieval historian, the historian who was more a craftsman than a philosopher. Yet, for all their 'errors and unfounded assumptions', they had deliberate historical or political reasons for making those assumptions.[206]

Overall, the basic structure of Islamic Almohad historical writing remained similar. As discussed at the beginning of this book, the main reason for this was that the creation of the Almohad historical myth occurred mainly in the context of Berber Almohad power. The root sources of the founding of the Almohads, the biography of al-Baydhaq, the *Mu'jib* of al-Marrākushī and the writings of Ibn al-Qaṭṭān were all written in a context that favoured the support of Berber power structures and the myth of the transformation of Berbers, once considered the least trained in Islam, as representatives of Islamic truths. All the sources, even those written under the Marinids, the rivals and successors of the Almohads, agree that the Almohads grew from a group of Berber mountain tribes.

As I shall discuss in Chapter 2, it was the Berber, North African, tribal context of Ibn Tūmart's message that the historical chronicles ultimately emphasized as the final basis of Ibn Tūamrt's support. These tribes were led by Ibn Tūmart, who claimed to be the Infallible imām and Mahdī. The main power behind Ibn Tūmart's claim was not his ancestry but the following of the tribes and the return to the sources of Islam. Unlike the Fatimids, who actively reconstructed history from the beginning of Islam to establish their main claim of legitimacy as descendants of the Prophet,[207] the focus of the Almohad revolution was more ideological than historical. The Almohads were creating a new Islamic community in the image of the original community of Muḥammad. The Berber tribes were not merely a means, as the Kutāma were for the Fatimids, but a core source of legitimacy and power behind and in support of Almohad doctrine. Almohad sources mentioned the descent of Ibn Tūmart, the founder of the Almohads, from the Prophet Muḥammad, but they did not dwell on it as the sole basis for his position.[208]

The way the histories of the encounter between the Mahdī and amir were written depended on each historian's context. The preconceptions and biases as well as the tribal and ethnic context of the primary source writers shaped the Almohads' history. Ibn 'Abī Zar', writing during the dynasty that defeated the Almohads, described Ibn Tūmart as sometimes petulant and unruly, but ultimately effective as a Berber tribal ruler. Al-Baydhaq described him as heroic and worthy. The chronicler may even have invented much of the encounter as a way of increasing Ibn Tūmart's status, emphasizing his power to command right and forbid wrong even against powerful rulers. Ibn Khaldūn used Ibn Tūmart to confirm his wider theories of history, tribe and religion.[209] This did not mean, however, that the history of this encounter was unreliable. If anything, the historians' contradictions and biases reveal the influence of the tribal, ethnic and religious forces on their writing. It was within the tribal milieu that Ibn Tūmart commanded right and forbade wrong against the Saharan tribes who formed the base of Almoravid power.[210]

Gender, Islam and Defining the Other

Gender often played a part in Ibn Tūmart's language of commanding right and forbidding wrong.[211] It was explicit during his encounter with 'Alī ibn Yūsuf.[212] The Almoravids were not simply breaking moral laws, they lived in a feminine state, an upside-down world in which men wore veils and women walked around uncovered. While the Almoravids only responded with feminized passivity, the one commanding right was masculine and active.

The Almoravid way of treating their women, which was probably based on traditional Saharan matriarchy,[213] was a particularly appalling and alien sight to him. The discrepancy between the Saharan and 'true' Islamic conception of women would present Ibn Tūmart with yet another opportunity to command right and forbid wrong in a political way. The Almoravid women's behaviour and haughtiness was, according to Almohad chronicles, further proof of the degeneration, immorality and heresy that needed to be extinguished.[214] Again, this was not simply a case of Ibn Tūmart commanding right and forbidding wrong. When he called the Almoravid prince a woman for wearing the veil, or insulted the amir's sister for riding high on her horse, he was proving the heretical nature of the Almoravid enemy.

The Lamtūna, like many Ṣanhāja confederations of the Sahara, were traditionally matriarchal tribes. In fact, the Tuareg, the present-day descendants of the Almoravid founding tribes, still follow matriarchal traditions despite the rise of modern Islamism in the African Sahara.[215] Unlike Arab women who gained status through adopting Islam, the rise of Islam in the Sahara forced women to give up many of their traditional privileges. Although a woman could no longer serve as the Almoravid ruler or expect to inherit the empire, Saharan matriarchal traditions remained, even in the heart of the empire at Marrakech. It was these traditions that Ibn Tūmart criticized. In his view, the Almoravids were weak because they did not follow true Islamic law. Allegedly blinded by legalistic Maliki texts and interpretations, the Almohad chroniclers of Ibn Tūmart made it appear as if they even allowed women like Sura to control the empire indirectly. If any more proof were needed in Ibn Tūmart's mind to demonstrate the supposedly feminine nature of the Almoravids it was that men wore the veil, a strong tribal custom rooted in Saharan identity. Women, by contrast, walked about freely with their hair uncovered so high and haughty it resembled Bactrian camel humps.[216]

Women were forced to surrender some of their traditional rights when the Almoravid Empire was formed and Islamic law superseded the old tribal customs. Nevertheless, many customs remained, including the practice of men, not women, wearing the veil. The male mouth veil was integral to the Almoravids' identity, culture and system of honour. In fact, most medieval chroniclers and geographers identified the Almoravid tribes as the *mulithāmūn* (the *lithām* or mouth-veil wearers).

Gender politics in twelfth-century North Africa was not confined to the clash between Islam and traditional beliefs. The Maṣmūda Berbers of the mountains, the founders of the Almohad movement, were largely patriarchal, whereas the Ṣanhāja nomadic herders were largely matriarchal. Yet both empires were Muslim; both achieved tribal unification; and both were revolutionary with radical pretensions to 'true Islam'.[217] There were fundamental geographic and cultural differences between the core tribal identities of the Almoravids and the Almohads.[218] One movement was started in the desert by a confederation of tribes, the other in the mountains. It was not Islam that separated these two empires: it was the way Islam was recreated, reshaped into a non-Arab phenomenon on the fringes of the Islamic world.

Defining the enemy with ethnic generalizations

The language of the Qur'ān and the *ḥadīth* was Arabic; and this applied not simply to the words, but also to the Arabs' culture, references and norms. It was for this reason that the study of Islamic sciences was called *ʿarabiyya*, literally 'Arab' studies in Arabic. Islam's early expansion and the invasion of Arab tribes led to the wide adoption of Arabic and Arab customs throughout most major cities and the Middle East. Some parts of the ostensibly 'Islamic' world, however, adopted Islam only as a superficial religious principle without implementing many of its cultural dictates, especially those coming from Arabia. This lack of exposure to Arab Islam was particularly pronounced among the nomadic desert and transhumant mountain tribes of North Africa.[219] Centuries after the dramatic conquest of the North African Berber Queen Kahina and the invasion of Uqba bin Nāfi in the seventh century, a majority of people in the Maghrib, especially south of the old Roman province of Mauritania Tigitania, still practised traditional beliefs, often with little or no knowledge of Islam.[220] Due to their geography, the tribes of the Atlas Mountains and the Sahara desert were both independent and proud. For these powerful tribes, Islam would have to be reinvented as a Ṣanhāja or Maṣmūda revolution, not simply an Arab one. Islam was in many ways a means to an end, namely to tribal unity.

The Almoravids had the idea first. They used Islam as the ideological framework for a massive trans-Saharan trading network that gave birth to cities like Marrakech from parched ground. Islam, not the tribe, was the new loyalty. The Almohads and the largely mountainous tribes, however, were not to be left out. Both Ibn Tūmart and the need to unify the tribes of the Atlas against a common enemy brought Islam to the tribes of the Atlas Mountains and turned early Almohad Islam into an ethnic struggle.[221] In their eyes the Almoravids were not real Muslims. In fact, they were almost worse than infidels because they corrupted the true religion. Ibn Tūmart called them 'worse than the Christians' and more deserving of *jihād*, in an address to the assembled Almohad tribes, he said: 'Apply yourselves in *jihād* against the veiled infidels for this is more important than combating the Christians and all the infidels twice or even more. In effect, they have attributed a corporal aspect to the Creator – May he be glorified! In rejecting *tawḥīd*, they have rebelled against truth itself!'[222]

Most of the time, commanding right and forbidding wrong was a simple, ordinary act, almost a civic duty performed by Muslims.[223] Yet, in the case of Ibn Tūmart, the objective was not simply commanding right and forbidding wrong, but defining right and wrong in revolutionary terms. Commanding right and forbidding wrong took on political, ethnic and even gendered tones. The Ibn Tūmart of the Almohad chronicles was not out to reform and improve Almoravid society. Rather, he used piety and commanding right as part of his language of revolution, unity and power. The alleged encounter with the Almoravid ruler and Ibn Tūmart, a masterful historical myth as portrayed by the Almohad historians, was more than an encounter between two rivals; it was an encounter between two different visions of Islam in two different cultural, geographic and ethnic contexts. It was the beginning of a conflict, not just about commanding right but also about defining right, defining morality and social norms, and hence, defining power. Despite inherent claims of universality, claims of the absolute unity of God, Islamic revolutions did not occur in a vacuum.

Almohad revolution developed in the intricate diverse political, ethnic and geographic landscape of the early twelfth century Maghrib.[224] It was in this varied landscape that Ibn Tūmart and his followers would reconcile belief, the demands of monotheism and obedience to the Mahdī, with identity, the demands of tribal loyalty and custom. In the next chapter I describe how Ibn Tūmart and his followers created a hierarchy, a systematic synthesis of tribes and religious institutions. This hierarchy allowed for this remarkable reconciliation of belief and identity, an army, and an effective government stretched across even the highest Atlas Mountain passes.

2

The Rise of the Almohads: The Tribal Roots of Monotheism

Abraham said, 'What are these images, to which you are so devoted?' They said, 'We found our fathers worshipping them.'

(Sūra, XXI: 52–3)

So when you have performed your devotions, then laud Allah as you lauded your fathers, rather a greater lauding.

(Sūra, II: 200)

And the brother shall deliver up the brother to death, and the father the child: and the children shall rise up against their parents, and cause them to be put to death.

(Matthew, 10:21)

THE ALMOHAD BOOK OF ANCESTRY

The Almohad revolution in the twelfth century Maghrib, built on the reconciliation of monotheism and Berber tribalism, established one of the largest and most influential empires in Islamic history. The most compelling primary source revealing the process by which tribalism was synthesized with the demands of monotheism, *tawḥīd*, was the *Kitāb al Ansāb* (Book of Ancestries).[1] The Book of Ancestries was instrumental in creating a founding historical myth, namely that Ibn Tūmart was able to accommodate both the religious demands of Islam and the power demands of the Berber tribes who accepted his call.

The *Kitāb al-Ansāb*, a compendium of early Almohad institutions and ancestries that confirmed and established the power of Atlas Mountain Berber tribes, opened with an apparent contradiction at the heart of the struggle between monotheism and tribalism. The text never, however, confronted the contradiction because it would have revealed a weakness in the construction of the Almohad historical myth as the foundation of allegedly pure Islamic principles among the Berber tribes. The treatise began with a list of reasons why the divisions of ancestry and blood should be abandoned. However, it ended with a long list of names and genealogies intended to bolster the power of the Almohad regime and hierarchy. Thus, while condemning ancestry and insisting on the universal application of belief, it also ironically revealed how the Almohads preserved and categorized ancestry.

The *Kitāb al-Ansāb* first invoked the 'arguments of the Book of God', the Qur'ān, against genealogy.[2] Both Arab and non-Arab, Atlas Mountains Berber and non-Atlas Berber, were hypothetically equal before God. (As other texts revealed, however, this was not actually the case.) Action and piety, not ancestry, were to determine one's place in heaven. As the *Kitāb al-Ansāb* revealed, Ibn Tūmart, like Muḥammad, wanted to preach a universal religion to humanity as a whole. At the same time he also constructed a hierarchy, a system that gave status according to a complex combination of tribal ancestry, politics and religious fervour.[3]

Ibn Tūmart implored his followers to reflect on the illustrious histories of pious people, like Abū Ṭalib the protector of the Prophet Muḥammad, who did good deeds but did not enter paradise. If genealogy were a guarantee, they would have entered the gates of heaven. According to Ibn Tūmart, the only use of genealogy was mutual recognition and identification. There should be only names, nothing else.[4] Yet, as Ibn Tūmart knew, ancestry was so much more important than he claimed. It was important to downplay divisive aspects of tribal identity, to make it more malleable, even as Ibn Tūmart and the Almohads used tribal identity and the Berber tribal system in their construction of the Almohad hierarchy. It was the manipulation of identities that led to the establishment of a new social paradigm even if that new paradigm (*tawḥīd*) used the building blocks (tribes) of the previous social model (segmentary society).[5] Abraham almost killed his son, but not really. Ibn Tūmart, like the Prophet Muḥammad, rejected ancestry formally but not in practice.

Muḥammad the Prophet was determined to integrate the Arab tribes fully into Islam, gaining not simply their traditional submission but also their individual souls. He wanted them to give up their ancestry and join the larger *umma* of Islam. In a strict sense Islam means to submit. However, the Prophet Muḥammad and religious revolutionaries like Ibn Tūmart wanted more than simple submission.[6] Muḥammad wanted to create a new community. In an ideal sense, he wanted that community to be open to the entire human race. The Qurʾān did not speak just to the Arabs or to the Muslims but to the whole of 'humankind' (*al-nās*) when it speaks of the universalism of God's judgement. Although Islam was defined as a universal religion, this did not mean that ancestry and tribal notions of lineage simply disappeared with its coming. On the contrary, these notions were simply reinvented to suit the new religious community. Genealogy was 'the accepted way of explaining pragmatically determined *tropus*, a structured framework to account for present reality.'[7]

So it was not surprising that immediately after an astonishing, idealistic appeal to the universal equality of humanity, the *Kitāb al-Ansāb* seemed to contradict its initial sentiment of genealogical equality before God. It was the apparent contradiction at the heart of monotheism; a rejection of ancestry even as it was embraced as

Figure 2.1: An ideal segmentary society expansion model

Each circle represents a field of loyalty and blood honour. Every step involves more allies and stricter disciplined agreements for the sharing of resources and the enforcing of justice. Monotheism/Tawḥīd is one more 'segmentary' circle, claiming to encompass the tribe, the 'brotherhood' of humanity.

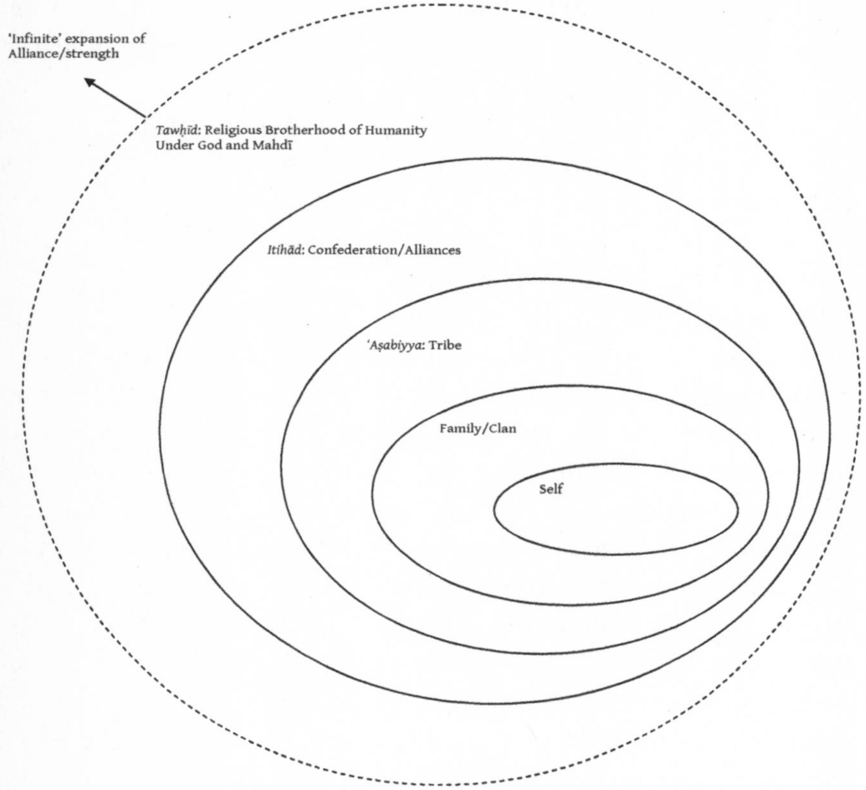

a pragmatic reality. The monotheistic imperative never really rejected ancestry to reject the father or son and embrace the will of God. Ancestry was only hypothetically subordinated to doctrine, to an eschatological ideal. The Almohad movement was not founded on an attempt to destroy tribal loyalty, but rather on an arrangement of those loyalties in a disciplined way, using native Berber tribal institutions.

The *Kitāb al-Ansāb* expressed a dual rejection and embrace of genealogy in a rapid and rather ironic shift. It spelt out the ancestry and genealogy of the Almohads right after arguing that genealogy was irrelevant. In truth, genealogy was not being rejected, but used for the formation of a new system – the Almohad hierarchy of Berber tribes.[8] Tribalism was a powerful part of forming monotheistic movements, so much so that it had to be reined in, made a part of the system.[9]

In fact, there was neither a wholesale rejection of tribal ancestry nor a wholesale embrace of pre-Islamic, Arab, or in the case of Ibn Tūmart, Berber traditions. Ibn Tūmart could not simply abandon tribalism for a pure and universal system of belief based on good works. Instead, he incorporated those aspects of the native Berber culture that would have the most popular appeal. At least in the way the Almohad sources portray him, Ibn Tūmart was not against Berber tribalism, he was against those aspects of tribalism and Berber culture that intrinsically supported the previous ruling elite. Despite the rhetoric at the beginning of the *Kitāb al-Ansāb*, Ibn Tūmart, like Muḥammad the Prophet, appeared in the Berber sources to appeal to the population at large, to co-opt the tribal elite when he could or to target them when he could not.[10] In doing so he had to compromise his absolute ideal of monotheism, of the irrelevance of genealogy, in order to appeal to the popular base. These subtle compromises were never admitted, they were simply folded into the new system.

The Almohads created a hierarchy by collapsing the tribal circles of loyalties, the segmentary system, into a pyramid social structure of loyalty to the Mahdī (see Figures 2.1–2.3).[11] The tribes were still the building blocks of that pyramid and maintained several powers.[12] The fact that Ibn Tūmart was able to accomplish the transformation of Berber society with remarkable speed and efficiency was testament to his charisma and the power of his doctrine. It was also a testament, according to the Almohad sources, to the effective use of pre-existing Berber institutions.[13] In a matter of years the Atlas Berbers were transformed from a segmentary society into a hierarchical society. The Berber *tamyīz* (the ordering of tribal confederations) the *mizwār* (allowing the enforcement of

Figure 2.2: A hypothetical representation of the complex state of pre-Almohad social loyalties

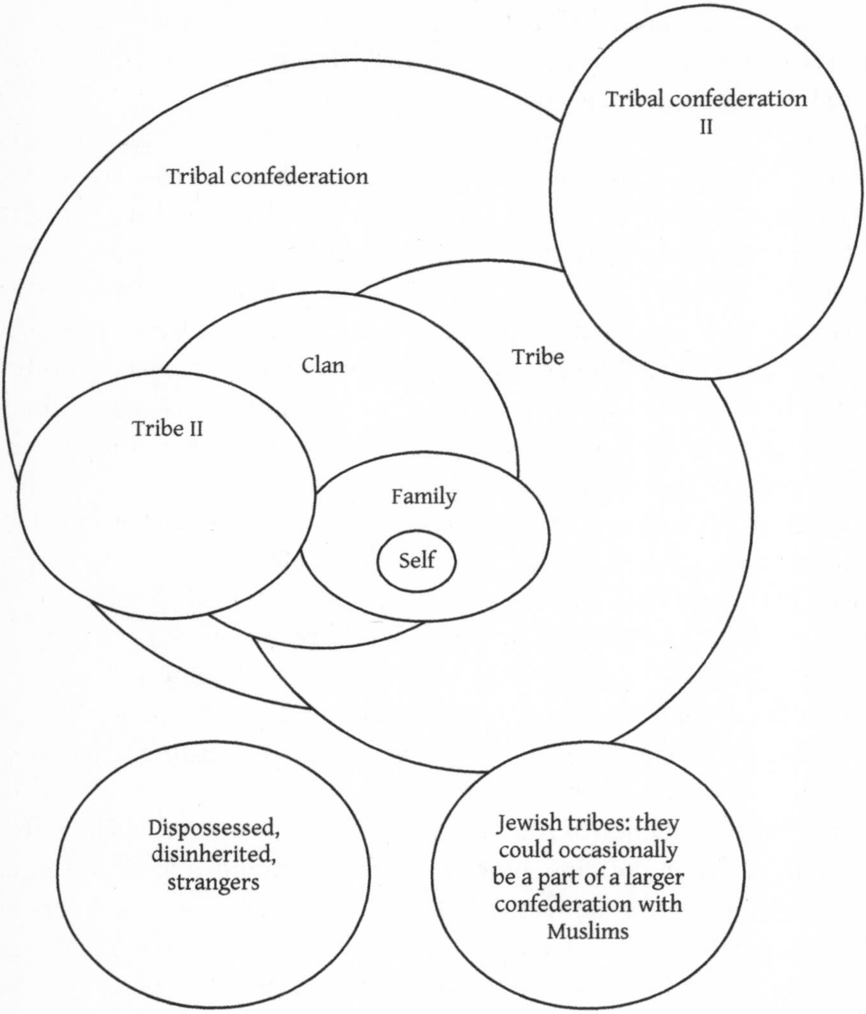

tribal rights), the *agrao* (the tribal council), the *āsmās* (a ceremonial meal to solidify 'new' blood relationships), in fact the entire segmentary system itself, based hypothetically on the absence of central control, was conducive to the rise of Almohad monotheism.

Figure 2.3: The Almohad social pyramid according to Ibn al-Qaṭṭān

Although, not all ranks on this pyramid were so equally divided, this diagram provides a generalized representation of the newly stratified nature of Atlas society under Ibn Tūmart.[1] A combination of tribal affiliation, good actions, prowess in *jihād*, obedience and proximity to the Mahdī determined rank in the community.

Above any rank and obeyed by all: the imām and Mahdī Ibn Tūmart

1. Council of ten
2. Council of fifty
3. Council of seventy
4. Ṭullāb
5. Memorizers: Ḥuffāẓ[2]
6. People of the house
7. Hargha (Ibn Tūmart's tribe)
8. Tīnmallal
9. Gadmīwa
10. Ganfīsa
11. Hintāta
12. People of the tribes: Hazmīr, Hīlāna, Hizraja[3]
13. The Soldiers
14. The Champions

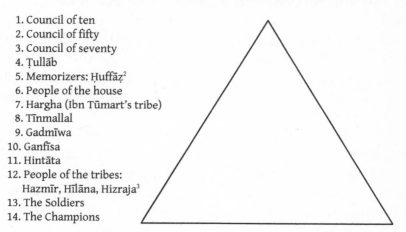

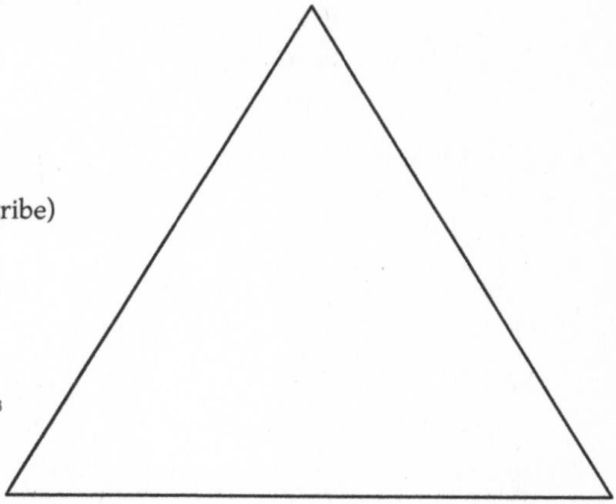

Notes:
1. For original list of 14 levels see Ibn al-Qaṭṭān, *Naẓm al*-Jumān, p. 28;
2. Memorizers of the Qur'an and the works of Ibn Tūmart.
3. These were various tribes around Marrakech.

A definition of segmentary tribal systems is required. The 'segmentary system' was an anthropological concept first expounded by Sir Edward Evans-Pritchard.[14] It is a simple, elegant, geometric theory that explains the relationship between members of a society governed purely by blood relations. According to this theory, concentric circles or orbits, each representing levels of loyalty and responsibility surround every individual.[15]

For example, if a close relative attacks an individual he need only call on closer relatives to defend his claim. If, however, a distant cousin attacked him, the clan or entire tribe might be mobilized (Figures 2.1 and 2.2). At the extreme, when there is an attack by distant strangers, he might call on the entire tribal confederation. These progressively larger circles of loyalty from family to clan, to tribe to confederation surround every individual in a segmentary tribal society (Figure 2.1). This regulates behaviour without the benefit of written rules. Yet it also risks the possibility of endless battles of honour between two equally matched circles of loyalty. As E. Gellner pointed out, 'The feud is a characteristic institution [of the segmentary system]: it means that the group of kinsmen are co-responsible for the conduct of any one of their number, sharing the risk of becoming objects of retaliation.'[16] It was because of the risk of feuding that alliances and the use of mediators between tribes, 'saints' as Gellner called them, *mizwārs* as they were called in the twelfth century, made sense.

Nevertheless, segmentary society was not always opposed to central, absolute, leadership. In the right circumstances it could actually be the basis for the development of a government, even of a new religious ideology: an ideology promising the end of the feud and the rise of a larger loyalty. This was especially possible when a large group of otherwise rival confederations and tribes were faced by a common enemy and were led by a charismatic leader. This was the case with the Almohad revolution.[17]

Ibn Tūmart used his influence over the tribes to create an even larger segmentary circle of loyalty. This circle would encompass all the tribes and all loyalties, eventually becoming the tribe of humanity itself, the circle of *tawḥīd* (Figures 2.1 and 2.2). Beginning from the confederation of tribes, Ibn Tūmart promised to create the ultimate alliance and the ultimate tribe – the brotherhood of humanity under God. Even the Almoravids, the worst enemies of the Almohads, could repent, be forgiven, and join this new encircling alliance. In his letter to the Almohads Ibn Tūmart said, 'If they respond to their invitation and return to the *sunna*, if they fight *jihād* against the infidels, leave them in peace, they are brothers in the religion of Allah, the *sunna* and the Prophet.'[18]

Yet, before establishing his universal tribe, Ibn Tūmart would have to defeat the Almoravids, a group that rose with similar claims to be the standard bearers of the *sunna*. To do so, he would need to use the strict hierarchy and discipline of the tribes, a discipline and system of local alliances that for centuries assured the peaceful movement of people between mountains and plains.[19] Thus, in both ideology and tactics Ibn Tūmart used pre-existing tribal structures to his advantage. The Almohad revolution was not an urban idea brought to the tribes; rather, it was a revolution at the heart of Berber culture.[20]

In using tribalism, the Almohad movement faced several challenges but also several opportunities. The segmentary system would transform rapidly, but not immediately, under the Almohad yoke. The endless blood feud between the Ūrīka and Hintāta tribes before the rise of the Almohads was an example of the divisive web of ancient honour. To confront the Almoravids, Ibn Tūmart had to resolve these ancient conflicts, reconstruct the web of relations and blood loyalties into a disciplined force, and unite them with a larger, religious sense of loyalty and unity. Thus, his main challenge was encircling a segmentary tribal system with *tawḥīd* or unity (see Table 2.1). His second challenge was to overcome the natural geographic isolationism of the Maṣmūda.[21] Just as the Alps divided Switzerland into cantons, the mountains of the Atlas divided tribes into independent, self-sustaining communities. For example, the Saksāwa Berbers were a remarkable, independent, self-sustaining community. The Saksāwa had an intellectual 'ruler chief', a mountaintop library, and successfully resisted all forms of taxation.[22] Ibn Tūmart needed to unify all this independent tribal spirit and warrior resistance and direct it towards one enemy: the Almoravids in Marrakech.

The Maṣmūda were already known for their fierce resistance to outside rule. During the Muslim conquests of North Africa, the Maṣmūda maintained a long war against ʿUqba ibn Nāfi[23] before adopting a form of Islam steeped in tribal traditions. They maintained their resistance against the rise of the desert tribes, the

Almoravids. The blue-veiled Almoravids built Marrakech near the High Atlas Mountains of the Maṣmūda to stop the 'audacious and endless raids' of the Maṣmūda.[24] Resistance, in the form of simple raiding, however, was never accomplished in a unified, systematic way. An individual tribe might rain down from the mountains to attack a settlement, a merchant caravan or even another Maṣmūda tribe. However, there was nothing very organized about these raids.

Ibn Tūmart needed to bring all the fierce and aggressively disunited tribes together. To do so, he would have to manipulate, but not completely abolish, the traditional 'segmentary system' of tribal society in the Atlas.[25] Ibn Tūmart did not wish to destroy the value of lineage and blood relations and replace it wholesale with strict monotheism. He was simply rearranging lineage and loyalty, creating a much more efficient and obedient society of tribes. He restructured and expanded and added flexibility to already existing Berber institutions to lay the foundations of empire.[26]

Integrating Tribal Traditions

The Almohads transformed tribal traditions into governing institutions using an ideology of disciplined monotheism represented in the person and authority of the Mahdī.[27] The *tamyīz*, traditionally a formalized process of forming alliances and organizing a confederation for war, the *āsmās*, a communal meal used to cement alliances, and the *agrao*, the tribal council, all became formalized Almohad institutions that were almost certainly adopted from existing tribal customs.[28] The Berber *agrao* was, and perhaps still is, the most important institution in the Atlas Mountain cantons, what Robert Montagne called *l'organisation républicaine*.[29]

Coming from the root m-y-z, to separate, *tamyīz* means distinction, distinguishing, segregation. The Almohad, Berber *tamyīz* described by al-Baydhaq involved the segregation and classification of the Almohad tribes. It generally meant the 'organization' or 'gathering' of the tribes but had several different meanings.[30] It could be a ceremony in preparation for battle, the ordering of different clans that had formed an alliance, or the killing of disloyal tribal members. Although used to describe the order of battle,[31] the *tamyīz* was more than that; it was the mechanism whereby tribes could maintain their identity while participating in a collective endeavour. The Berber tribes cemented alliances using *tamyīz*. The Almohad use of *tamyīz* to prepare for battle was an adoption of Berber custom. It was still being used with the same name in the 1920s when the mountain Berbers formed confederations of tribes to fight against common enemies.[32]

Traditional *tamyīz* usually involved lining up every tribe and tribal member into a specific hierarchy for the distribution of booty. *Tamyīz* could be used to adopt conquered peoples into the Almohad tribal order. New tribes were integrated into the hierarchy. This artificial extension of blood identity was sealed with a collective meal called the *āsmās*.[33] This ceremony made the adopted tribal member as much a member of the tribe as any other. The *āsmās* remains a living feature of Moroccan tribal life.[34] It is worth quoting Dale Eickelman's detailed description of the *āsmās*, a means of developing bonds between tribes that were not related through blood. He described the ritual forming of alliances between the Arabic speaking Wlād Khallū and the Berbers of the Aīt Bū Ḥaddū.[35]

> These alliances were concluded by different ritual means. In one case the groups involved had a communal meal, at the end of which all the men removed one of their slippers and placed them in a pile, one pile for each of the two groups. Slippers from the two piles were then matched at random. The men whose slippers were paired became companions with a special relation to each other. Whenever one needed permission for pasture rights or other matters, he approached his companion in the other group. In another case, the lactating women of the two contracting groups

> nursed the children of the opposite group after the men's communal meal. In a third case, the councils of the two groups had a communal meal in which the milk from lactating women of the two groups had been mixed in one of the plates, thus creating an enduring tie of milk brotherhood. Once such an alliance was concluded, any violation invited supernatural (as well as human) retribution.[36]

Eickelman described bilateral, horizontal pacts between tribes. The Almohads, however, used the *āsmās* not only to form alliances between individual tribes or to adopt new members into a tribe, but also to solidify loyalty to their system as a whole. Ibn Tūmart was proclaimed Mahdī during such an *āsmās*. Like the *tamyīz*, the *āsmās* was another example of how Ibn Tūmart used tribal traditions to legitimize his authority and organize the tribes around a hierarchy. Tribal identities were not static. They could be manipulated to meet the political and religious ends of the Almohad revolution. Ibn Tūmart and the Almohads not only adopted Berber tribal traditions, but they also refined them. They took these tribal forms to another level, the level of divine ideology. Thus, the communal meal, usually a simple means of solidifying alliances, became symbolic of the formation of Almohad ideology, the authority of Ibn Tūmart as Mahdī and the light and even the coming end of time.[37] Other tribal institutions and practices would undergo a similar transformation. What were once informal, unwritten tribal institutions and traditions became the formalized, written institutions of the empire.

The *tamyīz* allowed for the extension of Almohad tribal identities to occur in a systematic way. Several tribes, like the Haskūra and the Gūmiya, were simply 'entered into the *tamyīz*'.[38] Several individuals, even whole clans like the Inda Ou Zal, the Ida Ou Nadif or the Ida Ou Zekri were adopted as honorary Hargha or Tīnmallal.[39]

Like the *āsmās*, the *tamyīz* tribal tradition was transformed and expanded by the Almohads to take on a symbolic, ideological justification. The *tamyīz* would not mean the formation of alliances in the traditional sense of horizontal, bilateral loyalties; it would mean loyalty to a central ideology.

The Almohads seemed to have transformed the traditional process called *tamyīz* to cull and kill disloyal tribal members who did not submit to this ideology.[40] Often these were the older members of the tribe, chiefs who were against the new order or anybody suspected of disloyalty. Al-Baydhaq witnessed this form of *tamyīz* and provided an account in his memoirs. It is worth quoting him at length. Again, it should be remembered that al-Baydhaq was a close confidant of Ibn Tūmart and a loyal Almohad.

> A number of days passed and God gratified the Mahdī with the counsels of al-Bashīr.[41] He ordered the *tamyīz*. Al-Bashīr excluded all those Almohads who were dissidents, hypocrites or knaves such that the perfidious were separated from the good. The people thus saw the truth with their eyes and the believers redoubled their faith. ... The culling organized by al-Bashīr went on from Thursday to Friday forty days later. The people of five tribes were killed during this period at a place called Īgar-an-ūsannān where the Īsalayīn-an-uh-nā'in perished. Among the Hintāta, the Īmattazgā were killed. The Īn Mājūs were executed at a place called Īgar-an-Aīt Kūriyīt, as were the Āṣaddan and the Gadmīwa of Tākūsht. After this al-Bashīr called the loyal followers into review for an expedition[42] under the benediction of Allah.

The *Kitāb al-Ansāb* described how the blood *tamyīz* began after the dream of a companion of the Mahdī, Sheikh ʿUbaid Allah al-Haskūri,[43] a member of the council of fifty. The devil appeared to him and threatened to break the loyalty of the tribes to the Mahdī. From this strange dream the bloody form of *tamyīz* was justified.[44] The *tamyīz* and the enforcement of the *tamyīz* was a way of maintaining discipline and the strict hierarchy needed for military operations, even as it was founded on separate tribal identities. The *tamyīz* of al-Bashīr created a social transformation of Atlas society, pitting the generations against each other. According to the Andalusian writer Ibn Khallikān, most of those killed in the *tamyīz* were from the older generation. The old chiefs were 'afraid of the vengeance of the Almohads while the young and ambitious embraced the cause of the Mahdī'.[45] Yet it was not simply the Berber traditions of agrao, tamyīz and āsmās that were integrated into the Almohad system, it was the tribes themselves that became levels, institutions of Almohad government.

The Almohad Tribes

Modern historians have not described the Almohad tribes in any systematic way.[46] In this chapter I shall describe them as if one were passing in review along the row of tribes before battle. The tribes were transformed into levels of the Almohad hierarchy (Figure 2.3) and several of them remain so to this day. Others have changed their name, no longer exist or are severely weakened. The ties and prestige of kinship are never concrete or immutable.[47]

In his epic work on Berber genealogy, Ibn Khaldūn divided the Berbers of the Maghrib into three confederations – the Ṣanhāja of the desert, the Zanāta of the plains and the Maṣmūda of the mountains. This has become the commonly used, but artificial, categorization of the Berbers. Each group seemed to be divided by different economic, social and territorial conditions, and each played a major role as rulers of the Maghrib at various periods in history. Ibn Khaldūn explained how each of these groups had a common, mythical ancestor.[48] Although it was unclear how much loyalty or self-identification was associated with the Maṣmūda label, most of the tribes described below were at least nominally members of its confederation long before the beginning of the Almohad movement. Even so, Ṣanhāja were also represented in the Almohad system, as were the Zanāta – especially the Kūmya tribe of 'Abd al-Mu'min. The Berber dialect the Almohads used was some sort of combination of the modern Chleuh (Maṣmūda) and Saharan Ṣanhāja dialects.[49]

Although a majority of the Almohad tribes were Maṣmūda, not all were, nor were the tribes even uniformly Berber speaking. Below are descriptions of the particularities and remarkable diversity of each of the major Almohad tribes. Indeed, in the view of the Mahdī and the Almohad leadership, the Maṣmūda, Berber or Arab aspects of these tribes were no longer particularly important. What mattered were their loyalty to the Almohad cause, the order in which each tribe joined the movement and the resources each tribe had available.[50]

Before describing the main factions of the Almohad tribes, an important explanation of terminology should be made. The common way of introducing tribes in Berber was *Aīt*. In Arabic the word was *Banū*. Generally speaking, tribes carrying the label *Aīt* were Berber, and those with that of *Banū* were Arab. However, as tribal factions exemplified, many, if not most, tribal factions were simultaneously labelled Banū and Aīt. Just as Ibn Tūmart had both the genealogy of a Berber chief and an Arab *sharif* descended from Fatima, so too did many tribes have dual Berber and Arab identities. Referring again to the definition of tribe used for this book, this was further proof of the prevalence of the intermingled and imagined tribal ancestries, as described both by the modern anthropologist Jacques Berque and the historian Ibn Khaldūn.

The Hargha

The Mahdī Ibn Tūmart was born into the Maṣmūda Hargha tribe. The most loyal to the Mahdī, they were also the most devastated by the Almohads' many wars and expeditions. The small village of Igīlīz fairly near the Wādī Sūs was the fortified village of the Hargha and birthplace of the Mahdī.[51] They were not a very strong tribe except under the leadership of their charismatic kinsman, the Mahdī.[52] In fact, it was because of their relative weakness that the appeal of Ibn Tūmart's reforms of the traditional tribal hierarchy and the domination of surrounding tribes was so strong. Indeed, during the early Almohad period the Hargha went from being a slightly marginal tribe to becoming the elite at the height of empire.[53]

Despite weak beginnings, the Hargha tribe had an important role in the development of the Almohad hierarchy. At a great *tamyīz*, the Mahdī called the Hargha forward 'from among the other tribes, because they had a higher rank than the rest and they were the *anṣār*, the defenders of the Mahdī'. The Mahdī passed them in review 'faction by faction, clan by clan, the one after the other in the order in which they were named'.[54] Then their 'adopted brothers', members of other tribes who became honorary Hargha, were attached to each faction. Thus, Ibn Tūmart used his own tribal identity to cement the loyalty of his closest followers, inventing ties of blood and ancestry in the method described by Ibn Khaldūn.[55] The Hargha tribe became a model, a corps of honour. Thus, the story was told that when an envoy of the Hintāta tribe to the Hargha returned home, he said 'Oh Hintāta! The light is with the Hargha and you are all in shadows.' The Hintāta joined the Hargha in fealty with a communal meal.[56]

'Abd al-Mu'min was the most famous of the adopted Hargha before he became caliph and transported his own tribe, the Kūmya to Marrakech. He was a loyal, politically astute man directly below the Mahdī.[57] He was 'joined in the lines of fraternity'[58] and was invited to their communal feasts. Next was the Sheikh Abū 'Abd Allah Muḥammad bin Muhsin who was a part of the Mahdī's closest entourage. Sheikh Abū Zakarīyā, another honorary Hargha, was a propagandist of the Almohad cause.[59] The Mahdī made him a prayer leader. He was also a lieutenant of the famed general Abū Muḥammad al-Bashīr. He fought at the great battle of al-Buḥaīra against the Almoravids. On the day of battle 'an arrow pierced his eye while he was calling the prayer. He did not interrupt his call and continued until the end.'[60] Sheikh Ibrāhīm al-Hazmīrī and Sheikh Abū 'Īsā al-Guzūli, both members of the council of fifty were similarly made Hargha. Sheikh 'Abd al-Mālik bin Yaḥyā resided at

Igīlīz, in the *ribāṭ* of the Hargha, he remained there a hermit, 'always devoted until his death of sickness'. Yaḥyā al-Ṣanhājī was Ibn Tūmart's scribe. He worked with the Mahdī's secretary Sulaimān Āḥaḍrī and was probably involved in the actual writing of the Book of Ibn Tūmart, the doctrine and the praise poetry of the Almohads. 'He was eloquent and quickly learned new languages: he wrote in Syriac and in secret characters.'[61] The text also notes that his descendants were given title to land. His second son was the secretary to the caliph Ya'qūb al-Mansūr (d. 1199). Finally, there was Abī Bakr al-Dara'ī, a member of the council of fifty.

All these supporters of Ibn Tūmart, his inner cadre, were adopted into his family and line of blood. Originally outsiders, the Mahdī could trust them as close advisers and leaders. There were several motives behind the Mahdī's adoption of these loyal outsiders as members of his tribe. First, they may not have been as accepted by the other, great Maṣmūda tribes, like the Hintāta, unless they became fully one of them, part of the larger tribal confederation of the Maṣmūda and the high Atlas Mountains. Second, the Hargha had become more than simply a tribe; it had become the *Anṣar* of the Mahdī, bound to his blood and brotherhood. They were the first tribe, the first people to convert to the cause, to witness his emergence from the cave after three years of meditating. The Hargha could not remain a mere collection of blood relations; they had to become an institution, composing the upper hierarchy of the nascent Almohad state. There was no indication that these men of adopted blood were of lower status than those Hargha by birth. If anything, they had more power.

The Mahdī arranged the factions of the Hargha, like the factions of all other Almohad tribes, not only for military review but also for distributing the spoils of battle.[62] Some otherwise independent clans were conveniently integrated into this spoils system. For example, the Gudāna, otherwise a separate clan, was placed with the Banū Aīt Ḥamza for the distribution of spoils.[63] More than many other methods of control, the distribution of booty according to clan indicated Ibn Tūmart's desire not to destroy the tribal structure of clans and factions completely but to use it for larger ends. Just as each tribe was ranked according to its closeness to the Mahdī and the time since it had joined the movement, each clan was rewarded according to contributions to battle, status and prowess. The other Hargha factions were as follows: the Banū (Aīt) Tārīkt, these were the 'sons of the Sheikh',[64] Banū (Aīt) Zagzāla, Banū (Aīt) Makzāran, the Banū (Aīt) Wānnāmmar, who were found with the Banū (Aīt) Mallūl during the distribution of booty, Banū (Aīt) al-Malla, Banū (Aīt) Wāggānt, Banū (Aīt) Tashtūlīz, Banū (Aīt) Īkmītīs, Banū (Aīt) Mazākat, Banū (Aīt) Tūwīdāg, Banū (Aīt) Īdīkal, and the Banū (Aīt) Yūsuf who formed an independent group.

Interestingly, in addition to the individual adopted into the Hargha, there were also entire clans, from the Hargha region, but not strictly Hargha, who 'joined in the review' and the distribution of booty with the Hargha. This was another indication of Ibn Tūmart's ability to manipulate ancestry deftly, especially his own ancestry, to secure loyal alliances. These allied clans were the Banū Ūnīṭīf,[65] Banū (Īdā) Ūlīmīt, the Banū (Īdā) Ūfīnīs, the Īnad Wazāl (Īndāwazāl) the Banū (Īndā) Zaddūt the Banū (Aīt) Ūnīṣī, the Banū (Īdā) Zakarīyā, the Banū (Aīt) Tīn Ṣiddīq and the Banū (Aīt) ʿĪsā.[66]

The Ahl Tīnmallal

With the exception of the Hargha, the Ahl Tīnmallal had the highest zeal for the Mahdī; their centre was the fortified village of Tīnmallal, which was where the military organization of the Almohad movement began. The Ahl Tīnmallal would also be among the last of the Almohads to survive. If the *ribāṭ* of Igīlīz was the Mahdī's Mecca, then Tīnmallal was his Medina.

In his work on Almohad hierarchy, J. Hopkins espoused the theory that the Ahl Tīnmallal were not strictly a tribe at all. As they had no natural tribal loyalty of their own, they were automatically loyal to the Mahdī and the Almohad system.[67] Ibn al-Marrākushī mentioned in the *Muʿjib* that the Ahl Tīnmallal only had their place of living in common.[68] Unlike the other main Almohad groups, the Ahl Tīnmallal were not united by blood but by a vague sense of common loyalty, a common territorial identity. The Ahl Tīnmallal lacked the 'mythical genealogy' aspect of the previously mentioned definition of a 'tribe'. Further evidence of their non-tribal status was their name, *Ahl*, Arabic for 'people', instead of *Aīt*, Berber for 'tribe'. This did not make them sophisticated urban dwellers. They were most likely a type of proto-tribe, just beginning to develop a common tribal identity, when Ibn Tūmart appeared in their ranks and gave them an advanced doctrine, a purpose, to unite. The Ahl Tīnmallal gave Ibn Tūmart little, if any, resistance. He offered the Ahl Tīnmallal the opportunity to rise above the proud and close-knit neighbouring tribes. Only the Hargha would have a higher status. In fact, they formed the largest representation in the council of fifty (Table 2.1).

Table 2.1: Division of the council of fifty according to tribal affiliation

Tīnmallal	14	19
Famous Men of Various Tribes[1]	9	
Hargha	6	8
Hintāta	3	2
Gadmīwa	2	4
Ganfīsa	4	4
The tribes[2]	1	1
Haskūra	3	4
Ṣanhāja	3	
The champions[3]	5	5
	Ibn al-Qaṭṭān[4]	*Kitāb al-Ansāb*

Notes:

1. Men of standing who complete the 50.
2. Presumably this refers to the other tribes around Marrakech.
3. Al-Baydhaq does not mention them as part of the 50.
4. The sources disagree: thus the reason for different columns. The *Kitāb al-Ansāb* differs from Ibn al-Qaṭṭān over the exact number from each tribe. Possibly they represented different years or tenure.

The Ahl Tīnmallal were divided into 11 factions, which came from diverse geographic origins. Like Hopkins, Lévi-Provençal believed that their factional nature revealed their 'heterogeneity'. He was convinced that they were a type of random collection of 'partisans brought together to strengthen the *makhzen*: the central control. Their origins were not the pure Almohad tribes'.[69] Far from discouraging tribalism, Ibn Tūmart invented a tribe. He collected these small factions and individuals from random places under the name of Ahl Tīnmallal. They become a central corps, among the most loyal of the Almohads. The Ahl Tīnmallal could be viewed as a smaller example of a wider Almohad project of unification, of creating a 'people', a 'super tribe'. The Ahl Tīnmallal were not classically segmented according to ancestral loyalty.

Listed first among the Ahl Tīnmallal factions were the famed Masakkāla or Aumaskālan. This was the faction of Ibn Tūmart's mother.[70] Today they live on the plain of *Dīr* to the east of the Wādī Raghāya, north of the Ūrīka. Next were the Banū Wartānag, the Banū (or Aīt) Almās, the Saktāna,[71] the Banū (or Aīt) Wāwāzgīt,[72] the Banū (or Aīt) Ānsā, the people (Ahl or Aīt) of Tifnaut,[73] the Ahl (or Aīt) al-Qabila,[74] the Ahl Tadrārt, the Ṣanhāja of the Īṣnāgan group and the Ahl of the Sūs valley.

The geographic position of the Ahl Tīnmallal on a busy trading route may explain their proto-tribe nature. They exercised control of commerce and trade coming over the important Tizi-n-Test pass to Marrakech and the Atlantic. They also held the expansive, green valley of the Wādī Naffīs. Due to these geographic advantages and the legendary warrior strength of the Ahl Tīnmallal, it was little wonder that the Mahdī decided on Tīnmallal as the original political seat of his new movement, instead of his exposed birthplace at Igīlīz. From Tīnmallal the Almohads could manipulate, or even strangle, the traffic coming from Tarūdant and the south into Almoravid Marrakech. Surrounded by high mountains with only a few possible entrances, the valley formed a natural fortress, easily defended from Almoravid incursions; the only two passes into Tīnmallal from the east and west were treacherous and narrow; it was often necessary to dismount from one's horse and donkey to enter the valley. There was no need for the Almohads to build a sophisticated system of defences. Even so, they constructed a series of solid walls around the city. As added security, Ibn Tūmart also built the *Būrj Tidāf*, a tower high in the mountains where he put a sentinel with a drum who was charged to give prior warning of an Almoravid attack.[75] A century later, the remnants of the Almohads would spend their last decades holed up in this natural fortress of Tīnmallal, a small island repelling the changing tides of history.

Writing in the late fourteenth century, long after the Almohads had lost all political power, Ibn Khaldūn knew that the Tīnmallal still venerated the tomb of the Mahdī. Conceived by the Mahdī as a people, as a type of super-honorary tribe, this was but one sign of their fierce loyalty to the Almohad cause.[76]

The Hintāta

Down the Wādī Naffīs and Wādī Raghāya, on the foothills of the Atlas Mountains, the Hintāta were in an ideal position to intimidate Marrakech and the plains. From Marrakech, their lands could be seen rising dauntingly up the Atlas mountain range, peering down on the city. They were the largest and most powerful of the Maṣmūda tribes. As well as access to the plains near Marrakech and control of the trading routes after Tīnmallal, they had several geographic advantages. Their foothills and low mountains provided fortified depressions with rich soil. Closest to Marrakech and the plains the Hintāta were the most settled and sophisticated of the Maṣmūda. Although often partially controlled by the central authority in Marrakech, the Hintāta naturally had their own independent political ambitions. As a result, they adapted well to the Almohad revolution securing high positions of power in the empire.

Abū Ḥafṣ ʿUmar ibn Yaḥyā was from the Hintāta. His descendants founded the Ḥafṣid dynasty in Tunisia, which was originally a part of the Almohad Empire. As Abū Ḥafṣ was a leader of the richest tribe, Ibn Tūmart wisely chose him as one of his closest deputies. Other Hintāta chiefs would also play an important role in the Marinid period immediately after the Almohads.

There were nine factions among the Hintāta. These factions were much less geographically diverse than those of the Ahl Tīnmallal.[77] Unlike the Ahl Tīnmallal who are listed with their place of origin, the *Kitāb al-Ansāb* grouped the Hintāta geographically in generally the same location.[78] Again, like the Ahl Tīnmallal, the book lists them with both the Berber Aīt and Arabic Banū. They were the Banū (Aīt) Talwūh-rīt, the Banū (Aīt) Tāgurtant, the Banū (Aīt) Tūmsīdīn, the Banū (Aīt) Lamazdūr, the Banū (Aīt) Galgā'iya[79] and the Mazāla who were allies of the Hintāta, the Banū (Aīt) Wāwāzgit, the Banū (Aīt) Yīgaz and the Banū (Aīt) Taklāwwūh-tīn.

The Gadmīwa[80]

The Gadmīwa inhabited the Wādī Naffīs and the Āssīf al-Māl valley between the Hintāta and the Tīnmallal. During the Almohad period the family of S'ad Allah ruled them. There were two fortress villages, Tafargha and Tisakht, around Gadmīwa mountain. These fortresses served the Gadmīwa well against incursions. In modern times, tribes of the same name still exist in the valleys to the west of Wādī Naffīs.

Presumably, the Gadmīwa was a fairly large confederation because the *Kitāb al-Ansāb* listed 46 separate factions, 'each with its own *mizwār*'.[81] The *mizwār*, in the Berber context, was a type of chief, a moderator of disputes, an officer or an all-purpose authority figure. Hopkins seemed to assume that the *mizwār* was imposed on each group of the Gadmīwa with 'the authority delegated to him by the central government'.[82] However, there was no direct evidence of this being the case. More likely, the *mizwār* was already an institution of the Gadmīwa and possibly of most of the other tribes of the Atlas Mountains at the time. The *mizwār* maintained the identity, order and discipline of each subtribe or clan by wielding his special *baraka* or blessing.[83] He enforced the careful balance between grazing and agricultural rights. Some larger clans had more than one *mizwār* according to size. They seemed to be yet another example of a tribal tradition that Ibn Tūmart used to organize the Almohads.

Figure 2.4: The Gadmīwa context

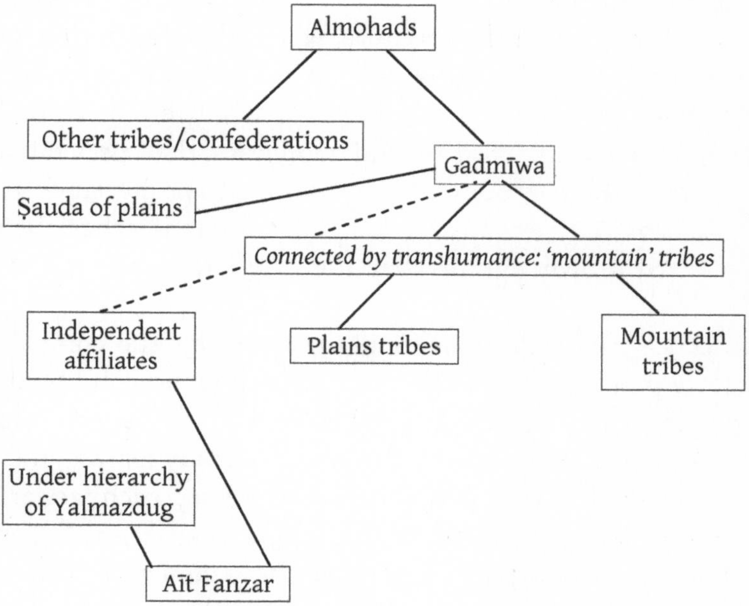

The Gadmīwa tribal confederation was in itself a remarkable feat of unity, a complicated collection of subtribes, allies and relations. They were roughly divided between the tribes 'of the mountain', the Banū Gartīt or Īnad Gartīt,[84] and the Gadmīwa of the plains (*al-faḥṣ*). There were also semi-independent tribes in the confederation like the Aīt Fanzar, who were under the hierarchy of the Banū Yalmazdug 'for purposes of distributing booty and in other circumstances'. The Banū Yalmazdug 'shared spring pasturage'

with one of the large factions of the Gadmīwa, the Māgūs (Īn Māgūs).[85] This sharing of spring pastures was an essential element of the tribal alliance. As is the case today, a complex system of unwritten rules over who could use the mountain pastures and when, was set up to prevent unnecessary conflict. A strong alliance would also prevent the invasion of prime pastureland by a stronger or larger tribe.[86]

The sources also mentioned tribes that 'emigrated to the Gadmīwa land'. These included Zanāta, not even part of the Maṣmūda confederation. From the evidence provided by the *Kitāb al-Ansāb*, it seemed that the Gadmīwa were a confederation of numerous transhumant tribes who moved between the plains and the mountains. The confederation may have been a mutual alliance between plains, pasture and mountain that prevented conflict between these groups as they moved their livestock in seasonal patterns. There were several other factions other than the 46 with their own *mizwār* that the *Kitāb al-Ansāb* did not mention.[87]

As with other tribes, Ibn Tūmart did not arrange the complex structure of alliances that suited Gadmīwa economic conditions. Rather, he took advantage of already existing alliances and integrated the Gadmīwa tribal structure, as it already existed, into his new order. To symbolize this, Ibn Tūmart passed each faction, sub faction and tribe in review during military exercises.[88] The *Kitāb al-Ansāb* spelled out the factions of the Gadmīwa in order, according to who was first in Ibn Tūmart's 'review' of the tribes and who was first to receive the spoils of war.[89]

The Ūrīka

Before the rise of Ibn Tūmart and the Almohads, the Ūrīka were the great rivals of the Hintāta. Like the Hintāta, they had control over an important river valley formed by the Wādī Ūrīka. They also had ambitions for power in the region as they laid claim to Āghmāt, the main trading town of the Atlas Mountains. The beautiful Ūrīka valleys still bear the name of this tribe. They inhabited a region to the north and east of the Hintāta. Ibn Khaldūn described the blood feuds between these two great Maṣmūda tribes, 'For ages these two peoples were at war, war in which much blood was spilt (in vain). Each party claimed victory alternatively. Many died until the Hintāta were invested as the tribe in command. They killed their adversaries *en masse*, with vengeance.'[90]

Ibn Khaldūn referred to the power the Hintāta gained during Ibn Tūmart's rise, as well as to the later Marinid period when the Hintāta also gained influence. The Hintāta took advantage of the Almohad movement to attempt an extermination of their traditional rivals. If so, Ibn Tūmart may have tacitly allowed this killing to gain the loyalty of the Hintāta, the marginally stronger of the two rivals. It was reasonable to believe that the Ūrīka were much less successful than most of their neighbours in securing the benefits of Almohad expansion. They may have simply been unlucky; the Hintāta found Ibn Tūmart first, the Ūrīka could not produce a reformer of similar stature and success.

Many Ūrīka were allied to, or at least sympathetic to the Almoravid cause.[91] They controlled a rich and prosperous region that supplied the capital city with produce and received the trade from Sijilmāsa. There may have been more to this feud between the Hintāta and the Ūrīka than ancient honour. The Almohad doctrine that Ibn Tūmart propagated would have been an ideal way for the Hintāta to outflank the Ūrīka by challenging the legitimacy of Almoravid ideology. It was not by chance that the Hintāta were among the first to join Ibn Tūmart.

The Ganfīsa (Saksāwa)

The Ganfīsa were the furthest west of the Maṣmūda tribes. They inhabited the Arella mountain pass southwest of Tizi-n-Test. Ibn Khaldūn had high praise for the fortitude of the Saksāwa, the main faction of the Ganfīsa. As the Almohads gained power, other

Maṣmūda tribes lost their tribal warrior spirit and fell into the decadence of settled, civilized life, but the Saksāwa maintained a high level of power and spirit. They dominated neighbouring tribes. 'Loving the advantages of the aggressive life, they never adopted the habits of luxury introduced among the other Almohad tribes; they never ceded to seductions.'[92]

Their fortitude was expressed in their geography. Their mountains were the highest and their forts inviolable. In a poetic flourish reserved for the Saksāwa Ibn Khaldūn said:

> Their geography personifies the virtue of independence ... their mountain escarpment touches the vault of heaven, hidden in a veil of clouds, its head crowned with stars. Its bosom serves as a retreat for storms; its ears hear the discourse of heaven, its face dominates the ocean, its back serves as the support for the desert of Sūs, and in its groin reposes the other mountains of Daran.[93]

The brave and knowledgeable Haddū bin Yūsuf was their chief during the Almohad period. Even as the Saksāwa joined the Almohads and followed the doctrine of unity, they never fully relinquished their legendary independence. The Saksāwa must have especially welcomed Ibn Tūmart's offer to abolish taxes for the Maṣmūda. Indeed, long after the fall of the Almohads, the Saksāwa stubbornly resisted the incursions of Marinid tax collectors.

For a remote, non-urbanized tribe, the Saksāwa were remarkably sophisticated. From his isolated tribal kingdom, 'Umar Ugallid (Ugallid means king in Berber), the son of Haddū, built a mountaintop library of law and poetry.[94] He even knew the sacred books of the Jews. He also dabbled in alchemy and white magic.[95] Learning was not absent from the isolated mountain tribes, especially among their elite. Ibn Tūmart was educated in the Atlas Mountains during his early childhood. This contradicted the classic view of Gellner that cities were the only places for education and learning.[96] Writing was not simply an 'urban' phenomenon. In fact, the cities were full of chaos and political intrigue that could prevent scholarship. Ibn Khaldūn himself wrote his *Kitāb al-ʿIbār* under the protection of a tribe in Tunisia. The tribes needed only the simple tools of writing, pen and paper. Pens and paper were not so difficult to trade or transport. The anthropologist Jacques Berque provided several examples of a rich, thriving native literature still alive among the Saksāwa in 1955. 'This society is in love with writing.'[97] Books were regularly transported across great distances, often on camels and donkeys, thus exposing even the most isolated tribal chiefs to written knowledge. Each major Saksāwa family probably had an archive, as it does today. 'It is rare to find somebody who does not have a collection of old papers in a leather bottle or even a large box. Every roll was a volume. ... In this dry climate the preservation was almost indefinite.'[98]

During Almohad times the Ganfīsa were allied with several smaller factions. Collectively they called themselves Ganfīsa after a geographic point, a mountain still called Ganfīs at the source of the Wādī Āgbār, or simply after their dominant clan, the Saksāwa.[99] Some of the Ganfīsa tribes did not seem to have a dual Arab-Berber identity like most Almohad tribes. They probably saw themselves as completely non-Arab. For instance, the Saksāwa were not called Banū in the *Kitāb al-Ansāb* but simply Saksāwa or the Berber Īsaksāwan. This was also true for several of the other 22 factions of Ganfīsa: the Zuddāga or Īdā wa-Zaddāg, the Mantāka, the Madlāwa, the Hassāna, and the Maṣgāla or Īn Maṣgālat. Some factions were called both the Arab Banū and the Berber Īn or Aīt including the Banū/Īdā Maṣāḍḍuāgag.[100] There were also those more loosely associated with the Ganfīsa, those who simply emigrated with them from plains to mountain. In this regard, the Ganfīsa were rather like the Gadmīwa, a collection of transhumant tribes who followed a similar route for mountain pasturage. This was excepting the fact that while the Gadmīwa were split into plains and mountain tribes, the Saksāwa was a much more dominant, core clan with an almost kingly chief who inherited his position as leader.

The Saksāwa remained a major mountain tribe in the High Atlas. The French anthropologist Jacques Berque wrote a classic study of them in 1955.[101] Much had changed in the Maghrib between the Almohad and modern periods but the Saksāwa remained fairly isolated.[102] Saksāwa migration patterns were somewhat disrupted under the Marinids, who fought against them and built a fortress at al-Qāhira in 1358. Later dynasties attempted, unsuccessfully, to control them.[103] Due to their strength and isolation, their basic movement patterns and social structures probably remained more or less unaltered even by 1955.

Although the Saksāwa were divided into semi-settled tribes of the mountains or plains, which often seemed isolated, mountain and plain were connected in innumerable ways. As Jacques Berque remarked, 'The rapport of the plain and the mountain could not be reduced to a simple dialogue. There were possibly a thousand connections between the two partners.' For instance, among the most important goods for the mountain people was salt, which the plains tribes could provide. The Saksāwa mountain was deprived of any salt deposits. The tribe also had to negotiate a way of sharing water resources, creating a network of surveillance and enforcement to ensure fairness. The important activity that united mountain and plains was the transhumant passage of mobile Saksāwa clans from the plains in the winter to the mountains in spring.[104] Most Saksāwa were not always nomadic or always sedentary.[105] Jacques Berque claimed that through a complex system of mutual regulation, shared sustenance and communal law, the Saksāwa successfully avoided one of the most difficult social problems: 'the rapport between the agricultural labourer and the pastoral migrant, a problem in almost all Semitic societies that was without a doubt the conflict between Cain and Abel'.[106] If Berque's thesis was true and if several of the social institutions of the Atlas Berbers have remained intact since Almohad times, the Ganfīsa, and other great tribal confederations like the Gadmīwa, existed mainly to prevent such conflict. Joining the Almohad cause would strengthen and expand their existing system of alliances.

The Kūmya

The Kūmya inhabited the maritime coast of present-day Algeria, around Tlemsan, far from the Atlas mountains and the heart of the Almohad movement. Most importantly, however, ʿAbd al-Muʾmin, Ibn Tūmart's successor, came from the Kūmya tribe. Ibn Khaldūn described them as 'formidable in number and in bravery. They were the strongest of the Almohad tribes.' Ibn Tūmart made a good strategic choice when he recruited ʿAbd al-Muʾmin from the Kūmya. He was from the Banū Abid, the most distinguished family of this powerful tribe. The future caliph was born in the fortress at Tagrart from where his family enjoyed considerable powers.[107]

The Almohad Hierarchy

Despite being published as long ago as 1958, one of the most comprehensive descriptions of the structure of Almohad hierarchy remains J. Hopkins's *Medieval Muslim government in Barbary.* Although he used nearly all known primary sources on the Almohad *ṭabaqat*, or social levels, Hopkins failed to mention the reasons for the construction of the Almohad hierarchy. He described how the structure came into place but provides no convincing reason why the Almohads used this structure. Also, despite devoting a chapter of his book to the Almohad system, he cast doubt on its very existence saying, 'One is entitled to wonder whether the whole system existed at all except on paper or in the minds of its inventers.'[108] Yet, given the nature of twelfth-century Arab chronology, focused as it was on military and political events, it was more than a coincidence that there were sometimes very detailed descriptions of the Almohad hierarchy in almost every major primary source.

Ibn al-Qaṭṭān and the anonymous author of the *Kitāb al Ansāb*, the two main sources on the Almohad hierarchy, provided a remarkable and unique description of the Almohads' long-term social structure, effectively breaking the mould of classical Arab historiography, which focuses mainly on chronology, not social organization. This focus on the hierarchy in the sources demonstrated the central importance of the hierarchical structure during the early rise of the Almohads. Although some elements of the hierarchy were in doubt, for the sources contradicted each other on minor points, there was no reason to question seriously, as Hopkins did, the hierarchy's very existence. It was true that as the Almohad Empire expanded into a vast territory, absorbed new peoples and was transformed into a dynastic state, the need for Ibn Tūmart's original hierarchal system seemed less pronounced. The chronicles suggest that the later Almohad caliphs centralized and bureaucratized power. Yet, the appearance of centralized power and the central importance of the personality of the caliph may have simply been because of the nature of the sources. It was a testament to the original power of Ibn Tūmart's hierarchy that elements, especially the men of the fifty and the bureaucratic descendants of sheikhs educated in Marrakech, remained powerful institutions and even checks on dynastic power. The original, tribal hierarchy formed the 'aristocracy' of the empire. They were the stewards of the Mahdī doctrine and they provided a cohesive military corps. They represented the original tribal alliances, the tribal traditions that united the mountains and formed the empire. Like the Atlas Mountains, they were the backbone of the empire, able to support or rebel, to cause division or secure unity and defence. In fact, only the Almohad hierarchy and the caliphs were allowed to discuss and interpret the Mahdī's doctrine.[109]

Recent descriptions of the original Almohad political structure, like Hopkins, do not explain why the hierarchy was so successful in such a short period of time; nor do they see the structure as part of a changing historical context. The conference papers of 'Los Almohades II: Organización Political y Militar' shed some light on the subject, but leave many questions unanswered, among which is that of how Ibn Tūmart used a combination of religious ideology, tribal co-option and military force to organize the tribes.[110] This was why the Almohads organized around a pyramidal hierarchy instead of a simple confederation, as was often the case with tribal societies. The manner in which tribes so quickly coalesce into a state, or in anthropological terms, how a structured hierarchical system arose from a decentralized, segmentary society played an important role in history. However, before these issues can be addressed, a detailed description of the Almohad hierarchy is in order.[111]

The Almohad pyramid[112]

Pre-Almohad tribal society in the Atlas Mountains was based on a 'flat' circular system, not simply in matters of loyalty and blood revenge but also in matters of authority (Table 2.2). Some tribes were more powerful than others, but each had a fairly equal claim to its own sovereignty and identity. Ibn Tūmart's doctrine, as well as exterior threats, gave Almohad tribal society a steep and organized peak by forcing tribal identity into the hierarchy and co-opting the most loyal members of each tribe into the upper echelons of power. Those who resisted Ibn Tūmart's new and radical reorganization of society were eliminated with bloody efficiency with the *tamyīz* – the culling of the disloyal as described by the *Kitāb al-Ansāb* and other sources.[113]

Accounts in the primary sources of the Almohad hierarchy were written with the model of the prophet and companions of the Prophet Muḥammad in mind. Indeed, Ibn Tūmart had his hijra to Tīnmallal and, as Hopkins observed, the people of Tīnmallal and Hargha may be an analogy of the *Ṣaḥāba* of Muḥammad. Nevertheless, it would have been difficult for Ibn Tūmart to claim that he was following the *sunna* of the prophet by dividing his followers into regimented levels. Although Prophet Muḥammad's followers organized themselves fairly rapidly, Muḥammad did not set up a hierarchy quite like Ibn Tūmart. The prophet's organization was based on who had fought at the famous battle of Badr, who had followed him on the hijra to Medina, who was a close companion, or who was a member of his family. There were no councils of ten, fifty or seventy, no established following of scholars and clerics who would defend his doctrine. The Prophet Muḥammad stood among his followers as he received the revelations of the Qurʾān and slowly established the basic foundations of Islamic society. Also, although Muḥammad's social system at Medina was fairly flat in nature, there was apparently no fear among the Almohads that Ibn Tūmart's regimented hierarchy would be considered a *bidaʿ*, or innovation, outside the *sunna* or example of the prophet. As Mahdī, Ibn Tūmart created his own *sunna*, his own life example. The new Almohad hierarchy was a means of assuring obedience as the community prepared for the ultimate triumph and the end of time. Extreme discipline was easier to enforce in an environment of expectation.

The two important sources for first-hand knowledge of the Almohad hierarchy were the *Kitāb al-Ansāb* and the *Naẓm al-Jumān*. These works were by authors who most likely would have witnessed the Almohad hierarchical structures in practice. First, because of its several unique features, I shall describe Ibn al-Qaṭṭān's insider's view of the regime. For the remainder of the section I shall use a combination of both sources.

The *Naẓm al-Jamān* (String of Pearls) was written by Ibn al-Qaṭṭān (d. 628/1231), the son of the distinguished head of the Almohad school at Marrakech, the first of the *ṭullāb*, scholar class.[114] Ibn al-Qaṭṭān provided a top–down perspective of Almohad society. As a high-ranking member of this hierarchy he had an interest in overemphasizing both the usefulness and extent of the hierarchy. His description of Almohad society should be seen more as an artificial ideal than as a completely accurate representation of a complex and fluid social process. One should not forget, however, that overarching ideals, not detailed compromise, was what drove the Almohad experiment. By formally solidifying tribal identities in written and hierarchical form, both Ibn al-Qaṭṭān and Ibn Tūmart could better control them. Rulership at the beginning stage of any major political or religious movement was not simply about having a monopoly of violence or enforcing rules. Rulership was about having a monopoly over identities, about defining the 'we' in a convincing way. That was the main purpose behind Ibn Tūmart's elaborate hierarchy of tribes, students and soldiers.

Ibn al-Qaṭṭān was a loyal believer in the Mahdī's message. He first established the central pillar of the Almohad system – the imām and Mahdī.

> Among the foundations of religion is the obligation of believing in the Mahdī who is the Imām. The Imāmate is necessary. ... Neither money nor birth is an issue. If one hears his call one must go out (hijra) towards him. [The] Imām [is] to teach the people the ways of religion and knowledge, what was necessary for belief and what one must obey.[115]

The imām and Mahdī was the ideal, the point at the top of the Almohad pyramid to whom all obedience and loyalty must be given.

Below the Mahdī, the pyramid was divided into 14 levels, or *ṭabaqāt*. Roughly speaking, each lower level had more members than its superior (Table 2.3).[116] Despite some variations this was roughly the same structure detailed in the other two sources. As al-Qaṭṭān noted, 'Every level among these levels was ranked according to its number.' He also noted that 'those who did not memorize their passages were rebuked.' This indicated that learning, as well as political and tribal considerations, determined rank. In fact, those who did not learn their verses were 'whipped' until they were sufficiently aware of both the Qur'ān and Ibn Tūmart's doctrine.[117] Although the transition from a fragmented tribal society to a regimented hierarchy may have been a more gradual process than Ibn al-Qaṭṭān claimed, it did occur with remarkable speed. One reason for this speed was the way some levels were organized according to tribe (Table 2.1). The highest levels, the ten, fifty and seventy, as well as the *ṭullāb*, had representatives from every major tribal group in the region. A balance of tribal representation and individual merit was achieved. The lower levels, including the 'Champions',[118] the 'Soldiers' and the various tribes in the lower levels, were divided into regiments according to specific military and social functions.

Many of the tribal names that survived in the hierarchy were not necessarily based on birth. Ibn Tūmart allowed his closest followers, including those who rallied around his cave, to become honorary Hargha, the tribe of Ibn Tūmart, even if they were not remotely Hargha by birth. The *Kitāb al-Ansāb* was explicit about Ibn Tūmart's positive harnessing of tribal identity, especially that of his own tribe, for political purposes. 'All those who, among the Almohads, were part of the immediate entourage of the Mahdī and who did not originate from the founding six tribes who formed the basis of Almohad power, the Imām and Mahdī gave them the favour of naming them Hargha.'[119] The famous al-Bashīr, the great general and martyr at the battle of al-Buḥaīra, was made an honorary Hargha. Thus, even those tribal names that remained in the hierarchy were less tribal than immediately apparent. For example, the Ahl Tīnmallal was more a collection of geographically diverse clans than a classic tribe. Yet, they also had honorary members.

The *Kitāb al-Ansāb* provided a different and more detailed description of the Almohad hierarchy and of the relationship between Almohad tribes and institutions. Like Ibn al-Qaṭṭān's the *Naẓm al-Jumān*, the book was almost certainly written after Ibn Tūmart's death. It attests to the lasting influence of the original Almohad institutions – even at the height of empire.[120] However, one must realize the potential for manipulation of the text. ʿAbd al-Muʾmin's followers and later caliphs would have modified the contents of the book for their own benefit.[121] The *Kitāb al-Ansāb* was used as a guidebook, an official compendium of the highest ranking Almohads and their relationship to the Mahdī. Several names and numbers are different from Ibn al-Qaṭṭān's account. It was not impossible that the names would have changed according to the rapidly mutable exchange of power and rank that characterized revolutions.

Even though it was likely to have been written earlier, the *Kitāb al-Ansāb* was not quite as explicit as al-Qaṭṭān about hierarchies: a slightly more flattened picture emerged from its pages. The book emphasized the importance of physical proximity to the Mahdī. The *Kitāb al-Ansāb* placed the *Ahl al-Dār*, the people of the house, the Mahdī's entourage, above all others. The people of the house were generally close companions of the Mahdī; there was little description of their specific functions.[122] Very likely, their purpose was to have no specific function, but rather to be available when needed for personal advice. They gained their power not out of formal positions but out of friendship and proximity to the Mahdī. The *Kitāb al-Ansāb* said that they were 'of those of the *aṣḥāb* who were the *ʿarīfs* and were specially devoted to the service of the Impeccable [Mahdī].'[123] Many of the same people mentioned as members of the *ahl al-dār* were also members of the fifty and the council of ten.[124] Although some seemed to hold a position of special honour, others were trusted servants. Abū Muḥammad Wāsnār, for example, was charged with the Mahdī's toothpick and ablutions. After the death of Ibn Tūmart, Abū Wāsnār guarded the Mahdī's grave.[125]

The Mahdī's family was an important element of the Almohad hierarchy that Ibn al-Qaṭṭān failed to mention as a distinct category. The Mahdī had three brothers – Abū Māsā ʿĪsā, Abū Muḥammad ʿAbd al-ʿAzīz and Abū al-ʿAbbās Aḥmad the blind, and one sister, Zainab, who was the mother of Abū Bakr.[126] The precise political role of the family was not mentioned in Ibn al-Qaṭṭān's work. Yet, each member of his family had a significant impact on the Almohad movement. Zainab played a crucial part in caring for Ibn Tūmart at his death. Two of Ibn Tūmart's brothers revolted in Marrakech against ʿAbd al-Muʾmin after he declared one of his sons crown prince in 1155.[127] They were later put to death. Their original role in the rise of the Almohad movement was obscured because of the threat they posed to the dynastic power of the descendants of ʿAbd al-Muʾmin. Ibn Tūmart's father ʿAbd Allah was known as Tūmart bin Ūgallīd. His role was only advisory, although he was highly respected up until his death.

The *Kitāb al-Ansāb* listed the companions of the Mahdī he met in Egypt. The purpose of this was to hasten the establishment of Almohad power in Egypt and the Levant. Lévi-Provençal believed it possible that several of these names and contacts were fabricated. Listing names of illustrious men who believed in him in Egypt created the impression of Almohad influence in the East, a type of Almohad cell ready to support what the Mahdī and his followers believed would be the inevitable expansion of Almohad power throughout the known world. These were the people among the tribes and groups of Egypt who came to the Mahdī and showed their sympathy to his cause. They were a ready and waiting source of support for the Almohads. They provided proof that 'the Imām was known in both the Maghrib and the Mashriq (West and East).'[128] These distant companions, fictional or real, were especially honoured as they followed the Mahdī even before gaining the protection and fervour of a large following of Berber tribes.

Council of ten

After honouring Almohad sympathizers in Egypt, the *Kitāb al-Ansāb* then lists those companions actually living in the Maghrib. First there was the council of ten. They were the highest and most elite, the people at the centre of Almohad power who met regularly with the Mahdī in council. In public they were never allowed to show *ikhtilāf*, differences in opinion, with the Mahdī. However, in private they may have provided Ibn Tūmart with the opportunity to discuss tactics and strategy without seeming weak, indecisive, or humanized to the common follower. The *Kitāb al-Ansāb* said the council of ten were chosen for their extreme and fervent loyalty to the imām and Mahdī. They were willing to fight 'all the people of the world, Western and Eastern, strangers and Arabs'[129] to spread the doctrine of the Mahdī. However the ten, like the fifty and the seventy, were chosen not only for their loyalty but also for political reasons. Ibn Tūmart neutralized powerful personalities by making them inner confidants and disciples. Their family names reappear regularly as rulers, caliphs and generals throughout the next decades of Almohad dominance in the region. The descendants of some even became founders of dynasties of their own. The men of the council of ten were mentioned in order to the writer of the *Kitāb al-Ansāb* by a former member of the fifty:[130]

1. The Prince of Believers (future caliph), ʿAbū Muḥammad ʿAbd al-Muʾmin bin ʿAlī al Qaisī. The Mahdī called him the man of the 'Master of Time'. He was the only follower allowed to ride a black horse.[131]
2. Abū Ḥafṣ al-Ṣanhājī, who was possibly related to the chronicler al-Baydhaq.
3. Abū al-Rabiʿ Ḥaḍramī, from the people of Āghmāt. Before his name was Arabized, he was known to the Berbers as Ibn al-Baqqāl and Ibn Tāʿḍamiyīt. He was the official letter writer of the Mahdī. He died a martyr at the battle of al-Buḥaīra.
4. Abū Ibrāhīm Ismāʿīl bin Īsallālī al-Ḥazrajī. He was a high judge of the people, installed by the order of the imām and Mahdī. Lévi-Provençal believed this was Abū Ibrāhīm Ismāʿīl Īgīg mentioned by al-Baydhaq as the companion present at Ibn Tūmart's cave of meditation in Igīlīz.
5. Abū ʿImrān Mūsā bin Tamārā al-Gadmīwī, who was called the *amīn*, the most trustworthy or upright, of the ten. He died a martyr at al-Buḥaīra.
6. Abū Yaḥyā Abū Bakr bin Yīgīt from the Hintāta tribe died a

martyr at al-Buḥaīra. He was among those present at the sermon of Ibn Tūmart in Igīlīz. His son was named the governor of Córdoba.

7. Abū ʿAbd Allāh Muḥammad bin Sulaīman came from the people of Ānsā, a remote oasis in south of the Anti-Atlas. He was originally a member of the Massakāla tribe. He was present at the sermon of Ibn Tūmart in Igīlīz.
8. ʿAbd Allah bin Yaʾlā al-Zanātī, originally from Tāza, was also known as Ibn Malwīya. He was condemned to death after the death of the Mahdī when he 'committed treason' against ʿAbd al-Muʾmin. He may have been a rival of ʿAbd al-Muʾmin. His claims to the caliphate were likely erased by historians of ʿAbd al-Muʾmin.
9. Abū Muḥammad ʿAbd Allah bin Muḥsin al-Wānshrīrī also known as al-Bashīr, commanded the forces at al-Buḥaīra where he was killed.
10. The Mahdī assigned Abū Ḥafṣ ʿUmar bin Yaḥyā al-Hintātī to carry the leather shield and to invoke divine blessings in its favour.[132]
11. Two other names are mentioned. These men were replacements or vice-members. Abū Mūsa ʿĪsā bin Mūsa al-Ṣaūdī and Abū Muḥammad ʿAbd al-ʿAzīz al-Ghīghāʾī.[133]

The council of fifty

Some 80 years ago the French anthropologist Robert Montagne made a series of observations about the structure of tribal councils, which revealed more evidence about the close relationship between the Almohad state institution and existing tribal systems.[134] According to Montagne, 'a Berber organization' was at the 'basis of the Empire'.[135] This parallel between tribal tradition and Almohad organization was most obvious with the formation of the council of fifty (forty plus the council of ten). The council was actually made up of 40 members, but became 50 when the council of ten was added. This is important because, according to

Montagne, 40 is the number of men in the Berber council, the *agrao* or *taqbilt*. The council of fifty was based on pre-existing Berber tribal councils.

While the Almohad *tamyīz*, or segregation of the tribes, opened up the Maṣmūda tribal system to a new generation, the councils of ten, fifty and seventy allowed Ibn Tūmart to integrate willing sheikhs and tribal leaders. This was an essential way of maintaining tribal identity even as tribes were integrated into the hierarchy. The anthropologist Paul Dresch observed the role of the sheikh in his study of mountain village tribes in Yemen similar to the Berbers:

> A section of a tribe has no 'face' as a man does, no ability to make undertakings or to commit its honour in a specific instance. It has, if you like, no legal personality. For all that, tokens such as rifles may in practice align tribes or sections ... they must be exchanged by individual men who act in an individual capacity. The men who do this are commonly sheikhs, who 'give their faces' on behalf of tribesmen.[136]

Similarly, the sheikhs of the Almohads 'gave their faces' on behalf of the Berber tribes as members of constant, representative unions, the councils. They were already 'representatives' in the limited, traditional sense. Ibn Tūmart simply transformed the negotiating role of the sheikh into a more permanent, representative role on the councils. He could thus maintain discipline and learn about the needs, desires and grievances of the various tribes.

Ibn Tūmart associated the council of fifty with his doctrine on the coming of the Day of Judgment in the *Aʿazz mā Yuṭlab*. He cited a *ḥadīth* recorded by al-Tirmidhī in which Muḥammad made a reference to 'fifty men'. The days of waiting and patience for the last judgement were like 'seizing hot coal in one's hand'. It required as much patience 'as the work of fifty men'.[137] The council of fifty was clearly an important part of Almohad mythology. It symbolized the fusion of Almohad ideology with traditional tribal forms. It was only natural that a council of fifty should be included in Ibn Tūmart's eschatological vision.

Unfortunately, there is little evidence on the actual role of the council of fifty, the *ahl khamsīn* in Arabic. Most of the deliberations of the council do not survive or were not written down, making it hard to see what they did or the amount of power they held within the hierarchy. According to the model of the Berber tribal council, Ibn Tūmart would have first consulted the council of ten for most immediate matters and used the council of fifty to relay orders and receive counsel.

Citing Ibn Ṣāḥib al-Ṣalāt, Ibn al-Qaṭṭān mentioned another council of seventy. Like the council of fifty, their precise role in the Almohad hierarchy remains something of a mystery.[138] Like the council of ten and of fifty, it had a diverse membership drawn from the tribes.

The Ṭullāb and the Ḥuffāẓ[139]

Originally, the *ṭullāb* were simply students, seekers or followers of the Mahdī Ibn Tūmart as he journeyed from the East. Inspired by his message and his learning, they gathered around the Mahdī and protected him from the machinations of wary rulers and governors. However, early in the development of the Almohad state, the Almohads required the services of trained functionaries well versed in Almohad doctrine. These became the formal levels of *ṭullāb* and the *ḥuffāẓ*. Yet, even this heavily bureaucratic and centrally trained element of the Almohad hierarchy was not completely divorced from traditional tribal structures. The councils of ten, of fifty and even of seventy were made up of high-ranking members of the tribes. The *ṭullāb* and the *ḥuffāẓ* were often the sons of tribal leaders and sheikhs. Most of the ten and fifty were themselves *ṭullāb*, thus showing that ranks, at least in the early Almohad period, were intermixed.[140] Many were original followers of the Mahdī and even if they professed almost complete loyalty to the Almohad state, they inevitably represented the interests of their own tribe. Rather than separating the state from the tribes, the *ṭullāb* were an important link between them. For example, in 1126 (AH 520), just as the Almohad state was taking shape, the original *ṭullāb* were sent out among the tribes, presumably to preach the Almohad message and to stiffen their loyalty.[141]

It was not until the disciplined rule of ʿAbd al-Muʾmin (d. 1163) that the *ṭullāb* and *ḥuffāẓ* became primarily government officials. ʿAbd al-Muʾmin set up a school at Marrakech to create a more uniform corps of bureaucrats. Even so, he maintained the doctrine of the Mahdī. The Anonymous Chronicler recorded: 'He ordered that the *ḥuffāẓ* be taught the *Muwaṭṭaʾ*, the *Aʿazz mā Yuṭlab* of Ibn Tūmart, and other works by the Mahdī. ... His aim was to educate them rapidly according to his designs.'[142] When they were ready ʿAbd al-Muʾmin sent the *ḥuffāẓ* to the ruling Maṣmūda sheikhs to replace the sheikh or provide advice. It was not clear to what extent the early Almohad tribal structure was superseded by these learned functionaries of the caliph. As Ibn Tūmart and ʿAbd al-Muʾmin exemplified, it was not unknown for the young descendants of amghars or sheikhs to go off in search of knowledge and return to replace their fathers as leaders of the tribe. ʿAbd al-Muʾmin may have only systemized and centralized a pre-existing process.

Other Almohad institutions

The *mizwārs* have already been mentioned as the enforcers of tribal custom. These men enforced tribal laws and maintained clan order. The *Kitāb al-Ansāb* also mentioned the *muṭtasibs*; those who were designated to perform *ḥisba*, to command right and forbid wrong. The *muḥtasibs* would have been specially trained to enforce Ibn Tūmart's interpretation of public morals in everyday life, in the market place, and after battles during the distribution of spoils. The *mizwārs* most likely still functioned as enforcers, but only of common agreements between settled Almohads and the semi-settled herders. They were internal, civil enforcers.

Meaning of the hierarchy

The overall meaning and function of the Almohad hierarchy was multifaceted. It was both simply a way of disciplining tribes into an army and the seed of a remarkable, elaborate, governmental system built successfully on tribal foundations. Later Muʾminid caliphs took more centralized control as the original doctrine and impetus of the Almohad movement began to lose steam, as the original tribes became a well-fed aristocracy.[143] Yet, they maintained much of the original character and doctrine of the Almohads. They formed the backbone of empire.

Beyond the survival of the tribal hierarchy at the height of empire, what was most remarkable about this system was its sheer structure and organization (see Tables 2.3 and 2.4). The *ṭullāb*, as well as the councils of ten, fifty and seventy, and the elite chiefs and leaders, the *ḥuffāẓ*, trained to memorize the sacred doctrine of the Mahdī. The incredible diversity of tribes with their different functions, the *mizwārs* and the soldiers; all these groups had specific levels and specific duties in the Almohad hierarchy. Before there was mainly a division of lineage, now there was a division of labour and a division of purpose. Before there were simply rival tribes fighting along ancestral lines, now there was a clear hierarchy, a line of battle. The introduction of a divinely inspired reformist and his enforcers created a systematic structure that would soundly defeat the powerful, if decadent, Almoravids and put fear in the hearts of Muslim rulers as far away as Egypt and Syria. By adopting tribal institutions and adapting them to a universalistic message by using strict discipline and appealing to a divine message, Ibn Tūmart and the Almohads created the foundations of an empire that would rule the western Mediterranean for a century.

The Almohad Tribal Economy: A Preliminary Sketch

One of the main reasons for the successful creation of the Almohad hierarchy was the economic condition of early twelfth-century North Africa. Although the economic conditions of the Atlas

Mountains before, and during, the rise of the Almohads cannot be described in any conclusive manner, several sources provide clues about the economic challenges faced by the Maṣmūda and the economic benefits of joining the Almohad cause. The economic conditions of medieval North Africa were used by Ibn Tūmart to encourage tribes to join. The Maṣmūda were a combination of transhumant and settled mountain tribes engaged in a wide variety of prosperous economic and agricultural activities. However, the Almoravids exploited them through their control of prices, which were managed by a complex network of trade. They taxed the Maṣmūda when they brought their goods to Marrakech or sent them to Salé for exportation to Spain. Some valued items from the Maghrib, like the fire repellent asbestos of the Sūs, were sent as far as Baghdad and the opposite fringes of the Islamic world.

The trans-Saharan routes were a primary source of Almoravid wealth and power.[144] The main route from Awkar and Awdagust in Ghana to Igīlīz, Tīnmallal, Āghmāt and Marrakech brought slaves, medicines, gold, rare woods and materials to the north for export abroad. The route was the backbone of the Almoravid territory. Ibn Khaldūn described the vast wealth that could be gained by engaging in this long distance trade, but also listed its perils:

> The merchants who dare to enter the Sudan country are the most prosperous and wealthy of all people. The distance and the difficulty of the road they travel are great. They have to cross a difficult desert that is made [almost] inaccessible by fear and beset by [the danger of] thirst. The distance of this road is braved only by a very few people.[145]

Ibn Khaldūn was writing in the fourteenth century when the political situation in the Maghrib was particularly unstable and when trading was at a low point. When the Almoravids ruled, however, the rich trading route was under their unified control.

The route went through the territory of friendly tribesmen who were familiar with the land and would have helped the caravans survive. As a result, the trade was much more frequent and prosperous during the eleventh and twelfth century.

A merchant travelling from Marrakech would have to allow a couple of months to reach Awdagust and Senegal. The distance between two watering holes could take as long as 11 days of travel. To protect against dangers, some of the caravans were quite large. Al-Idrīsī mentioned 100 camels under the proprietorship of a single merchant. There were even references to caravans as large as 6000 camels.[146] There may have been such large caravans during the Almoravid period. The Almoravid Saharan tribes were in a monopolistic position; they controlled the markets. Unusual economic conditions may have added to the success of ʿAbd Allah bin Yāsīn, the zealous, reforming founder of the Almoravids. The camels were bought at large camel fairs or markets on the edge of the desert where basic supplies were also acquired. Therefore, they controlled not only the major markets, but also the ability of caravans to obtain necessary trade goods. Guelmin, some 160 kilometres south of Agadir, remains a camel market to this day.[147]

Al-Idrīsī provided a colourful and atmospheric description of how the camel herders withstood desert conditions.[148]

> The travellers crossed this desert in autumn. This was how they made the voyage: One wakes up the camels well before daybreak and marches until the sun is high in the horizon, until the sand and air is permeated by insupportable heat from the sun. At this point they stop and release their camels. They set up tents to guard them from the heat of mid-day and stay there until the sun starts to descend. When the sun begins to fall into the western horizon they abandon their campsite and walk the rest of the day and follow the road until it becomes impossible to see. They camp where they arrive and pass the rest of the night there until just

before dawn. This was how the merchants that traded with the Sudan would travel. They would never wait as the sun would kill all those who were exposed to it in mid-day.

The most important items of trade were salt and gold. According to the eleventh-century geographer al-Bakrī, the king of Ghana gave a dinar of gold for every block of salt that entered his territory.[149]

Although seemingly confined to mountain hamlets, the Maṣmūda were not completely excluded from this trade network. The major routes passed through their territory, especially through Tizi-n-Test, the important mountain pass linking Tarūdant and Igīlīz to Marrakech. At first, the Maṣmūda profited as much from Almoravid expansion as the Lamtūna. The merchants would have been targets for raids by the Maṣmūda who may have also engaged in trade or transporting goods over the mountains to the markets in Marrakech. However, under the able leadership of the Almoravid amir Yūsuf bin Tāshfīn (1072–1106) the Almoravids consolidated their power and their trading routes. It was at this point that the Almoravids probably demanded taxes from the mountain Maṣmūda. It was also at this point that Almoravid rule was no longer economically advantageous to the Maṣmūda.

The single most important economic decision Ibn Tūmart made was to promise resistance to Almoravid taxation. In al-Idrīsī's colourful phrase, 'the people were forced into eating grasshoppers' because of oppressive Almoravid taxes.[150] Marrakech, the Almoravid capital and main trading centre through which all goods and merchants from the mountains had to pass, imposed heavy trade-stifling duties. A *qabāla* tax was levied on the souks, including markets for perfume, soap, refined or 'yellow' copper, and cotton and wool textiles. All these products originated in or passed through the mountains of the Maṣmūda. As the Almohads took over, they promised to abolish these taxes. They condemned to death anybody who attempted to raise duties on trade.[151]

The Andalusian geographer al-Bakrī wrote in 1068, just before the foundation of Marrakech. His description of trade around the Atlas region provided some idea of the Berbers' basic geo-economic situation. At each point along the route from Sijilmāsa to Āghmāt, new materials, from copper to knives to precious stones could be traded. Al-Bakrī followed the main trading route from Sijilmāsa, through the Wādī Draā to Āghmāt Ūrīka. There was a copper mine some two days away from Sijilmāsa. The banks of the Wādī Draā were covered with fruit trees. A tree found there called takūt, or tamarisk, was used in the preparation of leather. The Draā was so rich that 'every day there was a market day on the banks of the river ... some days [there] were two, such was the number of inhabitants.'[152] One walked along cultivated land for seven days.

The Haksūra, a minor Almohad tribe, lived in Ourzazat, a village on a route far down the slopes of the Atlas Mountains. Nevertheless, they provided significant support early in the movement. Al-Bakrī mentioned the fine stones and minerals that are still found in the Ourzazat region today.[153] 'They were good stones of every variety and remarkable for their good quality and the purity of their colours.'[154] Some of these stones were very sharp and could be used to 'slice the skin of the dog of the sea [whales]'. These stones were also used for the production of weapons and would have been traded as far as the sea for the purpose of cutting whale skin.

It took more than a week to travel from Ourzazat to the two Āghmāts – Āghmāt Ilan and Āghmāt Ūrīka. The two Āghmāts were at the centre of Almoravid power before the establishment of Marrakech. For various reasons, Āghmāt Ilan was closed to trade and to strangers. The Almoravids may have wanted to protect their exclusive hold on power; a forbidden space was a place of power. They may have also wanted to preserve the purity of their lineage by not permitting the intermixing with strange tribes and traders. The very fact that the Almoravids chose to close down a city to strange merchants may have only indicated the strength and diversity of trade in the region. Eight miles from Āghmāt Ilan and across the sweet waters of the Taghīrūt stream was Āghmāt Ūrīka, the vibrant mountain town where trade was permitted. Āghmāt Ūrīka was a thriving market centre, 'surrounded by gardens and forests of date trees'. Ūrīka was where the 'chief of the peoples' resided.[155] The Almoravids at Āghmāt claimed authority over a large region surrounding the Ūrīka, although it was unclear how much direct authority they had over the Maṣmūda tribes nearby.[156]

Al-Bakrī indicated that the Maṣmūda 'lived in fortified villages (*qusūr*) and ... in the places where they stopped their animals.'[157] The *Kitāb al-Ansāb* similarly described the combined transhumant, pastoral and settled economy of the Maṣmūda tribes.[158] They made as much use of the mountains, terraces and husbandry as they could. Although many lived in fortified villages, there was not always a significant distinction between migratory pastoralist and settled agriculturalist. Even so, the benefits of uniting around a single leader who could organize and enforce intertribal and trading relationships were clear.[159]

Economic benefits were one of the motives for the mountain tribes to unite and obey the Mahdī. The formation of the Almohad movement would have significantly improved these tribes' economic prospects. I shall now discuss how the Almohad hierarchy that resulted from this tribal, economic and religious unification showed that Islam and tribalism were not inherently in conflict.

3

The Doctrine of Muḥammad Ibn Tūmart: Mahdī of the Almohads

> I am Muḥammad Ibn ʿAbd Allah Tūmart. I am Mahdī of the end of time.
>
> (Ibn al-Qaṭṭān, *Naẓm al-Jumān*)

It was the month of Ramadan 1121 (AH 515).[1] Ibn Tūmart was meditating in the sacred Cave of Igīlīz. Then he emerged, filled with the light of inspiration. He stood under a tree and began to speak to spontaneously assembled followers. This speech was different from all previous ones. With powerful and inspired language, he silenced the crowd.[2]

He spoke of the obligation to follow and obey the coming Mahdī, a coming promised by the collected *ḥadīth*: sayings from the mouth of Muḥammad the Prophet. It was approximately 500 years after the death of the prophet; a time the *ḥadīth* predicted as the beginning of a new era.[3] After his speech about the characteristics of the Mahdī (see Table 3.1), a group of his closest disciples ran up to Ibn Tūmart and proclaimed, 'These characteristics are not seen in anybody but you. You are the Mahdī!'[4] Just as the Prophet Muḥammad proclaimed his message under a tree,[5] so too would the Mahdī Ibn Tūmart.

The following quotation is one version of what Ibn Tūmart may have said that inspired his followers to proclaim Ibn Tūmart Mahdī:

> He [the Mahdī] will be sent by God to command right and forbid wrong so that justice may take the place of injustice. His place will be the extreme Maghrib and his time, the end of time: his name will be that of the Prophet. He will reveal the injustice of the princes and rid the world of corruption. This is the end of the times: the name is the name, the lineage is the lineage, and the works are the works.[6]

Table 3.1: Necessary characteristics of an imam and Mahdī according to Ibn Tūmart's doctrine. The person of the Mahdī is the moral axis of the community, upholding right over wrong

	He must be free from (*ma'sūman min*) and stand firm against (*yathabatu*)	He must support and defend
1.	*al-baṭl*: falsehood	*al-ḥaqq*: truth
2.	*al-ḍalāl*: error, deception	*al-hadī*: true guidance
3.	*al-mafsadah*: evil, corruption	
4.	*al-jawr*: tyranny, oppression	
5.	*al-bida'*: innovation	
6.	*al-jahl*: ignorance	*al-nūr*: light
7.	*al-najāsa*: impurity	
8.	*al-ẓulāma*: unfairness, injustice	*al-'adl*: justice
9.	*al-'ikhtilāf*: disputation, difference	*al-'itifāq*: agreement
10.	*al-'īṣyān*: disobedience	*al-ṭā'ah*: obedience

Source: From Ibn Tūmart, *Kitāb A'azz mā Yuṭlab*, p. 345-55.

The message was clear. The Mahdī would be the hinge upon which the door of another age would open onto the end of time – blood loyalty, temporal power, nominal homage to the amir, and all the things so familiar to tribal life would be no more.

The question of why and how Ibn Tūmart and his followers made such extraordinary claims must be addressed. It was these claims that gave him the status of Mahdī and thus his power to enforce a new and extraordinary form of discipline and rule over the tribes. In this chapter I shall examine the nature, impact and meaning of Ibn Tūmart's doctrine as well as the development of an Almohad doctrine in response to the Almoravids, who represented 'the injustice of the princes' and the 'domination of the jurists'.[7] The specific historical background of the extraordinary Almohad claims was difficult to trace. Nevertheless, there were several precedents, several attempts by men to be declared Mahdīs in the past. Possible influences and doctrinal parallels will set the context for Ibn Tūmart's claim to be the Mahdī.

The Almohad Mahdī Doctrine: Possible Historical Precedents[8]

The Almohads cannot be easily categorized. They were not completely Shīʿite or Sunni,[9] orthodox or heterodox. Although influenced by different strands of Islam, Ibn Tūmart proclaimed a unique form of Islam, a form he believed would complete the call of the Prophet Muḥammad and fill the world with justice. At least in the way the Almohad sources portrayed him, Ibn Tūmart and the Almohads were not Shīʿite, Sunni Maliki, or Khārijite,[10] which are the three strands of Islam prominent in Middle Eastern and Arab history. Rather, the Almohad, Berber tribes, under the leadership of the Mahdī Ibn Tūmart, attempted to create a restored version of 'true' Islam in Maghribi Berber society.

Ibn Tūmart's claim to be the Mahdī was related to his claim to return to the original sources of Islam, to direct the Atlas Berbers on the straight path. Ibn Tūmart was a vehicle of salvation. An Imām or Mahdī was an essential feature of a successful Islamic *umma*. He was a pillar between this world and heaven. Patricia Crone provided an apt illustration of the need for an Imām.

> It helps to envisage the [early Muslim] community (*umma*) as a caravan. The early Muslims saw life primarily as a journey through a perilous desert in which one could all too easily go astray and perish. To survive, one needed to band together

> under the leadership of a guide (*imām, al-hudā, hādī, Mahdī*) who knew the right paths of guidance, that is the right things to do. ... The Imām performed two tasks indispensable for the achievement of salvation. First and most fundamentally, he gave legal existence to the *umma*. Without him there was no caravan, only scattered travellers ... the second task of the Imām was to lead the way. He did not simply cause the caravan to exist: he also guided it to its right destination.[11]

However, as Patricia Crone explains, the early Muslim community quickly lost faith in temporal leaders as the Prophet Muḥammad's true successors. The ʿAbbāsid caliph in Baghdad did not really represent the true leader of the Muslim community.[12] According to the Shia, there was no true imām, only a puppet controlled by political forces in the east.[13] By the twelfth century, Ibn Tūmart had refused to recognize not only the ʿAbbāsid caliph but also the legal tradition of Sunni Islam that had developed during the 500 years since the Prophet's death. In his remarkable book of doctrine, Ibn Tūmart claimed to be the illuminated, promised imām and Mahdī of the entire Islamic *umma*. He would make this claim not in tribal Arabia but in tribal Berber lands on the westernmost fringes of the Islamic world.

One of the reasons Ibn Tūmart and the Almohads were successful was because of their relative remoteness from historical developments in the geographic 'core' of Islam. This allowed the Almohads and Ibn Tūmart to develop a distinct doctrine without interference or contradiction from established centres of theological learning in the East. Nevertheless, Ibn Tūmart and the Almohads were not completely divorced from history. Historical precedents influenced the creation of Almohad doctrine. The Almohad doctrine was influenced not only by the Mahdī's journeys in the Islamic East but also by the immediate spiritual, social and historical context of twelfth-century North Africa. The Almohad movement emerged in a political, economic and religious milieu that seemed particularly suited to the rise of Mahdī figures of all sorts. As I shall explain, the eleventh century and early twelfth century was an 'Era of the Mahdīs' in Andalusia and the Maghrib.

DEFINING THE MAHDĪ

Generally speaking, the term Mahdī referred to the 'rightly guided one' who will lead the Muslim community before the Day of Judgment. Yet, throughout Islamic history, there have been several uses of the word Mahdī that have different meanings in different contexts.[14] There was some evidence that Islam originated as an apocalyptic movement and that Muḥammad was the first Mahdī, even if he was never given that label.[15] S. A. Arjomand, a specialist in the early Islamic period, made a convincing argument for the apocalyptic origins of Islam. Muḥammad the Prophet was preparing the Muslim community for the coming of the end of time.[16] Some caliphs were called Mahdī and Umayyad court poetry clearly uses redemptive language, promising salvation through obedience to the caliph. Caliph 'Umar II (AD 717–20), for example, was called a Mahdī who would fill the earth with peace and righteousness.[17] Al-Mukhtār (d. AD 687) was possibly the first Shī'ite to use the term Mahdī when he preached in Kufa and identified himself as the helper of the promised Mahdī Muḥammad b. al-Ḥanafiyya, a son of 'Alī by a slave girl who lived in Medina.

Even these few examples from the Islamic East show that there were many different ways of using the word Mahdī. There were, in fact, many different definitions of the word depending on the religious, political and social objective of those who were called Mahdī and those who called them Mahdī.[18] Although a strict classification or definition of the word would be artificial, and every different Mahdī has different combinations of characteristics, there are essentially three types of Mahdī depending on the context.[19]

The word Mahdī can refer to a simple, ordinary believer who

sets an excellent example to other believers. This type of Mahdī does not have a large group of followers or the ambition to change the political status quo. This was the most common type of Mahdī who worked quietly within his own small community of believers to command right and forbid wrong, almost always by example. These Mahdīs were virtually unknown to history but were well known to their own community. They set a moral example and deserved great respect. Yet, they did not usually have much impact on political events. If they did command right or forbid wrong to a ruler they were quickly dispatched or imprisoned by the amir.[20] Sometimes political figures or amirs asked them to join new, reforming movements. The Mahdī Ibn Yūsuf al Jiznai who lived in Meknes and whom the Almoravid Yūsuf bin Tāshfīn asked to participate in the conquest of Fes was an example of this simple, urban, populist Mahdī.[21]

There was also the more extraordinary type of Mahdī whom God elected to command right and forbid wrong and to lead a Muslim community. This sort of Mahdī had political ambitions to change the state, though often on a limited scale in a specific, urban context. These more politically active Mahdīs are occasionally mentioned in historical texts. If they did not have much tribal support they were similarly silenced by the ruling power, though this was far more difficult to do than with the simple, individual Mahdī. The Shīʿites, for example, identified the Ḥasanid Muḥammad b. ʿAbdallāh as the Mahdī before the ʿAbbāsid revolution. His remit was simply routine redemption, not the apocalypse and the conquest of the world.[22]

Finally, there was the Mahdī who not only laid claim to lead the Muslim community but also heralded the coming of the Day of Judgment.[23] This was *al-qāʾim*: a term used even before Islam to refer to the one who would not die but would live on in the promise of redemption.[24] The Mahdī Ibn Tūmart was such a revolutionary and apocalyptic Mahdī who proclaimed the beginning of a new era.

The Mahdī Ibn Tūmart's life, even his emergence from a cave in

Igīlīz, followed a progression from simple, ordinary, individual Mahdīsm to political leadership and the expectation of apocalypse.[25] When he returned to Igīlīz and gained the loyalty of a diverse group of tribes he achieved another type of Mahdīsm. This last type of Mahdī, almost always arising from tribal lands and tribal support, aimed not only to reform the political state, but also to create an entirely new nation.

The apocalyptic, era-changing Mahdī was the subject of contentious debate in the Islamic community.[26] There was no mention of the Mahdī in either the Qur'ān or the most reliable *ḥadīth*. In fact, the idea of the Mahdī is still an issue debated today.[27] Despite the importance of Mahdī movements and eschatological expectation in the foundation of dynasties, overthrow of regimes, and foundation of new empires, the vast, complex and confusing theological source material on the Mahdī remains almost unexplored by modern scholarship. Researching and translating this vast literature would be a life's work.

The Shī'ite concept of the imām and Mahdī[28] relied heavily on the right and necessity of hereditary leadership after the death of Muḥammad.[29] Although Ibn Tūmart claimed an ancestry reaching back to Fatima, the daughter of the Prophet, his doctrine did not dwell on the perceived injustices inflicted on 'Alī and his son Ḥusayn. There was no substantial mention of either of these figures in his doctrine. Nevertheless, the necessity of an imām and the role of the Mahdī in restoring Islam had several parallels in Shī'ism.[30] The Shī'ite hero 'Alī, the Prophet's cousin and son-in-law, gained leadership of the Muslim community as the fourth caliph only to be overthrown by the governor of Syria, Mu'āwīya, a descendant of the Meccan elite and founder of the Umayyad dynasty. Seen as a political liability by the Umayyad caliph Yazīd, 'Ali's son and Muḥammad's grandson, Ḥusayn, and his band of about seventy followers, were massacred at Karbala in Iraq. Out of these historical and political events grew a religious doctrine of continual resistance to the Sunni majority. In Shī'ism 'Alī gained a prominence as high, or even higher than, the Prophet himself.[31] Various descendants of ʿAlī, most famously Ibn al-Ḥanafiyya, willingly or sometimes unwillingly, became the imāms or leaders of the Shīʿites as they struggled under Sunni rule. In several Shīʿite sects the imāms eventually went into 'occultation', a type of hiding that concealed their identity. The imām and Mahdī would come out of occultation on the Day of Judgment to restore the rightful rule of the Prophet's family and herald the end of injustice.

Yet there was little reference to ʿAlī or Ḥusayn or to the battle of Karbala in the Book of Ibn Tūmart, or in any of the Almohad sources, as one would expect from an essentially Shīʿite movement. Al-Baydhaq referenced a book of divination, *al-Jafr*,[32] which ʿAlī supposedly left to the sixth imām Jaʿfar al-Sadiq.[33] Even so, Ibn Tūmart did not attach himself closely to the Eastern Shīʿite or Fatimid claims. Unlike the Shīʿites of the East, the Almohads did not develop their doctrine out of centuries of being a minority under rule by a religiously different majority. Although the Almoravid rivals claimed to be orthodox Sunni, they had themselves only recently converted to a more strict approach to Islam after centuries of pagan practice in the Sahara. The Almohads did not need to develop a complex system of *taqiyya* or concealment or an underground movement. Ibn Tūmart seemed very open about his claims, even in front of the Almoravid amir himself. The Ismāʿīlī Shīʿites in Egypt may have had some influence on Ibn Tūmart, but few direct or deliberate connections between the Almohads and their Fatimid predecessors could be proven.[34]

Ibn Tūmart's Mahdī claim had a historical and social basis in North Africa and Andalusia, as well as the traditions of Eastern Islam. Although the Almohads rejected any association with them, in outward form their movement was not very different from the Fatimid revolution. Towards the end of the ninth century, the Kutāma, a group of mountain tribes somewhat similar to the Maṣmūda, revolted against their Aghlabid rulers in present-day Tunisia. They were led by the Prophet Abū ʿAbd Allah, who came to herald the appearance of the Mahdī.[35] Like Ibn Tūmart, Abū ʿAbd Allah demanded absolute obedience, consolidated his power, organized the stateless tribes into a coherent army and overthrew the Aghlabids in AD 909. The new dynasty was known as the Fatimids, future rulers of Egypt, and one of the most powerful dynasties in Islamic history.[36]

While similar in their beginnings, the Fatimids had no significant influence on the Almohads. That the Almoravids called Ibn Tūmart a Khārijite was simply an indication of how the religious establishment viewed him at the time, namely as a heretic who had exited from orthodox Sunni doctrine and killed other Muslims as sinners.[37] Interestingly, the eminent scholar of Khārijite history, Wilfred Madelung, suggested that there may indeed have been remnants of a North African, that is non-Ismāʿīlī, form of Shiism that could have survived Almoravid persecutions, even as late as the advent of the Almohads. The Almohad sources contain no specific mention of these Khārijite survivors, so it is difficult to speculate on the directness of their influence on Almohad doctrine, especially the notion of the Mahdī.[38] The Almoravids associated the Almohad movement with Abū ʿAbd Allah and the Fatimids, a dynasty that began with a puritanical, apocalyptic rebellion. The Khārijite label, which also attached to the Fatimids, so enraged the Almohads that Ibn Tūmart decided to label the Almoravids as well; he called them anthropomorphists – *mujisimūn* or *zarājina* in Berber.[39] Although it was unclear how much Shiism, either North African or Eastern, influenced them, the Almohads wanted to distance themselves from any association with the Fatimids or the Khārijite label. Although there were many interesting similarities between the Fatimids and Almohads, Ibn Tūmart's chroniclers gave few indications in his writings of a direct Fatimid influence.

Despite the Almohad desire to distance themselves from the Fatimids, several parallels between their doctrines of the Mahdī existed. This shows there was probably some influence from the Fatimids, despite Ibn Tūmart's vigorous denial.[40] A central tenet of

Ismāʿīlī thought was the return of the truly guided one (*al-Mahdī*), or the one who arises (*al-Qāʾim*).[41] While the early Shīʿites and Sunnis initially believed the Mahdī to be a good or righteous caliph or successor, the Ismāʿīlīs developed a more eschatological view of the Mahdī. They also believed that the Mahdī would not simply bring a renewed Islam, but would reveal the original, hidden doctrine of Islam by preaching 'true religion'. Yet, while the predecessors of the Ismāʿīlī Mahdī were based on Shīʿite tradition, Ibn Tūmart claimed Moses, Jesus, Muḥammad and Abū Bakr as his predecessors: there was no reference to the usual, exact Shīʿite chain of descent. In fact, Ibn Tūmart traces his lineage through Arab Berber ancestors to Idrīs, who came to Morocco in the eighth century. Also, al-Ghazālī, who was the intellectual inspiration for the Almohads, actively rejected the Ismāʿīlī movement, though there was little indication of how much the Almohad sources were aware of his position.

Occultation and *taqiyya*, hiding one's beliefs to avoid detection, were not a major part of Almohad doctrine. Nor did Ibn Tūmart base his authority on esoteric, mystical knowledge. The Fatimids, in contrast, had developed a large body of literature dedicated to the secret meaning of the Qurʾān.[42] Unlike Fatimid doctrine, which was obscurantist and reserved for the elite, Almohad doctrine was meant for everybody in the community. One of Ibn Tūmart's reasons for success was his populism, his appeal to the tribes.

As well as the Fatimids, another Maghribi historical precedent for Ibn Tūmart's Mahdī claim was found in the Berber heresies that emerged after the briefly successful Arab conquest. One group of Berbers, the Barghwata, developed their own Qurʾān and were led by a charismatic prophetic figure by the name of Ṣāliḥ. Like Ibn Tūmart, Ṣāliḥ established a distinctly Berber form of Islam. Both Ibn Tūmart and Ṣāliḥ refused to follow any single eastern school of Islam or to implement Sunni law. Yet, unlike Ibn Tūmart, who fiercely defended *al-uṣūl*, and the central importance of the Arabic Qurʾān, Ṣāliḥ and the Barghwata wrote their own Qurʾān in

Berber.[43] They ruled south of Rabat for centuries until they were finally defeated and dispersed by the Almoravids. The Barghwata also relied on messianic claims. Their long history in the Maghrib exemplified how independent the Berbers could be from Arab influence and Arab interpretations of Islam. Although he used his eastern education to full advantage, Ibn Tūmart would also reject classic models and schools of doctrine and law. However, he did not go as far as the Barghwata in rejecting the whole Islamic tradition and being loyal only to an altered, Berber Qur'ān.[44]

There was also a precedent for the divinely inspired leadership set by ʿAbd Allah ibn Yāsīn, founder of the Almoravid dynasty, the great Almohad rival. Although Ibn Yāsīn did not claim to be Mahdī, he did demand personal obedience. This 'holy man on a donkey'[45] travelled to southern Morocco to reform the pagan tribes.[46] Like Ibn Tūmart, who also rode a donkey, he commanded right and forbade wrong in explicitly political ways. The geographer al-Bakrī, the major source for the rise of the Almoravids, described Ibn Yāsīn as a strict reformer who rallied the tribes around him. After enforcing strict moral standards and controlling pagan desert customs 'he massacred all those who declared themselves against him'.[47] He became 'master of the entire desert' and all the tribes of the region rallied to his cause. He demanded absolute obedience to a new revolutionary doctrine. Thus, a mere 'holy man on a donkey' was able to control the fate of Maghribi Islam. The theme of the righteous leader, bringing the tribes back into the fold of Islam, was repeated throughout Maghribi history.[48]

The Era of the Mahdī in the Maghrib

The particularities of Maghribi society and geography, especially in the medieval period, were conducive to the rise of prophetic figures.[49] Mohamed Zniber from Muḥammad V University in Rabat argues that the very cultural, ethnic, geographic and even economic landscape of the Maghrib has encouraged the rise of spiritual leaders and Mahdīs throughout history. He speaks of the 'psychological disposition' that is found in Moroccan society throughout history – 'the appeal to a miraculous solution'.[50] Discussing the inconsistent nature of the climate, the harsh realities of the desert and the mountains, he made a direct link between Morocco's geography, hagiocracy (the rule of saints) and Mahdīs in Moroccan history. 'In a country where the rain is not always faithful in its visits, where tribal discord can maintain a state of insecurity and economic crisis, Morocco's history has been shaped by those critical moments when charismatic chiefs emerge with enough prestige to resonate through an entire dynasty.'[51] Maintaining power in the Maghrib was a difficult undertaking that required a heavy and consistent application of spiritual charisma, obedience and unity: exactly the nature of Ibn Tūmart's doctrine. As Georges Gurvitch reflects in an essay on Moroccan sociology, Moroccan rulers were charged with 'simultaneously maintaining the natural order, the social order, and the divine order'. This often immobilized dynasties and rulers and made them weak because 'these three orders could easily come into conflict'.[52] The need to maintain natural, spiritual and social obligations provided opportunities for the revolutionary. Whenever Moroccan leaders lost the careful social balance, revolutionaries were able to use those breaks to make claims that the social order was wrong and needed to be corrected. This was the case with Ibn Tūmart and the Almohads. The scholar Madeline Fletcher claimed that Ibn Tūmart 'simply provided the formulation of the leadership role traditionally granted by Berber custom to the holy men'.[53] Although Ibn Tūmart's Mahdīsm was not an exclusively Berber concept like the Barghwata Qur'ān, it was a product of his immediate environment rather than adopted from a Shīʿite or Sunni model.

Several 'Mahdīs' in the Maghrib before the rise of Ibn Tūmart held charismatic, messianic claims.[54] One was Mahdī Muḥammad al-Nafs al-Zakia, who was related to the Prophet Muḥammad and lived during the time of the Idrīsīds, an Arab sharifian dynasty that ruled large parts of Morocco from Fes (789–828). Interestingly, the actual ruler of the Idrīsīds, Idrīs I, was Mahdī Muḥammad al-Zakia's brother-in-law. He was proclaimed as Mahdī after his military exploits routed the ʿAbbāsids from Morocco. Idrīs I often used the language of Mahdīsm, exhorting the Muslim community to follow his guidance (*huda*) and restore the true *sharīʿa* laws of Islam, which the invading ʿAbbāsid had wrongly applied.

Besides al-Zakia, several Mahdīs with political power emerged immediately before the rise of the Almohads.[55] There was the Mahdī Ibn Yūsuf al-Jizani who ruled from Meknes and who supported the Almoravids and their conquest of Fes. The Mahdī Ibn Talal built a fortified castle near Ifrane in the Middle Atlas. The Almoravids attacked him. Finally, Maribel Fierro described the influence of Ibn Qasī from southern Portugal. He started a revolt and claimed to be Mahdī, but without a strong tribal base he was eventually engulfed by the more broadly successful Almohad movement.[56] An interesting parallel could be made with Muḥammad the Prophet and the increasing number of prophetic figures that emerged in Arabia during the sixth and seventh centuries.[57] In both the case of Muḥammad the Prophet and the Mahdī Ibn Tūmart the time seemed ripe for their rise. It could have been the very presence of so many different Mahdī figures with varying claims and levels of power that inspired the search for the true Mahdī. The late eleventh and early twelfth century was the era of the Mahdī in the Maghrib.

A New Religiosity

The Islamic world as a whole was approaching a turning point; the ʿAbbāsid caliphate was falling into disarray, the great focal point of Muslim culture in al-Andalus was losing control to the Christians, the Normans were conquering Sicily and the Italian city states were beginning to emerge. The Mediterranean, though largely Muslim, was no longer a predominantly Islamic sea. The year 500 seemed to herald news of a new coming.[58] There were other natural and economic phenomena linked to important trade routes that led the region into certain turmoil and a desire for newly inspired leadership and change.[59] Finally, a new ethos was emerging throughout the Muslim world, an ethos that grew out of a need to deal with fragmentation and political crisis, an ethos linked to a more mystical view of the world and of God.

Tilman Nagel called this new era '*die neue Frömmlichkeit*', the era of a new religiosity.[60] It was an era in which the seemingly opposed Sufī and Ash'arite trends came together. Maribel Fierro similarly identified the eleventh and twelfth centuries as a period when 'blind acceptance of doctrine was to be rejected'. There was a new need to find proof of God's unity (*tawḥīd*). The Ash'arites used reason; the Sufīs used techniques of mystical union. Thus, both methods, the rational and the mystical, became threats to the old styles of rule and authority; they removed individual Muslims from obligations to the human authority and legitimacy. In particular, the Sufī literature from the period spoke of the individual developing a way, a *ṭarīqa*, in which to find God without the intervention of the state. This newly developed relationship between the individual soul and God could exist even in the midst of profound political crisis and change. This new religiosity, religious individualism, posed a threat to the established order because it removed belief from human authority. The separation of belief and authority led to an overwhelming desire to replace the old system of rulers and jurists. The jurists and rulers had lost their religious legitimacy and failed to sustain the Muslim community against a variety of internal and external threats. Caliphal authority was no longer sufficient. 'Spiritual personalities, be it theologians or Sufī masters', filled the gap.[61] Ibn Tūmart was one of these personalities.

Ibn Tūmart was successful because of his ability to harness the spirit of the new religious awakening to focus on the realities of establishing the foundations of a new empire. Even as al-Ghazālī attempted to unify the mystical and rational in his theological and philosophical works,[62] Ibn Tūmart attempted to unify individual spiritual awakening with obedience to temporal power and absolute social order. This ability to unite the obligations of the temporal with the hopes and expectations of the spiritual was the basis of a revolutionary Mahdī's power.

Ibn Tūmart and the Almohads were proclaiming a new era of Islam, a new political expression of this religious awakening. Whereas the Seljuk Turkish invaders of the Middle East and the desert Almoravids of North Africa and Andalusia gave the ʿAbbāsid caliph symbolic leadership, the Almohads claimed their own spiritual head in the Mahdī Ibn Tūmart.[63] Unlike the Almoravids, Buyids, Seljuk Turks and a host of other invading peoples of Islamic history, the Almohad tribes were not merely *de facto* invading rulers who maintained the caliphate's legitimacy. The Almohad movement was among the first true attempts not only to imitate, but also to reinvent and recast Muḥammad the Prophet's call. With the Almohads, *sultan* (effective power) and *dīn* (religion) were merged yet again. The Almohads, under the infallible guidance of the Mahdī Ibn Tūmart, claimed to achieve the religious and political unity of Islam in this world, a unity that had been a goal of the Muslim community since the death of the Prophet Muḥammad.[64] According to the *ḥadīth*, 'Religion and [temporal] power are twins.'[65] A Mahdī proclaiming a new era could bring these twins together again.

The Almohad Doctrine of the Mahdī

> It has been (accepted) by all Muslims in every epoch, that at the end of time a man from the family (of the Prophet) will without fail make his appearance, one who will strengthen Islam and make justice triumph. Muslims will follow him, and he will gain domination over the Muslim realm. He will be called Mahdī. Following him, Satan will appear, together with all the subsequent signs of the Day of Judgment.
>
> Ibn Khaldūn

Divine expectation, the expectation of an era of divine rule unmitigated by the fallibility and contradictions of humanity, was the fuel of revolution and of change. It was the struggle for an ideal, divine society, finally united with the will of God, which provided a pretext for rebellion against an unsatisfactory economic, political or social status quo. In his recent book, *The court of the caliphs,*[66] Hugh Kennedy described the fervent pitch of divine expectation that brought the ʿAbbāsid to power. He described mysterious men dressed in black, fanning the sparks of divine expectation. This was the small group of ʿAbbāsid revolutionaries who, like Ibn Tūmart in the Atlas Mountains, organized the remote tribes of Khurusan in the mountains of Persia and sacked the magnificent power of the Umayyads in Damascus. The Almohad movement and the notion of the Mahdī was another example of this combination of tribal revolution and divine expectation.

As Ibn Khaldūn noted, almost all Muslims accepted the Mahdī idea. Yet there was no clear reference to the Mahdī in the Qurʾān. The Qurʾān made many suggestions about the end of time, but there was never a specific reference to a Mahdī or any clear indication of who this Mahdī would be. In fact, the term Mahdī did not even appear in the Qurʾān.[67] The root of Mahdī, h-d-y, occurred often in the Qurʾān referring to divine guidance *huda*. 'Mahdī' was a verbal noun meaning the divinely guided, but no such word appears in the Qurʾān. Without any clear direction from the Qurʾān about the Mahdī, and with the salvation of the world at stake, the Mahdī idea has been an especially divisive issue for Muslims.

Even in early Islam there was a wide variety of interpretations about the Mahdī. Muḥammad ibn Sīrīn of Basra (d. 728) believed that the Mahdī would come from the Kahtani tribe, which was to lead a righteous revolt. Another early scholar believed that the Mahdī would find hidden versions of the Torah and Gospel in Antioch.[68] This confusion and wild speculation about the Mahdī only increased with the passage of time and the failure of the much-predicted day of reckoning to occur.

It was ironic, given that there was no specific reference to the Mahdī in the Qur'ān or the most established *ḥadīth*, that Ibn Tūmart advocated a strict interpretation of the revealed scripture.[69] Thus, when Ibn Tūmart advocated a return to the roots, *al-uṣūl*, of Islam he was basing his authority on a concept that had little basis in the original sources. Yet, it was never Ibn Tūmart's intent simply to promote the original texts. His claim to be an advocate for the return to the origins of Islam was only one step in a much more ambitious theology of unity, conquest and salvation, a theology that had about as little basis in the Qur'ān as the trifling discussions of the Almoravid Maliki jurists he so despised.

One of the main appeals of the 'Mahdī idea' was the promise that the Mahdī would usher in a new era of unity throughout Islamic lands. This concept was especially appealing after the invasion of Islam by the Mongols and Turks and the division of the Islamic world into several competing states. As the Islamic world fractured, centres of power shifted and the Ismaili movement and other Shī'ite movements, with their concentration on the Mahdī, gained political prominence in key parts of the Islamic world. The term 'Mahdī' was associated with those who claimed to lead Muslims at the end of time. As part of this divine expectation in the midst of turmoil, books of divination, like the book of *al-Jafr*, promised a new, fated era, a renaissance of Islamic unity and power.[70] An infallible Mahdī would lead this new era: a man who would restore the relationship between fallible human society, which had gone astray, and God.

Despite divine expectations, no Mahdī ever succeeded in uniting the entire Islamic world under his rule. Nevertheless, as discussed previously, several Mahdīs achieved greater ends, starting movements that brought dramatic change and unity to their region. Throughout Islamic history, various tribal and religious leaders emerged to claim the title of Mahdī, herald a new era of justice, Muslim unity and the end of time. These messianic figures appeared in tribal regions at the margins of established legal schools, doctrines and governments, sweeping in change and reform with their dramatic message of unity, salvation and Islamic revivalism. Near the end of the fourteenth century, Ibn Khaldūn refers to these false Mahdīs as they appeared in the medieval period.

> The common people, the stupid mass, who make claims with respect to the Mahdī and who are not guided in this connection by any intelligence or helped by any knowledge, assume that the Mahdī may appear in a variety of circumstances and places. They do not understand the real meaning of the matter. They mostly assume that the appearance will take place in some remote province out of the reach of the dynasties and outside their authority. ... Many weak-minded people go to those places [outside ruling authority] in order to support a deceptive cause that the human soul in its delusion and stupidity leads them to believe capable of succeeding. Many of them have been killed.[71]

Like other Mahdīs, Ibn Tūmart failed to bring justice to all of Islam and, as I have discussed, the historical chroniclers favourable to the Almohad movement attempted to deal with this fundamental problem. Yet, his Mahdīsm sparked the beginning of the Almohad Empire. In this sense, Ibn Tūmart's claim to be Mahdī was among the most successful in Islamic history.[72] Such was the power of his message that with Ibn Tūmart the promise of salvation and renewal seemed to shift from the centre of Islam to the perimeter with new legends claiming that the Mahdī should appear in the West.

Obedience and infallibility

A central tenet of Ibn Tūmart's doctrine was obedience to the Mahdī. The imām and Mahdī, the true leader of the Muslim community, was free of all forms of sin. He must be *ma'sūm*, or incapable of error. For, 'error does not destroy error. Thus, the one who errs does not destroy error.'[73] The imām upheld the virtues of truth and righteousness and is truly guided. These were the personal characteristics and requirements of the infallible imām. Yet, the imām also required certain behaviours and virtues from his subjects, most importantly, strict obedience. The tribes of the Atlas Mountains had not only to follow his teachings and law, they had also to purge themselves of all differences (*'ikhtilāf*) and be in agreement (*'itifāq*) with the imām. Moreover, they must physically imitate the way of life of the infallible Mahdī, watching his every move and following his example, like the *sunna* of the Prophet Muḥammad.[74] To justify this strict code of obedience and the strict forbidding of disagreement, it was useful for Ibn Tūmart to refer both directly and indirectly to the example of the Prophet Muḥammad; the original rise of Islam thus enforced unified action in an environment of divided tribal loyalties.[75]

The sequence of events leading to Ibn Tūmart's rise as imām and Mahdī seem deliberately depicted to bear a striking resemblance to the life of the Prophet, with a cave similar to the cave of Muḥammad and a hijra from Mecca (Igīlīz) to Medina (Tīnmallal). Ibn Tūmart and al-Baydhaq seemed actively to cultivate such comparisons between his life and the life of Muḥammad. But there were crucial differences, especially regarding the extent of the claims of the Mahdī. First and most striking, while Muḥammad was a prophet, Ibn Tūmart was a Mahdī who would bring the end of time. Ibn Tūmart described himself as 'the central tent pole that supports the heavens and the earth'.[76] Where Muḥammad claimed to be only human,[77] Ibn Tūmart claimed that there would be chaos without himself as imām. The 'heavens will crash onto earth' when the imām loses his authority.[78] Thus, one must believe in the Mahdī, the imām with the 'innermost blood of the heart'.[79] The blood of the tribe, *'aṣabiyya* (tribal solidarity) and factionalism will have no relevance at the end of time. The *A'azz mā Yuṭlab* was clear about its purpose, 'This book is about the truth of believing in the

Imām. This belief is a basic principle of religion. It is a basis of religious law (*sharī'a*).'[80] It would seem that the 'doctrine' of the Almohads was not simply a doctrine of ideas; it was also a command to follow and obey the imām and Mahdī.[81]

The Day of Reckoning

In the *A'azz mā Yuṭlab* Ibn Tūmart exhorted the Berbers, the chosen audience, to 'believe in Allah and the last day for this is the way of God'.[82] The end of time was a central theme in Ibn Tūmart's preaching. There would be a time when the earth was ruled by sin, depravation, avarice and jealousy: this implied the rule of the decadent, anthropomorphist Almoravids. In this time of depravation 'the knowledgeable go and the ignorant remain, the righteous go and scum remain, the believers go and the distrustful remain.'[83] At the end of time the Mahdī, 'the pillar of religion', would reverse these sins and bring victory to the religion of God. Wrong will be replaced by right, tyranny by justice, sin by good works and the Mahdī will 'establish the firmly grounded law' based on *al-uṣūl*, the roots of religion, and demolishing *al-furū'*, change, innovation and sin.[84] Obedience to the Mahdī, not to any idea, or sect, or person, was the way to realize divine expectations of the last day.

Ibn Tūmart claimed to be the Mahdī, the man who would usher in the end of days. This assertion gave Ibn Tūmart the ability to gain immediate power and influence. First, despite his relatively low birth, he could claim direct descent from the Prophet Muḥammad.[85] Second, he could command the absolute obedience of his followers, which is essential when organizing a loose tribal clan to fight against the Almoravid desert warriors and their Spanish mercenaries. Third, Ibn Tūmart could attribute the sins and problems of the world to the Almoravid leaders and their faulty doctrine. Finally, he could provide his often less than literate followers with a simple way of approaching God. Most importantly, the North African context, the audience of Berber followers, shaped, inspired and influenced Ibn Tūmart's doctrine.

When Ibn Tūmart met his closest follower and deputy, ʿAbd al-Muʾmin, and learnt that he was going East in search of knowledge, Ibn Tūmart told him that all he would need to know was here in the West, in the Maghrib.[86]

The Doctrine of the Aʿazz mā Yuṭlab: The Book of Ibn Tūmart[87]

A primary purpose of this study has been to answer the question of how a new form of Islam, envisioned by the Mahdī Ibn Tūmart, transcended deeply divided, blood loyalties to produce the foundations of the Almohad Empire in North Africa. Having discussed the historical, economic, geographic and social circumstances of this stunning burst of Islam among the divided Berber tribes of the Atlas Mountains, Ibn Tūmart, leader and founder of the Berber Almohad Empire took advantage of these circumstances to articulate a new and revolutionary vision of Islam. This vision would be a force to unite the tribes of the Atlas, even as Muḥammad originally united the tribes of Arabia in the seventh century. In his inspired book the *Aʿazz mā Yuṭlab*, Ibn Tūmart created a doctrine suited to the Berbers of the Atlas Mountains. He used his theology to challenge the legitimacy of the ruling Almoravids and to justify *jihād* against other Muslims. In this book, Ibn Tūmart established his title of Mahdī, bringer of the end of time. Most importantly, he used his doctrine to construct a vision of unity and imperial destiny in the face of tribal differences.

Like the writings of most religious revolutionaries, Ibn Tūmart's book challenged the status quo and did not fit easily into a previously existing school or category of Islam. It was difficult to determine whether his ideas were influenced by al-Ghazālī of the East, the Malikis of the West, the philosophical Muʿtazila or literalist Ashʾari, the Shīʿites or even the radical Khārijites. In some ways Ibn Tūmart was rejecting all established precedents, attempting to create a fresh, unique message, a message that attempted even to exceed the words of the Prophet Muḥammad.

Ibn Tūmart's political theology was a selected amalgam of

different influences and revolutionary concepts. Although heavily influenced by thinkers of his time, especially al-Ghazālī, Ibn Tūmart was not from any one school. Instead, he adopted a variety of theological arguments that would most support his claim to power and spiritual authority. He created an 'Almohad Qur'ān', a book of doctrine that was memorized, studied and respected almost as much as the Qur'ān itself.[88] Mirroring the Qur'ān, it had three fundamental purposes: a guide for a way of life, a justification for fighting against disbelief and a promise of salvation through the guidance of the Mahdī, himself, at the end of time.

Before summarizing the book of Ibn Tūmart, in this chapter I shall introduce four concepts that were the foundation of Ibn Tūmart's doctrine. First, *tawḥīd*, or the absolute unity of Allah, was the most important point of Ibn Tūmart's book. God was one and only one: any attempt to divide his essence or to think of him in a limited physical manner was *shirk*, blasphemy. The very name Almohad, a French corruption of *al-Muwaḥid*, comes from the Arabic root, *waḥid*, meaning one, the Almohads defined themselves as believers in the oneness of God. Second, Ibn Tūmart devoted the first part of his book to discussing difference between *al-uṣūl* and *al-furū'*. The roots or fundamentals of Islam were *al-uṣūl*. Later judgements and embellishments, the focus of Almoravid jurists, were *al-furū'* the 'branches' of law. The third major component of Ibn Tūmart's book was an attack on *tajsīm*, anthropomorphism. Any physical embodiment of God was wrong. Lastly, Ibn Tūmart devoted a portion of his book to the discussion of himself as the infallible Mahdī, as has been discussed above.

Tawḥīd[89]

There was perhaps nothing more difficult for the believer than to think about the nature of God. Today, an educated person born into postmodern society is most likely to question the existence of God at some point in their lives. In twelfth-century North Africa, as in most of pre-industrial world history, a person was more likely to question the nature of God, as opposed to his existence. The existence of God was evident in daily life and practice. The nature of God, however, was constantly in dispute and in flux. People sought to define God in many different ways according to their immediate cultural background. Some defined God according to the traditional beliefs and practices of ritual, coming of age, death and birth that dominated tribal society. Some defined him using mystical notions of spirit. An educated few used philosophy to discover the nature of God. The issue of the nature of God inevitably emerged even in the minds of the most uneducated and isolated people. Ibn Tūmart sought to address this issue through a strict doctrine of *tawḥīd.*

Soon after the foundation of the Almohad Empire, the Almohad doctor and thinker Ibn Ṭufayl wrote the story of a man named Ibn Yaqẓān, created alone on an island. He was isolated from humanity but still able to transcend the world, to know and believe in a single, monotheistic God.[90] Ibn Ṭufayl's main argument was that *tawḥīd* was a part of human nature; it was a sense of divinity that exists from birth itself.[91] In some ways the story of Ibn Yaqẓān, the spiritual Robinson Crusoe of the Almohads, mirrored the birth of the Almohad Empire. In the rugged and isolated island valleys of the Atlas Mountains the notion of God absolutely detached from the world but also encompassing and controlling the world and everything in it, emerged.

This overwhelming sense of God as completely free of a worldly nature, in the mystical Sufī sense,[92] but also completely in control of human will in the rational Ash'ari sense, was Ibn Tūmart's doctrine of *tawḥīd* – a word that is difficult to translate that meant the divine unity and singularity of God without attributes. For Ibn Tūmart, *tawḥīd* was an expression of the synthesis of mystical and rational experience.

The idea of a completely separate but all-encompassing God was a powerful one. However, it raised the question of how they could know God if he was completely separate, not only from human nature but also from the nature of the universe. Such a question required the skills of the Mahdī. Great minds and thinkers like al-Ghazālī and Ibn Rushd could think of God completely in the abstract within the confines of their study and the inspiration of the pen. The people in general, however, did not have access to this depth of philosophical and spiritual training.[93] The Mahdī was able to provide the direction, guidance and discipline necessary to prepare the common, tribal people for the coming judgement of this both distant and omnipotent God.

'There is no God but God.' This statement was not only the first pillar of belief and a requirement for conversion to Islam, but it was also the very core of the original Islamic concept of society and the universe. It was a powerful, direct, straightforward message, meant both to unify believers and to solidify a society of divisive Arab tribes. Yet, even so simple a statement as 'there is no God but God' was subjected to the vicissitudes of history and interpretation. Although this central belief in the oneness of God was meant to unite a religious community, it became the source of divisive arguments about the true nature of God. Questions arose about what exactly was meant by there being no God but God, whether God had an image and whether this statement meant that all the universe was God, which would make ourselves a part of God. This divisiveness in the community, inspired by the conflict over the meaning of God's unity, gave Ibn Tūmart an opportunity to use his own version of *tawḥīd* to revolt against other Muslims.

With deeply simple, poetic language, similar to the last sūras of the Qur'ān, Ibn Tūmart described the Almohad meaning of *tawḥīd*.

> Allah, our guide (in life), declares that it is necessary for all to be instructed that Allah, the Great and Almighty, alone in His rule, created the entire universe, above and below. ... There is nothing before Him or after Him, nothing above Him or below Him, nothing to the left or to the right,

> nothing in front of Him or behind Him, not all, not some. He is not specified by the consciousness, not figured in the eye, not pictured in dreams, nor fashioned in the mind ... thoughts cannot represent him at all. He is the All-Hearing and the All-Knowing. There is no other Creator than He.[94]

Ibn Tūmart also summarized his doctrine of *tawḥīd* in a letter written to his followers. He proclaimed to the assembled Almohad tribes the threat of damnation for idolaters who did not follow *tawḥīd* and the award of paradise for true believers in *tawḥīd*. The believer of Ibn Tūmart's conception of absolute *tawḥīd* would return to the state of innocence that existed 'the day his mother bore him':

> Occupy yourselves with understanding *tawḥīd*, for this is the base of your religion. One must not allow any comparison or association with the Creator, all ideas of imperfection, diminution, limitation, direction; he is not situated in a place or a direction for the Highest exists before places and directions! Those who situate him in a place or a direction give him a corporal form; and those who give him a corporal form adore him like an idol. And those who die with these beliefs end up in eternal flames! But those who understand *tawḥīd* will become pure of sin like the day his mother bore him: he will die in this state, he will sojourn in Paradise![95]

With native fluency in Berber, Ibn Tūmart would have astounded his audience with these simple phrases declaring God's unity. Tied to matters of tradition, tribe and patriarchy, the inhabitants of the Atlas Mountains would have been struck, possibly scandalized and riveted, by the powerful force of his words. There was no God but God. He could not be seen, touched, heard, or even imagined. He was inconceivable to the human mind. His power was far beyond the human sphere. In fact, this power to communicate a simple concept beyond the struggles and concerns of everyday life would break through the barriers of history, ancestry and geography. What had once been important concerns were irrelevant compared with this ultra-monotheistic idea of God. The processes of breaking through history, of questioning human perception and of affirming eternity were what characterized the birth of the Almohad movement.

For Ibn Tūmart, *tawḥīd* meant a pure and absolute conception of God as God. This was no theological debate about the nature of God. Ibn Tūmart was not making a technical point, but emphasizing the fundamental basis of humanity's relationship with God. God was not at a place, in a location, or part of something. God 'existed before places and locations'. One was to believe in God as 'one believed in God at the day of your birth' without association or symbol or difference or representation.[96] Any idolatry, any attempt to associate God with the world, merited the punishment of eternal damnation. God must be believed as God. He sought a God that would be the most basic expression of human spirituality, belief as 'at the day of birth'.

The notion of belief 'at the day of birth' was an integral part of Islamic philosophy and law. According to the *ḥadīth* of Abū Ḥusayn Muslim, Muḥammad said, 'Every infant is born in the natural state. It is his parents who make him a Jew or a Christian or a heathen.'[97] For 'the soul in its first natural state of creation is ready to accept whatever good or evil may arrive and leave an imprint on it.'[98] This was the *tabula raza*, the blank slate of Muslim belief. Humans were born to be Muslims. They were simply corrupted to be otherwise. For Ibn Tūmart, humans were born to be Almohad Muslims, believers in the most perfect notion of *tawḥīd*.[99]

This powerful message struck at the heart of human belief and rallied even the tribes of remote and inaccessible mountains to a common cause. The purity of belief became eminently radical, an excuse to destroy or demolish all experience, all attempts to understand God. It became a convenient way of condemning those who used association and difference to describe God. God's presence was not of any 'body'. Only the Mahdī could express this message of God's unity. Through promotion of the doctrine of *tawḥīd*, many of Ibn Tūmart's practical political objectives were given religious force and legitimacy.

The challenge for Ibn Tūmart and his successors was to maintain the original fervour of religious revelation. Other spiritual leaders had ventured into the Atlas Mountains before, but their light was quickly extinguished both by internal division and impossible odds.[100] Ibn Tūmart had to do more than express the unity of God, he had to express the unity of God as something known only to those who followed the Almohad movement. He made a simultaneously universal and exclusive claim. God was universal. *Tawḥīd* transcended tribe, time, dimension and space. But *tawḥīd* could only be understood though Almohad doctrine and the leadership of the Mahdī, excluding the Almoravids and non-Almohads.

Anti-anthropomorphism

Spiritual eloquence and power were insufficient to form a government out of tribes. To translate the unity of God to the unity of the tribes, Ibn Tūmart's doctrine spoke to the economic, political and tribal conditions of twelfth-century North Africa, mainly the domination of the Almoravid rulers. The Atlas tribes were already aware of the economic and political advantages of destroying the domination of their old rivals. However, Ibn Tūmart was able to give powerful spiritual justification to reaping those advantages.

In addition to expounding on the ethnic differences from the mountain tribes, Ibn Tūmart accused the desert Almoravids of a grave heresy – anthropomorphism, *al-mulithāmūn al-mujisimūn*.[101] *Al-tajsīm*, or anthropomorphism, was the practice of embodying or incarnating Allah. Ibn Tūmart was not accusing the Almoravids of worshipping idols. They were even greater sinners. Through their narrow, scholastic reading of the Qur'ān, the Almoravids had transformed the perfect and inconceivable unity of Allah into a physical idol.

To avoid anthropomorphism, the Qur'ān could not be taken literally. Ibn Tūmart referred to unbelievers who 'interpret the words of the Qur'ān out of context'.[102] Although he advocated a return to the sources, Ibn Tūmart was far from being a literalist. Certain passages of the Qur'ān suggest that Allah acts with a human form. Sūra LV *Raḥman* says: 'All that is on earth will perish: But will abide (for ever), the Face of thy Lord, full of majesty, bounty and honour.' This could be read as meaning that God had a face. Ibn Tūmart, like al-Ghazālī, believed that these passages must be read in their figurative sense. If God were unbounded, a force of pure unity, there could be no human-like face of God. The face of God in this passage symbolized the bounty and power of God. The Almoravids, according to Ibn Tūmart, read these passages in their narrow, literal sense, therefore giving God a human, anthropomorphic image.

According to Ibn Tūmart, this was the Almoravids' cardinal sin, for it was limiting the nature of God. For this reason, and for all the various 'faults' of the Almoravids, Ibn Tūmart condemned them to the same fate as the unbelievers and the ignorant. Indeed, the Almoravid period was worse than the *jāhiliyya*, the period before Muḥammad's time. At least the pagans of Arabia did not defame the very being of God. Thus, in Ibn Tūmart's words, 'the necessity of waging *jihād* against the unbelievers and anthropomorphists'.[103] In this manner, Ibn Tūmart gave the force of theological certainty to the mountain tribe's vague sense of distrust and economic envy towards the nomadic Saharans.

Ibn Tūmart declared it necessary 'to detest them, because of the wrongs that they do ... their eating and drinking of what is forbidden by God.'[104] Their women 'wore their hair high'. They violated the truth of Islam every day. Their culture, their desert way of life as portrayed here was counter to the truth of Islam. While Almohads knew that God could not be seen, touched, conceived of, or imagined, the Almoravids believed that God could be contained. They contained God not only in their interpretation of the Qur'ān, but also in the interpretations of lawyers and jurists, in the writings and commentaries of those who lived centuries after the life of Muḥammad. They even favoured *al-furū'*, later legal accretions, over the very words of God and the most reliable *ḥadīth*, or sayings of Muḥammad.

The trunk and its branches

Ibn Tūmart's purpose was to wrest *mulk*, temporal power, away from the Almoravid jurists and rulers, restoring a theocratic ideal to the Muslim World.[105] The scene where Ibn Tūmart confronts 'Alī bin Yūsuf in Marrakech was the most dramatic display of this purpose. Therefore, it was not surprising that the exclusive use of *al-uṣūl* (the original sources of Islam: literally in Arabic the 'roots') over *al-furū'* (later legal texts and interpretations: the 'branches'), was an important part of Ibn Tūmart's doctrine.

Although Ibn Tūmart wanted to restore the 'fundamentals' of Islam, it would be inaccurate to call him a fundamentalist in the modern understanding of fundamentalism as a literal interpretation of revealed texts. In fact, as the dispute between Ibn Tūmart and the Almoravid jurists at Āghmāt exemplified,[106] the issue was often much more complex than literalism verses symbolism. On the question of God's image, Ibn Tūmart was a prime example of an anti-literalist who was wholeheartedly 'fundamentalist' in several other ways. For example, he declared that a strictly literal interpretation of certain passages of the Qur'ān led to anthropomorphism, the great sin from which a whole host of other sins followed. He called for the interpretation of these passages as figurative speech. Yet, he also commanded the exclusive use of *al-uṣūl*, the 'roots' or fundamental scriptures of Islam, along with his guidance as Mahdī. He rejected the narrow, Maliki law books and the exclusive club of jurists who interpreted them.[107] In this sense, he was a non-literalist fundamentalist, rallying tribes and marginal groups against elite, literalist scholars who seemed to keep the spirit of Allah and his word to themselves.[108]

This problem of literalism, knowledge, interpretation of popular verses and of elite understandings of religion, was predicted in the Qur᾿ān, in Sūra III, 7, the Family of ᾿Imran:

> He it is who has sent down to thee the book:
> In it are verses basic or fundamental (of established meaning);
> They are the foundation of the book: others are allegorical
> But those in whose hearts is perversity follow the part thereof that is allegorical,
> Seeking discord, and searching for its hidden meanings
> But no one knows its hidden meanings except God.
> And those who are firmly grounded in knowledge say,
> 'We believe in the Book; the whole of it is from our Lord:'
> And none will grasp the message except men of understanding.

It seemed simple – nobody knew the hidden meanings of the Qur᾿ān except God. Nobody should interpret the Qur᾿ān allegorically, but should follow the basic meaning of the verses. Nevertheless, the verse was not as straightforward as it seemed. The most contentious part of the verse was not the part that required acceptance of the basic meaning of the Qur᾿ān. Rather, it was the last phrase: 'and none will grasp the message except men of understanding'. Debate and disagreement arose over who were the men of understanding and what qualified them to grasp the message of God. Some felt this excluded the common people from knowing the inner meaning of God's message. Ironically, this Qur᾿ānic verse, clearly intended to pre-empt a literalist versus allegorist dispute, was itself a great source of dispute. It commanded against 'seeking discord', but was itself the source of much discussion. Working under the patronage of the Almohad caliph Abū Yaq῾ūb Yūsuf (reigned 1163–84), Ibn Rushd (Averroes in

Latin) wrote about this verse in his defence of philosophers who, in his view, were 'the men of understanding' or 'those firmly grounded in knowledge'.[109]

For the Almoravids, it was the Maliki jurists who were the 'men of understanding'. The position of the Malikis in Maghribi Islam had a long, established history. There were several historical reasons for the position of the Maliki jurists, with the full backing of the Almoravid rulers and chiefs, the 'men of understanding'. The Maliki school dominated the Maghrib. The Malikis were one of the schools or ways (*madhāhib*) of Sunni Islam attributed to Mālik ibn Anas (d. AD 796).[110] His works were spread from Medina into Egypt and North Africa by a variety of commentators, disciples and scholars, including ʿAbd al-Raḥman ibn Qasim, whose *Mudawana* (code or codex of law) became the standard book through the efforts of ʿAbd al-Salām.[111] By AH 448 (AD 1048) the *Mudawana* of the Malikis had come fully to dominate the Maghrib.[112] The necessity of these law books was more practical than intentional.[113] The Qur'ān was considered the foundation of Islamic law, but by itself it did not provide a practical reference to all legal problems that arose in a complex system of government and enforcement. The *Mudawana* condensed the Qur'ān, the *ḥadīth* (the statements of Muḥammad) and the *sunna* (the way or example of the Prophet Muḥammad), into actionable laws.

However, over the centuries, jurists began to focus more on the codex, the *Mudawana*, and its many commentaries, precedents and accretions and less on the fundamental texts, *al-uṣūl* that Ibn Tūmart so vehemently revived without, of course, accounting for the practical difficulties of applying Islamic law. The revolutionary, especially the tribal revolutionary, often had an advantage in not needing to address the practical issues of statecraft that consumed the ruling authorities. As discussed previously, Ibn Tūmart could unify his followers around the repeal of odious laws like the taxation on trade going through and coming from the Atlas Mountains. Most importantly, however, Ibn

Tūmart could appeal to the same simplicity of purpose that unified the Arab tribes around Muḥammad on the fundamental texts of Islam. The *Aʿazz mā Yuṭlab*, which was relatively thin compared with the voluminous books of Maliki law, was the new guide to the community and an explanation of the true nature of God. It was not the mere dictates of lawyers and jurists.[114]

By removing the intermediary of the lawyers and jurists, Ibn Tūmart mobilized the tribes in a struggle that would similarly appeal to the common people. According to the Almoravids, farming tribes and people working in the coastal plains, were deemed not to be 'men of understanding'. As a result, it was the common people who joined the Almohads as they conquered Spain and North Africa. In this sense, the rejection of the jurists was the rejection of the present economic, social and political order and a rejection of the barriers placed between the common people and the truth of the scriptures, barriers meant to consolidate power and create a class of learned elite. It was this class that Ibn Tūmart seemed particularly to despise on his journey back to the Maghrib.

Ibn Tūmart rejected, with particular vehemence, the way Almoravid jurists seemed even to despise the original, fairly egalitarian concepts of Islam, the equality of believers and the *umma*, the community of believers. Ibn al-Faradi described how most Maliki jurists, including the chief *qāḍī* at Córdoba, Ashbagh bin Khalil, rejected several of the *ḥadīth*, even the accounts of the Prophet's closest companions. He said he would prefer 'the head of a pig than the head cushion of Ibn Abī Shayba in [his] coffin'.[115] Ibn Abī Shayba, like the more famous Ibn Ḥazm, was part of a much despised minority supporter of *ḥadīth* in al-Andalus. It was a minority tolerated only because of the extraordinary protection of a few caliphs and small kings.[116]

Most *faqihs* and Maliki *qaḍāʾ* before the rise of the Almohads were fervent supporters of law books, of secondary sources, *al-furūʿ*, over the primary sources of faith, *al-uṣūl*. They even considered a return to *ḥadīth* as retrograde backtracking. They saw no reason to return to the *ḥadīth* when so much progress had been made in the law books since the time of Muḥammad. Al-Marrākūshī, the Almohad chronicler, declared that, before the coming of the Almohads, 'the only knowledge they assigned the prince of the Muslims to memorize was the knowledge of *al-furū'*, the *al-furū'* of the Maliki school of law.' They often taught like this 'until they forgot the view of the book of God [the Qur'ān], the sayings [the *ḥadīth*] of the Prophet of Allah.'[117] For Ibn Tūmart, by contrast, the *al-uṣūl* were much more important than the *al-furū'*. '*Al-uṣūl* means, in the Arabic language, the trunk of the tree, *al-furū'* are merely the branches ... *al-uṣūl* are the *sharī'a*, the holy book and consensus (*ijmā'*).'[118]

Interestingly, Ibn Tūmart explained these terms 'in the Arabic language', implying that parts of the book were proclaimed in Berber. Instead of leaving religious matters to the established elite, Ibn Tūmart spoke to the tribes as a whole. He relied on his popular appeal, charisma, and the power of a message kept secret by ignorant, close-minded jurists. In an interesting turn of fate, it was no longer the rough, mountain tribes who were *jāhilīn* (ignorant). Rather, it was the learned clerics who thought they knew the truth, but could only grasp at the branches of the tree and ignore its roots. The tribes were made to give up the divisions of their ancestral traditions. They had to 'give up following the ways of our fathers and stop the worship of idols'.[119] The idols of the jurists and the Almoravids were their law books and their narrow anthropomorphism. The idols of the Atlas tribes were their fathers and traditions that divided them and caused ancient blood feuds. Ibn Tūmart attacked both of these 'idols' simultaneously as he attempted to reveal the roots, *al-uṣūl*, of Islam.

Law and Society

To Ibn Khaldūn, the fourteenth-century North African philosopher of history, law that had developed outside the *sharī'a* (Islamic law based on *al-uṣūl*) was an inherent problem of settled government.

The triumph of the Almohads over the Almoravids and the Maliki jurists was a reason for Ibn Khaldūn's belief that the 'reliance of sedentary people upon laws destroys their fortitude and power of resistance'.[120] Regarding limits to the law, he wrote:

> man must by necessity be dominated by someone else. If the domination is kind and just and the people under it are not oppressed by its laws and restrictions, they are guided by the courage or cowardice they possess in themselves. They are satisfied with the absence of any restraining power. Self-reliance eventually becomes a quality natural to them. They would not know anything else.[121]

For Ibn Khaldūn, self-reliance and character were more essential than the dictates of the law. If laws were imposed too harshly or forcefully this sense of self-reliance would be threatened. 'If, however, the domination with its laws is one of brute force and intimidation, it breaks their fortitude and deprives them of the power of resistance as a result of the inertness that develops in the soul of the oppressed.'[122]

When Ibn Khaldūn referred to the laws, he referred to the 'derived' Maliki law books, not to the fundamental laws of Islam contained in the Qur'ān and the recognized *ḥadīth*.[123] 'Governmental and educational laws destroy fortitude, because their restraining influence comes from outside. The religious laws, on the other hand, do not destroy fortitude because their restraining influence is something inherent.' Belief in *al-uṣūl*, the foundations of Islam, the 'religious law' was 'inherent' from birth. True religion, true belief in the oneness of God, was found not only at the beginning of creation, but also at the birth and beginning of every human. This was the doctrine of Ibn Tūmart. It was the Mahdī who would inspire a rebirth, a return to the true intentions of Islam. As Ibn Tūmart proclaimed, 'those who understand *tawḥīd* will become pure of sin like the day his mother bore him: he will die in this state, he will sojourn in Paradise!'[124] Ibn Tūmart not only restored the 'fundamentals' of religion, but he also restored the true intentions of creation.

Ibn Khaldūn was no anarchist. Rather, he described a historical pattern found in most tribal Islamic revolutions. This pattern was exemplified by the Almohads with their rejection of pragmatic, but often oppressive and politicized, laws of the ruling authority in favour of an idealistic, rarefied version of Islamic law, based on the *ḥadīth*, *sunna* and the Qur'ān. Although it might be assumed that the imposition of laws would strengthen the government's hold over tribes, it may cause a serious rift if done with 'force and intimidation'.[125] The Almohad tribal revolution, like most revolutions, was an attempt to return to principles, *al-uṣūl*. It was an attempt to fight against the decadence and ignorance of government and power, to prove that those who claimed to be 'men of understanding' were in fact blinded by their own specialized, materialistic view of Islam. Their positions were almost completely governed by political will, not by theological understanding.[126]

Summary of the Book of Ibn Tūmart

Title: *Aʿazz mā Yuṭlab* or The Greatest of What is Sought, the Most Excellent of What is Earned, the Most Precious of What is Preserved, and the Best of What is Done.[127]

The passage below was on the front page of the original manuscript:

> A book containing collected sayings of the Infallible Imām, the Known Mahdī, may God be pleased with him, which were dictated to our ruler the Imām Caliph, Prince of Believers, ʿAbū Muḥammad ʿAbd al-Muʾmin bin ʿAlī, may God protect them and assure their victory and strengthen their fortune.

[The last page of the book similarly praises Ibn Tūmart and ʿAbd al-Muʾmin with the colophon dated to hijra 579 (AD 1182–83).]

The contents were written as follows:

The Greatest Thing One Seeks: *Aʿazz mā Yuṭlab*
(Includes a lengthy discussion of *al-uṣūl*)

On prayer:
Proof that *sharīʿa* is established in the mind

On the general and the particular
On theological science
Information (Human Personal Relations)
Creation
On service
The profession of faith (The Creed)
The two revelations
The two anthems
The Imāmate and Characteristics of the Mahdī
The law
Catalogue of the liars
A section on the end of the world
Book on the forbidden nature of wine
Book of *jihād*

Under these chapters there are approximately 131 subheadings.

The book begins with the full title, 'To strengthen what one seeks, to improve what one beholds, to reveal what one remembers, and to better what one does: (this is) the knowledge brought about by God because of his guidance to all good. He is a strength of the seeker, an improvement of the one who beholds, a revelation of the one who remembers and a betterment of the one who acts.'[128]

There are roughly four main parts to the book, representing different periods in the life of Ibn Tūmart and the Almohad movement. The first part addresses the heated ideological debate over the authenticity of the sayings of the Prophet and the proper way of distinguishing true from false *ḥadīth.* The purpose of Ibn Tūmart's arguments is to show how Islam has been misrepresented and improperly practised. By restoring the true rules, Ibn Tūmart claims to restore Islam as it was originally intended. So, although the legal discussions of authenticating *ḥadīth* or proper methods of prayer may seem dry and technical, they are also steeped with revolutionary significance. This section of the book is written in legalistic prose although several sections do seem to inspire visceral reaction. The second part of the book is much more philosophical and rationalist, the *ʿaqīda* or profession of faith sets out to prove the absolute, single unity of God with Aristotelian logic. This book is to address the philosophers and the learned elite, although the language can also be stirring to the common listener. The third part, the revelations and the anthems, the section on the Mahdī and imāmate is specifically oriented towards recitation and memorization by the wider public. Finally, the rest of the book is devoted to a catalogue of reasons why the Almoravids must be punished for their sins against 'true' Islam.

These parts are only rough approximations of a collection of writings and sayings that do not exhibit any great internal coherence. Yet, certain key phrases, concepts or words seem to be repeated very regularly throughout the book, seemingly to the point of redundancy. Overall, the book is very challenging and difficult to translate, with words masked as deeper philosophical concepts that must be explained to be understood. This may be one of the main reasons why few sections of the book have been translated into any European languages despite the prolific efforts of E. Lévi-Provençal on other manuscripts. Even though it is important for understanding the rise of the Almohads and the influence of Almohad doctrine on important adopted European thinkers like Averroes,[129] this book has remained a largely underappreciated, even unknown document.

Introduction: The introduction of the book begins with a stark description of a universe divided into good and evil. God created the world with both sin and righteousness, evil and good. Yet he provides the knowledge, *ʿilm*, to distinguish right from the wrong, to discover what is hidden, the inner light of the heart. Following the true path leads to success. There is a thin boundary between good and evil. Straying from the path in any way will lead one to wrong, to the path of sin and misinterpretation. This would be the charge levelled against the Almoravids later in the book. The introduction was written in simple prose form, not verse. However, there does seem to be an attempt to mirror phrases and words with an opposite or counterpart. The opening passage of the introduction is important, for it expresses the intention behind the book.

> For what God created on the higher earth, and the middle, and the lower world is divided between doubt and certainty, truth and sin in equal proportion. And the one who follows God is a seeker of the knowledge that opens what is closed, discovers the true intent and grasps the law and the false claims about the intent and desire of God in *guidance* and success.[130]

Guidance and the necessity of guidance are mentioned throughout the book.[131] Again, the reference to the Mahdī, Ibn Tūmart, even in these first lines is unmistakable. It is through him that the truth can be known, even if it is obscured.

Knowledge is light, a light in the heart that determines the right and the wrong. It is through this light of knowledge that truth can be distinguished from falsehood.

Determining the true and the false in law, in life, in the universe as a whole, required the light of inspiration. 'Knowledge is a light in the heart that distinguishes in it the true, the particular, and the darkly ignorant.'[132] Truth and falsehood, light and shadows, ignorance and knowledge: from the introduction it is clear this is to be a book of dichotomies.

After this stirring description of moral absolutes, the book enters into a discussion of the proper transmission of *ḥadīth*:

distinguishing the true sayings of the Prophet from the false or weak sayings must be done properly to avoid straying into falsehood. The first section of the introduction ends with short sections on ignorance, idolatry and thought, meaning wild or wrongful interpretation.

The rest of the introduction continues with the science of *tawātur* – determining the validity of the sayings of the Prophet Muḥammad. The foundation of this science is the ability to distinguish *al-uṣūl* from *al-furū'*, the roots of tradition from the many false branches. *Al-uṣūl*, the fundamentals of religion, was the right path. Ibn Tūmart discusses how to confirm *al-uṣūl* and the evidence needed for this confirmation. Then he discusses the need to know *al-furū'*, its weakness, and the evidence needed to know what is *al-furū'*.[133] He discusses the importance of distinguishing sayings of the Prophet that are mentioned only once in unreliable sources, the *al-ahād* coming from the word for 'one', those found in multiple reliable sources, 'The way to distinguish what is weak and false *ḥadīth* and what is strong *ḥadīth*.'[134] The book focuses on reasons why the rigorous science of *ḥadīth* should be standard practice. In attempting to create an alternative to the Maliki legal interpretations, Ibn Tūmart does make convincing arguments for more careful reform of the law and the *sunna*. The beginning of the introduction itself reads as a type of invocation, a *fātiḥa*, or opening, summarizing the main arguments and setting up a picture of the absolute moral universe that was the basis of Almohad doctrine: the thin edge, how easy it was to fall into darkness. This leads, at times, to a type of theological paranoia, a cataclysmic view of the cosmos that could only be alleviated by the leader and Mahdī. The rest of the section is focused on technical discussions of various methods used to verify *ḥadīth*.[135]

Prayer

Prayer, as opposed to the intricacies of the science of *ḥadīth*, was something for all Almohads to practise. There can be no more powerful physical act of religious unity than the collective act of prayer. Ibn Tūmart entreated in one of his letters to bring the entire household: the entire tribe, slave or free, man woman and child, to prayer.[136] Prayer was a physical expression of unity. In the next section of the book the focus is on prayer, which was, as Ibn Tūmart pointed out, 'one of the pillars of Islam'.

The proper method of prayer was a common concern. The emphasis here is on doing prayer properly, implying of course that the Almoravids did not know how to pray in the way of the Prophet Muḥammad. This made their prayers invalid. In contrast, leading the Almohads to proper prayer five times a day could provide an important force for unity in the daily routine of the Almohads. This routine of the true Almohad, provided exceptionalism, security and a sense of loyalty, not only to the religion, but to the system established by the very person of Ibn Tūmart, the guide and Mahdī who guaranteed the right way of prayer and therefore guaranteed that God was listening.

There are two forms or meanings of prayer, the legal form and the verbal form. There is what Ibn Tūmart calls the well-known physical action of 'standing, kneeling, sitting, prostrating',[137] which was well established in the *ḥadīth*. Irrelevant speaking, however, was another matter. No speaking from the people will be allowed. Speaking or mumbling during prayer was an outward sign of pride and arrogance.

Ibn Tūmart justifies this from *ḥadīth* saying that understanding is 'hindered by speech during prayer'.[138] Speaking or mumbling blocked the mind from contemplation of meaning. Speaking was a mere surface act, a ritual tradition that, according to Ibn Tūmart, was not followed in the time of the Prophet. Ibn Tūmart wanted to encourage understanding of the Qur'ān and the prayers, not a surface reading. This was one of the main ideological bases of the Almohads. Whereas the Almoravids viewed the scripture as a surface ritual and did not probe into the meaning of words, the Almohads maintained the unity of God through meaning. In fact, the theme of meaning over mere perception is used throughout the book. Again, the Almoravids are compared with the *jāhiliyya*, 'When the Arabs spoke during their prayers, the Prophet, may peace be upon him, said unto them nothing from the words of the people is permitted for it is boastful and prideful.' Ibn Tūmart does not forbid the recitation of the Qur'ān itself, but seems to condemn any speaking outside proscribed prayers.

Ibn Tūmart then explains various incidents and parables at Muḥammad the Prophet's mosque in Medina that clarified the proper method of prayer. As mentioned before with regard to Ibn Tūmart's declarations in the cave and his attempts to mirror his own life with that of the Prophet, the purpose of following this *ḥadīth* so strictly was to create in exact detail the actions of the Prophet and his followers, to recreate seventh-century Medina in the Atlas Mountains. For example, a follower of the Prophet Muḥammad came into the mosque to pray once. When he got up to leave he greeted the Prophet. However, one prayer was insufficient. It was only after praying three times that the Prophet permitted him to take his leave. This established the necessity of repeating the section of the Qur'ān being read, three times. Ibn Tūmart says, 'God prospers those who pray humbly.' This section of the book explains why. It is not simply a matter of humility, although that is important. It is a matter of grasping the meaning of the Qur'ān and the scripture. Going into great detail and citing various *ḥadīth*, he continues with a long description of the proper way to pray, the time, the number of repetitions and the method.[139] For example, he cites Ibn Abdallah who witnessed the specific way Muḥammad divided the prayers throughout normal days and during the holy month of Ramadan.[140]

Proof or guidance

Returning to the idea that silent understanding is better than boastful display, the *sharīʿa*, too, must be interpreted and understood in the mind, rather than from the surface. Ibn Tūmart discusses what he believes is the proper use of *qīyas*, analogy: using the *sharīʿa* and the life of the Prophet, to address issues not encompassed by the *ḥadīth* or the law.[141]

The general and the particular, the free and the shackled

In this section and the next three chapters Ibn Tūmart delves into the legal and theological arguments of the Mashriq (the Muslim East). Abrogation was a persistent issue for Muslim scholars, the issue of whether or not to abrogate earlier Qur'ānic verses with later ones. Obviously, it was difficult to accept contradictions in the text and Ibn Tūmart seems to take a more conservative view of the issue while also stating the need to follow the deeper meaning of the scriptures. Ibn Tūmart also discusses particular legal issues like the need for circumcision and the treatment of the people of the book, Christians and Jews. He was quite strict in demanding the payment of special tax from the people of the book. He also calls for an aggressive campaign of conversion.[142]

On service: a discussion on service, its necessity and conditions

This chapter begins with a simple question and its answer. 'What is it that I must do? Serve the Lord of the worlds.'[143] For Ibn Tūmart, the obligation of service and good works was far from a simple task. It was not enough to perform a random set of apparently good works. Human judgement and reason could not be relied on to determine the validity of good works. Rather, the good works must first be combined with faith, will and knowledge; and this knowledge must be based on the true *sharīʿa*, the law of God. God sending an infallible Prophet proved the truth of the law of God. The Prophet's truth was then confirmed by the miracles of God, the direct intervention of God into the affairs of the world. It is easily implied that Ibn Tūmart seems to be with the Prophet at the apex of this ladder of truth as infallible imām.

In religion, truth and salvation were sources of dispute. There was a long-running theological debate raging in the East between the philosophers who believed that reason and intellect were the bases of good works and the orthodox Ashʾaris who rejected human freedom and reason in favour of an all-powerful God.[144] Unlike these, and many other schools of thought, Ibn Tūmart does not attempt to confirm his position with complex theological language. He does not support his position with any one school or theological system, but through a simple statement of fact: faith was not genuine without good works and good works were not genuine without faith. Thus, Ibn Tūmart claims to reconcile faith with action. The most crucial links between faith and action are the Prophet, the Qurʾān and the Mahdī. Ibn Tūmart simply ignores many of the thorny theological issues of justice and the reconciliation of divine and human will that so vexed the great minds of the Orient. Ibn Tūmart was not writing a commentary or engaging in a technical, theological discussion. He wrote this text to revive the depths of Islamic moral life, 'the greatest thing that one seeks'. Transcending the debate, Ibn Tūmart reproves those who argue fruitlessly over whether faith or knowledge is first needed to serve God properly. 'One faction says the first obligation is faith, another says it is learning and knowledge (*ʿilm*). Each sets up a system of proof, defends their position and negates as sinful the position of their counterpart such that every good becomes refuted.'[145] In their effort to negate each other, these two factions lost sight of the unity of God and his will for humankind. Reason was neither against faith nor faith against reason. Instead, they complemented each other. According to Ibn Tūmart, these theologians and philosophers 'exited from the [true] path of inquiry'.[146] They created differences where there were no differences.

Ibn Tūmart claimed to revive the perfect origins of Islam, before the theological splits that plagued the community after the death of Muḥammad. He demanded perfect adherence to the conditions of service and faith. According to Ibn Tūmart, service to God is worthy only if specific conditions are met. 'For when any one condition is violated, all aspects of service are disturbed.' For example, one of the most important services to God is the service of prayer. When one prays one must 'cover one's privates and pray [exactly] towards Mecca.'[147] If this is not done, the prayer is invalidated. 'If anything is scattered, all is scattered.' Also, one must not simply pray, one must pray with consistency, with knowledge, understanding and belief. In this sense, Ibn Tūmart demands a simultaneous adherence to basic formal rules and an interior understanding of faith: both of which are possible by the living example of the Mahdī. Ibn Tūmart is the bridge between faith, action and knowledge.

The ʿaqīda

The *ʿaqīda*, the basic Almohad creed, begins with three sayings of the Prophet that demonstrated the Prophet Muḥammad's notion of God's unity, *tawḥīd*.[148] This firmly grounds the rest of the creed in the sound sayings of the Prophet – *al-uṣūl*. The next section explains that 'it is by necessity of reason that the existence of God, Praise to Him, is known.'[149] The meaning of 'necessity' is what is 'independently present in the minds of all who are endowed with reason'.[150] The third section makes the logical argument that 'from the fact of his own creation man knows the existence of his creator, since he knows his own existence after having been nonexistent'. This was supported by the Qur'ān 19: 10: 'I created you from a previous state when you were nothing.'[151]

Next was an argument of cause and effect and the necessity of creation. This argument suggests that God exists because of actions in the world.

> By the first act the existence of the Creator is known, Praise to Him, and in the same way the second and third all the way to limitlessness. ... And if the creation of the first body is known, the creation of all other bodies is known since they are the same in extension in space, mutability, positioning, particularity, adventitiousness and need for a creator.[152]

What was created cannot itself be the creator. If even the most rational of created things, humans, cannot turn back time or 'put back a single finger after it had disappeared', it would be impossible to think that inanimate things could do better.[153] God is thus the only logical creator of all things. As such he cannot be like anything else. He cannot have attributes and signs. God is of a separate 'kind' from his creation. 'And if God is known to be the Creator of all things it is known that he is not like anything else, since nothing resembles anything except of its kind. ... If He were of the kind of created things, then He would be incapable as they are incapable.' Again, the Qur'ān (16: 17) was used to support this argument 'Is He who creates like he who does not create? Will you not remember?'[154]

The human mind and imagination has a limit on its ability to understand God. Minds cannot describe or limit the nature of God. 'Minds have a limit at which they stop.' As for those sacred texts that describe God 'sitting himself upon a throne' (Qur'ān 20: 4), it was wrong to 'imagine comparison or modality'.[155] God has no limit. God is capable of 'all his wishes'. For 'Not so much as the weight of an atom in heaven and earth escapes him, nor anything smaller than that or greater' (Qur'ān 34: 3). The impossibility of knowing the complete truth and the limitless power of God: this was the main argument of the *'aqīda*. God knows what is predestined for all. And all things take place 'according to His knowledge in a way that is incalculable and with an organization that cannot be puzzled out'.[156]

The *'aqīda* speaks in very logical, systematic and Aristotelian language that is meant to prove the existence of God and the divine unity. Madeleine Fletcher argued that the *'aqīda* Almohad creed was written primarily as a way of taming the original Almohad doctrine for an elite Andalusi audience based at the new Almohad capital in Seville.[157] Fletcher speculates that because of the dense philosophical nature of the prose, the philosopher Averroes was the 'author' of the *'aqīda*.[158] Yet, it would have been possible for Ibn Tūmart to develop an advanced understanding of theological issues. There seemed to be nothing in the manuscript to suggest that different hands wrote it. There is little reason to dispute the book's claim that it was 'a book containing collected sayings of the Infallible Imām, the Known Mahdī, may God be pleased with him, which were dictated to our ruler the Imām Caliph, Prince of Believers, ʿAbū Muḥammad ʿAbd al-Muʾmin bin ʿAlī, may God protect them and assure their victory and strengthen their fortune.'[159]

Ibn Tūmart had already stated the basic concepts of the *ʿaqīda*, namely the notion that God had no limit and that it was impossible to attribute signs and characteristics to God. Ibn Tūmart proclaimed in a letter to his followers that:

> One must not allow any comparison or association with the Creator, all ideas of imperfection, diminution, limitation, direction; he is not situated in a place or a direction for the Highest exists before places and directions! Those who situate him in a place or a direction give him a corporal form; and those who give him a corporal form adore him like an idol.[160]

This perfectly reflected the *ʿaqīda* found in the *Aʿazz mā Yuṭlab*. 'And if God is known to be the Creator of all things it is known that He is not like anything else, since nothing resembles anything except of its kind. ... If He were of the kind of created things, then He would be incapable as they are incapable.'[161] The simplest explanation makes the most sense; Ibn Tūmart was the author of the *ʿaqīda*. Averroes interpreted Almohad doctrine. He may even have altered elements of the doctrine. But he most likely did not create it from scratch as Fletcher suggested. It would seem extraordinary that so much of this essential part of the doctrine could have been altered without notice by the Berber sheikhs.

The anthems

These were the songs chanted at ceremonies involving the Mahdī and the Almohad leadership. As such, they were probably memorized by the full Almohad cadre, including the illiterate and semi-literate, as a type of popular, basic profession of faith in the movement. The anthems would have been sung before and during battle, or to mark the occasion of a major campaign. They summarize many of the basic aspects of the Almohad doctrine of unity and the Almohad idea of the Mahdī. Whereas most of Ibn Tūmart's doctrine could not possibly be repeated by the common follower, these anthems were almost certainly a profession of faith and of membership in the movement.

The first anthem praises the wonders of God's creation. The anthem is reminiscent of the early mystical sūras of the Qur'ān meditating on the power of God's will. The hymn praises the absolute will of the one and only God. It is also provides a glimpse into Ibn Tūmart's view of the cosmos, a view that was undoubtedly influenced by the philosophers he met in his travels to the East. Ibn Khaldūn comments on the position of the earth in his *Muqaddimah*:

> In the books of philosophers who speculated about the condition of the world, it has been explained that the earth has a spherical shape and is enveloped by the element of water. It may be compared to a grape floating on water. ... The water withdrew from certain parts of the earth.

This explains why Ibn Tūmart praised God who 'lays out the dry land of the earth'.[162] Ibn Tūmart then described the world using scenes known to the common and the elite Berber alike. He praised the mighty heights of the land, the fruit of the soil, the oil and juice presses. It was as if the hand of God were in the very landscape and geography of Berber life. The second anthem, beginning with 'Praise who you showed the leadership and the signs' is a concise summary, in verse, of the most important points made by Ibn Tūmart in his book: overcoming death, rejecting weak sources, revealing a true vision of Islam and following the leadership of the Mahdī.

The imāmate[163]

The Imāmate and the Mahdī is a central tenet of Almohad doctrine. The Mahdī doctrine and its historical background were explained previously in this book.

The catalogue of lies

This was 'the catalogue of the lies of the sinners, the *Lithām* wearers, the anthropomorphists and their scholars'.[164] In other words, it was a diatribe against the Almoravids. Ibn Tūmart begins with a frontal attack on the Almoravid *'ulamā'* whom the Prophet will 'throw into the fire of hell'.[165] He then outlines their sins, for doing what is *ḥarām*. They 'drink and eat what is forbidden'.[166] He forbids 'helping them in their sinful ways or befriending them'.[167] The main reason for this was their anthropomorphism. They believed they could limit and form God around their literalist interpretation of his attributes.[168] It was necessary 'to perform *jihād* against them', for not only do they try to confine and limit the power of God, they reverse God's true intentions. They 'keep their women's faces exposed' even as the 'men wear veils'. They are worse unbelievers than 'the Jews and the Magians'.[169] In this long catalogue of sins and accusations against the Almoravids, Ibn Tūmart builds the justification for war against his powerful enemy. One of his most powerful arguments was that God would smite them before the coming of the end of time; because of their sins, they 'will not see the Day of Reckoning'.[170]

The end of the world and the Day of Reckoning

Revolutions are often successful more for the extraordinary ideals they promise than for what they actually achieve. Excitement, change and miraculous promise are all enemies of the status quo. For Ibn Tūmart, the Almohads, and perhaps most of the Islamic world, the Day of Judgment seemed overdue. Not only was it 500 years since the hijra of Muḥammad, a date significant for its eschatological meaning, but the Islamic world seemed to be on the brink of a new era, the old, established unity of the ʿAbbāsid caliphate in the east was disintegrating. The Almoravid promise proved false and heretical, and the rulers and jurists were mere shadows in the light of the coming judgement. The imminent coming of the end of time gave Ibn Tūmart an exceptional amount of legitimacy, a legitimacy he needed to consolidate the power of the Maṣmūda tribes. Indeed, it was the hope and ultimate promise of the Almohads to consolidate the entire Islamic world, to return to the true belief and original intent of Islam, to prepare all Muslims for the coming of God's judgement. It is only natural that the book of Ibn Tūmart should discuss the end of time and claim that the coming judgement will originate in the Maghrib. It was as much a rallying cry for ideological unity as a statement of religious doctrine. Ibn Tūmart wanted to make clear that with the end of time the Almohads as true believers have nothing to fear. Only the enemies of God need be afraid.

First, in his typical fashion, Ibn Tūmart links his own time to the time of Muḥammad. He compares 'the exile of Islam during the first days and its exile during the last days'.[171] He cites a *ḥadīth* from the writings of Tirmidhi, one of the reliable *ḥadīth* writers, about the '50 agents' who will be rewarded by God. There is a clear reference here to the 'men of 50' who compose the highest ranks of the Almohad power pyramid. He also speaks of the 'sect from the Maghrib that will fight for truth at the end of time'. This is from the 'true' *ḥadīth* of al-Muslim. According to al-Muslim, the Prophet said, 'the people of the Maghrib shall not know the truth until the end of time'.[172] Just to strengthen his point, he refers to a whole list of *ḥadīth* traditions that speak of the 'group of Muslims' at the end of time who fight for truth. Obviously, this group of

Muslims was supposed to mean the Almohads. Interestingly, Ibn Tūmart does not provide much, if any, interpretation of the *ḥadīth*. Perhaps the connection between the Almohads and the sayings of the Prophet seems so clear to him that it does not need explanation. It is possible that some of Ibn Tūmart's writings were edited out by the scholars who completed inscribing this edition. Many of Ibn Tūmart's more immediate prophecies may not have come true. This was a possible embarrassment to ʿAbd al-Muʾmin, Ibn Tūmart's successor.

Ibn Tūmart's idea of a band of righteous Muslims gathered at the end of time is taken directly from the Qurʾān. 'None shall have the power of intersession, but such a one as has received permission from God the Most Gracious' (Sūra XIX 85–7). The one with 'the power of intersession' would be the Mahdī, Ibn Tūmart. The day of reckoning or resurrection signified the power and immediacy of the one and only God. It showed he had a direct interest in human affairs. An entire new world will come into existence. A world where there is nothing to separate the human soul from God. 'At length, when the sight is dazed. And the moon is buried in darkness. And the sun and the moon are joined together. That day will man say: Where is my refuge? ... Before the Lord (alone) that day will be the place of rest' (Sūra LXXV: 7–12).

The prohibition on wine drinking

Ibn Tūmart overturned wine jugs, threw them, broke them, and, in the midst of parties at the risk of personal harm, demanded that all drinking cease. Wine and alcohol was so abhorrent to Ibn Tūmart that he devoted a chapter of his book to the numerous *ḥadīth* verifying Muḥammad the Prophet's wine-drinking prohibitions.[173]

Jihād

According to the Qurʾān, one must 'fight in the cause of God those who fight you, but do not transgress limits for God loveth not transgressors' (Sūra II: 190). There is the call for *jihād* but also moderation, for 'if they cease, let there be no hostility' (Sūra II: 193). Ibn Tūmart, however, does seem to emphasize this more moderate or limited approach to *jihād*. He calls *jihād* a pillar of religion. Using selected sayings of the Prophet Muḥammad, he focuses on aggressive and unforgiving battle against the Almoravid oppressor. Unlike the Prophet who fought the pagan tribes, Ibn Tūmart was fighting against other Muslims. Also, the power and extent of Almoravid power was even more encompassing than the localized power of the Quraysh in the city-state of Mecca. The Almoravids were rulers of an empire, an empire of wealth, of trade and sophisticated cities from Spain to Ghana. They had the Almohads surrounded. Initially, at least, Ibn Tūmart would need as much fervency from his followers as he could get to break the spine of Almoravid domination.

Ibn Tūmart needed to call his people to war and reveal God's promise of rewards to those who sacrificed their lives to the cause of true Islam. In his chapter on *jihād*, Ibn Tūmart provides almost no original commentary. Rather, he stitches together a collection of authoritative *ḥadīth* describing Muḥammad the Prophet's promise of heavenly reward to those who fought in battle against the enemies of Islam. Perhaps Ibn Tūmart found the parallels too obvious for comparison. He had already listed the sins of the Almoravids. The chapter on *jihād* merely added more legitimacy to Ibn Tūmart's cause. Most crucially, it motivated his followers with the promise of heavenly reward, a promise coming directly from the words of the Prophet Muḥammad. Even the way he selects and edits the *ḥadīth* changes their meaning and significance; and when Ibn Tūmart refers exclusively to the saying of the Prophet Muḥammad and the accomplishments of the first Muslims, he subtly creates an original form of Almohad *jihād* to rally the tribes against the Almoravids, the rebels of God. One of Ibn Tūmart's most repeated *ḥadīth* is the promise that those who go on *jihād* will either go to heaven or return home with great booty and honour.[174] He includes several different versions of the same *ḥadīth* told by different companions of the Prophet just to back up the argument. *Jihād* in the path of God was just as important as fasting, prayer, *zakāt* and the *ḥājj*.[175] Jihād was a pillar of religion for the Mahdī. He quotes a *ḥadīth* describing the 'levels of heaven' and that 'the distance between the levels of heaven is like the distance between heaven and earth'. The way to a higher level of heaven was through *jihād* against the Almoravids.

4
The Rise of the Almohads in Context

> Characteristically, the tribe is both an alternative to the state and also its image, its limitation and the seed of a new state.
>
> (Ernest Gellner, *Muslim society*)

> Islam originated in a tribal society, and any attempt to explain its appearance must take this fact as its starting point.
>
> (Patricia Crone, *Meccan trade and the rise of Islam*)

In this book I have described several reasons for the rise of the Almohad movement as portrayed in Berber Almohad sources. Economically, the Almohads had a material incentive to overthrow the Almoravids and their taxes in order ultimately to impose their own, even more systematic, system of taxation. As the Almohad sources put it, the Almoravid cities were rich with booty, and trade in gold and salt was especially lucrative. The Almohads even famously replaced the Almoravid round dirham with the uniquely shaped square dirham as a symbol of their new domination of lucrative trade in the western Mediterranean and across the Sahara desert.[1] Yet, despite the obvious material advantages to overthrowing the Almoravids, economics alone cannot explain the remarkable development of the detailed Almohad hierarchy, or the specific and compelling content of Almohad doctrine. The Maṣmūda lived under Almoravid taxation and rule for several decades before the rise of Ibn Tūmart. Like millennial cults and movements throughout world history, a charismatic figure, a Mahdī, inspired the Almohad movement.[2] Ibn Tūmart clearly fits into Max Weber's definition of a charismatic figure. His charisma was a major reason for the rise of the Almohads. He had 'a certain quality of an individual personality by virtue of which he is set apart from ordinary men and treated as endowed with supernatural, superhuman or at least specifically exceptional powers or qualities'.[3] However, as compelling as he was to the Maṣmūda, and as important as his life, his *sīra*, was to the development of Almohad doctrine, Ibn Tūmart's individual charisma could not in and of itself explain the rapid rise and success of the Almohads. Similar charismatic leaders arose throughout the Maghrib at this time. Ibn Tūmart lent a charismatic spark, inflaming already existing economic, social, ethnic and historical conditions. He did not create those pre-existing conditions himself.

Perhaps, as the Berber myth about the Almohads' foundation suggested, the most important reason for the successful rise of the Almohads was probably, given that we are dealing with tribes, anthropological. The specific, informal, pre-existing structures of the Maṣmūda tribes, including the *asmās* or communal meal used to cement loyalties, the *agrao* or tribal council, the *tamyīz* or ordering of otherwise egalitarian tribes for battle, even the segmentary, ancestor-based system that encouraged united defence against outside threats, all existed prior to Ibn Tūmart's return from the East.

It is not my aim in this book to claim that any one of these elements – economic, charismatic, social or historical – was, on its own, the primary cause of the rise of the Almohads. Rather, it was the mixture and combination of all these different factors that led to their rise. Although any analogy is inherently imperfect or even facile, it may be illustrative to envision the Almohad rise along the same lines as the building of a mosque, which was something that Ibn Tūmart did throughout his travels. To build a sanctified mosque, certain elements must exist; first, there must be the right type of stone, the actual material that is to be transformed. This material, of course, has its own character and shape. For the Almohads, this basic material was the tribes and the Maṣmūdas' tribal institutions.

In myths of founding narratives, there must also be an architect to design the appropriate elements and bring them all together in a balanced way that follows 'true' Islamic principles. Ibn Tūmart himself was portrayed as that 'architect' of the Almohad structure. The specific economic and historical conditions pertaining to the Maṣmūda tribes provided the mortar with which to bind the tribal building blocks together; in other words, they provided the conditions under which the raw materials, the tribes, were able to come together. Had any of these elements – the tribal building blocks, the charismatic architect and the economic mortar – been missing, no structure could have been built. It was not that the economic conditions necessarily *caused* the tribal alliance or that the desire for such a tribal alliance *caused* the rise of the Mahdī, or vice versa; rather, all these elements – economics, leadership, pre-existing social organization and history – came together simultaneously to produce the right conditions for the rise of the Almohads. Just as the artist is limited by his canvas and the colour of his paints, and the cook by the availability of certain ingredients, so too were Ibn Tūmart and his doctrine limited, coloured and shaped by certain specific historical, social and ethnic factors. As Ernest Gellner claimed in *Muslim Society*, 'The tribe is both an alternative to the state and also its image, its limitation and the seed of a new state.'[4] My purpose in this chapter is to provide a brief theoretical and comparative basis for the concomitant tribal, social, economic and charismatic causes of the rise of the Almohads, an ascent that arose from a perfect storm of social, charismatic and economic causes.

SOCIAL FACTORS: WHAT IS A TRIBE?

To understand the social factors that led to the rise of the Almohads from among the Maṣmūda Atlas tribes it is important to define the word tribe. Tribes were the building blocks of the Almohad system. Although I have no intention of delving into the specifics of the protracted, anthropological debate on the exact nature of a tribe, the question of what comprises a tribe is at the core of anthropological studies and has engendered a considerable amount of debate and uncertainty.

Nevertheless, some frame of reference for the term 'tribe' is in order. The anthropologist David M. Hart and the historian of Islam Akbar S. Ahmed provide a useful definition of a tribe that, with some modification, will provide the framework I use for this study. 'Tribes are rural groups that have a name and distinguish between members and non-members, which occupy a territory and which within that territory assume either all responsibility, or at least a significant proportion of the responsibility for the maintenance of order.' Tribes 'can be said to possess political and military functions'. They also possess 'some kind of tribal genealogical charter' that 'assumes almost mythical importance and is memorized from generation to generation'.[5]

A tribe has four crucial characteristics – a distinguishing name, a specific territory, a responsible power and a semi-mythical genealogy. The vast majority of Berbers and Arabs who joined the Almohad movement easily fit this definition, as do most of the tribal groups that joined Muḥammad the Prophet in the first decades of Islam. Ahmed and Hart, however, go too far in excluding non-rural, village or even urban people who display all the characteristics of rural tribes apart from their physical surroundings.

It was the semi-mythical that defined the history of the rise of the Almohads in general. The manipulation of 'semi-mythical ancestry' in tribal society for wider political ends led to the creation of a coherent and organized Almohad army and government. Tribes were not completely isolated from the state milieu and, in the case of the Almohads, were part of its creation. From his broad view of Maghrib history, Jamil Abun-Nasr observed that 'Maghribi history would be difficult, if not impossible, to explain if the tribes were not viewed as political units and tribalism as a form of political organization.'[6] This study described how Ibn Tūmart manipulated his own ancestry and the ancestry of others by bringing them into his own tribe, the Hargha.

Modern anthropology confirms the practice of modifying ancestry for political ends. Describing the Haūz, a tribe near Marrakech, Paul Pascon observed how ancestry was simply an emblem of a common identity and territorial status.[7] In his seminal article that questioned the very nature of the tribe in the Maghrib, 'Qu'est-ce qu'une "tribu" nord-africaine', Jacques Berque claimed that most tribal notions of common descent were, in fact, illusions. A tribe is 'in part artificial'.[8] The anthropologist William Lancaster, who lived among the Rwala Bedouin in Arabia, made similar observations. He called the bedū system 'the generative genealogy'.[9] Some 700 years before the development of modern anthropology, Ibn Khaldūn had made the same observations about the often-mythical ancestral relationships of tribes. 'When the things which result from (common) descent are there, it is as if (common descent) itself were there, because the only meaning of belonging to one or another group is that one is subject to its laws and conditions, as if one had come into close contact with it.'[10] If Ibn Khaldūn and the consensus of most modern anthropologists of the Maghrib are to be believed, ancestral descent was primarily the mythical basis of an imagined identity. In fact, it was the ability in tribal societies to adjust to new identities that partially explained the rapid adoption of Islam in tribal societies. Tribes were based on imagined ancestries and identities that could encompass almost any group or tribe, often regardless of ancestry.[11]

To refine the definition of a tribe further, it is necessary to look at the nature of its organization. The political system of a tribe was often contained by what anthropologists call inherent 'segmentary' limitations. There were few or no written rules in tribal society. Therefore, small circles of loyalty often maintained social structures and justice. Evans-Pritchard, the anthropologist widely credited with developing segmentary theory, explained:

> Each section of a tribe, from the smallest to the largest, has its Sheikh or Sheikhs ... and political leadership is limited to situations in which a tribe or a segment of it acts corporately. With a tribe this only happens in war or in dealings with an outside authority.[12]

Tribes form alliances of wider and wider ancestral inclusiveness when they feel threatened by outside groups. This tendency towards alliances, which occurs naturally in tribal organizations, with or without religious inspiration, helped form the Almohad system. The Almohads and the Almohad idea of *tawḥīd* was simply a wider circle of confederation and loyalty, if not the ultimate circle, the ultimate tribal alliance in the minds of the Maṣmūda.

According to the Almohad's own version of events, Ibn Tūmart and his followers were able to transform this random, mosaic collection of diverse and sometimes even warring tribes into a coherent picture, a stratified pyramid that was the basis for Almohad expansion and rule. This feat was portrayed as even more remarkable than the tribal unification their Almoravid predecessors achieved. The desert tribes were not separated by high mountains and passes blocked by winter snow.[13] In the words of Huici Miranda, 'One is surprised by the complicated and rigorous organization implanted by Ibn Tūmart during the birth of the Almohad state.'[14]

The rapid formation of the Almohad hierarchy was made easier by the fact that there were pre-existing mechanisms and traditions for forming larger alliances within the tribes themselves.[15] Alliances were based on power. Depending on the strength of the sheikh or tribal chief, some tribes were stronger than others. Not all tribes were purely isolationist in nature. Intermarriage and a confluence of tribal identities probably produced a vague sense of Maṣmūda identity even before the rise of Ibn Tūmart. Ibn Tūmart used a combination of military action, co-option of tribal traditions and tribal leaders, and persuasive indoctrination to transform this vague sense of unity into a solid government and army.[16] Despite some easily transferred resistance of older generations and allegiances, it was Ibn Tūmart's irresistible doctrine of absolute monotheism that won over the largest following. His doctrine not only expressed discontent with Almoravid rule. It provided the means for tribal unity. It replaced ancestral practices with religious discipline and allegiance to the infallible Mahdī.[17]

Charisma and the Mahdī

In *The Trumpet Shall Sound*, an anthropological study of Melanesian millennial cults, Peter Worsley described the limitations of charismatic, millennial leadership. Worsley observed that effective charisma, charisma that enjoys loyalty and obedience, does not exist without social support. According to him, 'the followers, then, in a dialectical way, create, by selecting them out, the leaders, who in turn command.'[18] There were plenty of people with inspired messages and ideas. As the history of the Maghrib in the medieval period reveals, there were plenty of potential Mahdīs. The message, however, must be relevant to its audience, to the society in which it is preached.[19]

As discussed in the chapter on doctrine, specific parts of Ibn Tūmart's message were tailored against the Almoravid rivals of the Maṣmūda. The doctrine of the *Aʿazz mā Yuṭlab* was written in a

Berber, Maṣmūda context. Almohad Islam originated in a specific, Berber tribal society and any attempt to explain the appearance of Almohadism must likewise take this fact 'as its starting point'.

The chapter against anthropomorphism in the *Aʿazz mā Yuṭlab* was essentially a tract of typical Maṣmūda prejudices against the desert, Almoravid tribes. There were also plenty of instances in Ibn Tūmart's description of the end of time in which he mentions the importance of the council of fifty, a traditional form for Berber confederate assembly. Ibn Tūmart's charisma and his specific personal experiences and theological influences in the East did not single-handedly determine the shape and nature of the Almohad movement. Although parts of his message were admittedly shaped in the East and in urban contexts, the audience, the society in which it was preached, was Berber and tribal. This naturally had a profound effect on the content and reception of his doctrine.

Just as the architect must shape his plans according to what materials are available, so too must the social architect, the Mahdī, shape his message to fit his audience; and this audience, namely the Almohad scholars who wrote the history and biography of Ibn Tūmart, followed this ideology.[20] While the Mahdī's personality played a central role in the creation of the Almohad Empire, it was not enough to explain the transformation of the Atlas people into the Almohad state. The role of the tribes and people of the Atlas, coupled with their decision to follow this leader, cannot be ignored. The tribes and their traditional practices of *tamyīz*, *āsmās* and *agrao*, along with the natural organizing principles of segmentation, were not primitive or inherently weak institutions demolished by the Mahdī's charismatic presence. Instead, the tribes of the Atlas had developed a highly sophisticated system of regulating their own affairs, especially the often uneasy interaction between migrants and settled villagers. In his social anthropology of the Atlas Berbers Robert Montagne observed the oscillation between tribal republics governed by assemblies of elders, the *agrao*, and the temporary rulership of strong men, sometimes inspired leaders.[21] Like *'aṣabiyya*, or collective action, charismatic leadership and religious prophecy were often the products of a tribal society (see Table 4.1). As Worsley demonstrated in his study of the Melanesians, in almost every case the successful Mahdī needed to shape his message according to his audience.

Table 4.1: Draft representation of Ibn Khaldūn's hierarchy of social cohesion (*'Aṣabiyya*)

	Highest Form of Cohesion: Religious or Prophecy-based Cohesion
a.	Must be combined with tribal cohesion for success but can also occur among more settled tribes
b.	Most successful when new religious movement rallies around saint or messianic figure (Ibn Tūmart, 'Abd Allah)
	Second Form of Cohesion: Blood-based Tribal Cohesion
a.	Increases inversely as decadent, 'urban' influences decrease (most powerful among nomadic Bedouin of the desert)
b.	Limited to fleeting raids and enforced tribute without religious prophecy
	Third Form of Cohesion: Urban Cohesion
a.	Based on loose economic interests and weakened by the division of labour but the streets and bazaars can still be an important source of authority
b.	Strongest when cities set up municipal councils independent from strong dynastic control
	Fourth, Least Powerful Form of Cohesion: Forced Dynastic Control
a.	Prone to decadence and the whims of dynastic succession
b.	Based on forced compliance, not common interests
c.	Constantly vulnerable to the rise of new dynasties based on a combination of religious, tribal, or even urban dissidence

Rather than being a hindrance to state formation, or a stumbling block to charismatic leadership and inspired monotheism, the tribal structures of the Atlas Mountain people could form a basis for the Almohad social system and doctrine. Like any truly social movement, the Almohad hierarchy was not purely the invention of Ibn Tūmart or his followers. The architect alone does not make the building. Charisma alone, no matter what its source or specific content, does not make a society. Although often written that way, history is not the exclusive realm of great personalities and prophets. Events are shaped by the many daily decisions and opinions of those who choose to follow, not just those who choose to lead. The Mahdī demanded obedience, but his followers chose to obey and support him, not despite, but because of their tribal affiliations (Figure 2.3).

Possible Economic Incentives for the Rise of the Almohads

Charisma and existing tribal structures do not completely explain the rapid rise of the Almohads. The Almohads also had specific economic and materialistic reasons to unite and revolt against the Almoravids. A united coalition of tribes, no matter what the economic conditions, is always more efficient at obtaining economic resources from the urban core. A confederation of tribes is much more successful, both at obtaining large amounts of booty and at scaring away the tax collectors sent from the city.

Friedrich Engels, the famous companion of Karl Marx, observed this relationship between economics and the Almohad tribal revolution in an article published in *Die Neue Zeit* in 1894/5.

> Islam suits Orientals, especially the Arabs, that is to say, on one hand townsmen practised commerce and industry, on the other hand, nomadic Bedouin. But there is in this the seed of a periodic collision. Townsmen, growing opulent and ostentatious, become lax in the observation of the law. The Bedouin, poor and hence austere in their manners, contemplate the wealth and enjoyment with envy and lust. They unite under the direction of a prophet, a Mahdī, to punish the faithless. ... A hundred years later, naturally, they find

> themselves at exactly the same point as their predecessors; a new purification is required; a new Mahdī emerges; the game restarts. So it has come to pass since the wars of conquest of the Almoravids and the African Almohads in Spain, till the latest Mahdī of Khartoum.[22]

Engels saw in this cycle, which Ibn Khaldūn who was his probable source also described, the basis of 'Islamic Marxism'. The collective nature of tribes, with their shared ownership of land and property, predisposes them to impose equality in the name of morals and beliefs. In fact, they end up enslaved by the very decadence and amoral inequality they originally sought to destroy. Although Engels possibly goes too far in attempting to fit a Marxist interpretation to Ibn Khaldūn's cycles of history, the general notion that tribes could unite around a leader for economic motives initially seems sound.

Yet, the Maṣmūda did not revolt immediately in a united way after the imposition of taxes. They embarked only on minor, ineffective raids as separate clans. The specific charisma of the Mahdī Ibn Tūmart, an excuse for rigid obedience, inspired the tribes into united action. The Almohad hierarchy was not an ideal egalitarian Marxist collective, far from it. As 'architect' of the Almohad revolution, Ibn Tūmart manipulated the existing tribal social structures even as his message was directed towards the tribes. Economics was an important incentive to the tribes, but it would be facile to claim that it was their only reason for giving up their previous independence to join the Almohad cause.

There is no price to be put on the apocalypse. No amount of gold can satisfy the appetite of religious expectation. In Peter Worsley's account of the millennial cargo cults in Melanesia, individuals and tribes will actually dispose of their 'cargo', their material possessions in expectation of the end of time.[23] Likewise, the Hargha and the Almohad leaders gave up their horses and their possessions at the great *āsmās*, the ceremonial meal at the cave of

Ibn Tūmart. It could be argued that this material sacrifice was only done in expectation of greater material reward, reward gained from collective action. Nevertheless, the spiritual expectations were genuine. Religion was not merely the opiate of the tribes, but the inspiring flame. The Almohad sources made this clear when they described tribesmen and chiefs giving up their old ancestral lineages and joining the new lineage structure established by Ibn Tūmart.

The role of tribes and tribal social organization in human civilization has recently been the subject of vigorous scientific debate. Several genetic and anthropological studies have revealed a fascinating tendency in humanity to break into tribal groupings. It was only with the advent of complex forms of language and culture that tribes could organize around a civilizing idea. What the rise of the Almohads demonstrated, however, was that this process could happen rapidly and almost instantaneously if the right social, charismatic and economic conditions existed.

Conclusions

In his endeavour to establish the absolute unity of God on earth, Ibn Tūmart was expressing Almohad ambitions.

> There is no God but God as is attested by all creatures. His existence is absolutely necessary without limitation or determination by time or place or direction or limit or class or form or figure, nor by volume aspect or state. ... He cannot be defined by thought or imagination: he is neither determined by ideas nor qualified by reason. He is singular in his eternity.[1]

God had no attributes or signs. Humanity must submit to a universal and completely separate creator with no attributes. The founding principles of the Almohad movement were based on the endeavour to create a universal society, a universal, all-inclusive tribe, led by the spirit and energy of Ibn Tūmart and his successor, ʿAbd al-Muʾmin. The doctrine of *tawḥīd* meant not only the absolute unity of God, but also the absolute unity of God's community.

Yet, as the Almohad historical sources made clear, Ibn Tūmart did not construct the foundations of the Almohad Empire out of nothing. Credit, especially in the writings of al-Baydhaq, was given as much to the Berber tribes as to the Mahdī's inspiration. He used existing, informal and often unwritten tribal institutions, *tamyīz* (the process of preparing for battle), *āsmās* (the ritual alliance meal), *agrao* (the tribal council), the *mizwār* and other tribal social structures as the foundations of a disciplined hierarchical system.

Rather than being the antithesis of Islamic government, as has often been assumed, tribes formed the ranks of the new Almohad hierarchy. As the rise of the Almohad Empire demonstrated, understanding how tribes were transformed from a loose, segmentary system into a structured hierarchy that conquered previously impenetrable territories was key to understanding the history of identity and belief in Islam.

It was possible to have a strong, ancestral, tribal identity and loyalty (a feature of many Middle Eastern and Muslim societies) and still believe in a God who subordinated ancestry, a God whose nature can only be defined as *tawḥīd*, absolute unity. Berber Almohad historians and early Almohad documents, like the *Kitāb al-Ansāb*, supported the myth that Ibn Tūmart and the rise of the Almohads proved that it was possible to reconcile the apparent contradiction between identity and belief. Instead of destroying tribalism, however, Ibn Tūmart and the Almohads redefined the meaning of tribal identity, manipulated blood loyalties, and made God and his Mahdī the focus of a new identity, a newly unified tribe. The result of this reconciliation was an empire, an era of unity and power that began to break down as soon as the contradictions between equality and tribal hierarchy were challenged. In fact, several new Mahdīs emerged after the Almohads to attempt again this reconciliation of tribal blood loyalty and allegedly universal apocalyptic vision. These movements created their own attempts to rewrite history, to mythologize the reconciliation of the symbols of social differences and the ideals of religious unity in a way favourable to their own particular tribal, economic and social contexts.[2] Yet, none were quite as successful as the Almohads. The Almohad Empire was an Islamic empire whose myth of unity continues to be a distant hope for North Africans today.[3]

The keystone that held this remarkable reconciliation between belief and identity, this remarkable tribal hierarchy, together was the doctrine of the *Mahdī Maʿṣum*, the infallible Mahdī.[4] As a 'column between heaven and earth', as the chosen leader of a new era, as the leader who was destined to transform the Islamic world from the outside in, the Mahdī, the one who must be obeyed, the one who never erred, was the physical promise of God's plan for humankind. He was the final, needed proof that would inspire the tribes to maintain their unity, to fight the enemies of God's true nature: the Almoravids. They were the heretics who degraded God into a physical being, the elite jurists who despised the sources of God's word (*al-uṣūl*), who wanted to own God's law. Just as important as the Mahdī was the society that embraced his message and became the warriors for his cause: the Berber tribes of the High Atlas Mountains who, even until the fourteenth century when Ibn Khaldūn was writing, held some sway over the way the history of the Almohads was written and portrayed. In the myth of Ibn Tūmart portrayed by medieval North African sources, the making of the Almohad Empire was the making of an all-inclusive community of God.

Notes

Introduction

1. Roger Le Tourneau, *The Almohad movement in North Africa in the twelfth and thirteenth centuries*, translated from French, Princeton: Princeton University Press, 1969, p. 95.
2. On the role of Christians in Almohad Marrakech, see Allen Fromherz, 'North Africa and the twelfth-century Renaissance: Christian Europe and the Almohad Islamic Empire', *Islam and Christian-Muslim Relations*, vol. 20, no. 1, January 2009, pp. 43–59.
3. Huici Miranda, *Historia política del imperio Almohade*, vol. 2, Tetuan, 1957, p. 472.
4. See Le Tourneau, *The Almohad movement.*
5. A recent conference publication edited by Patrice Cressier, Maribel Fierro and Luis Molina entitled *Los Almohades: problemas y perspectivas* (2 vols, Madrid: Consejo Superior de Investigaciones Científicas, 2006) contains important contemporary research on the Almohads conducted and orchestrated by the scholars Maribel Fierro and Mercedes Garcia-Arenal from the Consejo Superior de Investigaciones Scientificas (CSIC) in Spain. Muhammad V University in Rabat, Morocco is also leading the way with important research on social and religious life under the Almohads by Halima Ferhat. See *Le Maghrib aux XIIème et XIIIème siècles: les siècles de la foi,* Casablanca, 1993.
6. Ibn Khaldūn, *Histoire des Berbères*, translated by de Slane, Paris, 1927, vol. 2, p. 53.
7. Vincent J. Cornell, *Realm of the saint: power and authority in Moroccan Sufism*, Austin: University of Texas Press, 1998, p. 193, a specialist in the history of sufism in North Africa, discussed the cult of Ibn Tūmart upheld by the Saksyūwa amirate. As he put it, there were 'tribally based movements that espoused mahdist beliefs and relied for legitimacy on inspirational or 'revealed' texts ... [they] regarded Maliki ulama as unbelievers.'

8 Mercedes García-Arenal, *Messianism and puritanical reform: Mahdis of the Muslim west*, translated by Martin Beagles, Leiden: E. J. Brill, 2006, pp. 157–64; Huici Miranda, 'La leyenda y la historia en los origenes del Imperio Almohade', *al-Andalus*, vol. 14, no. 2, 1949, pp. 339–76. David J. Wasserstein, 'A Jonah theme in the biography of Ibn Tūmart', in Farhad Daftary and Josef Meri (eds) *Culture and memory in medieval Islam: Essays in Honour of Wilfred Madelung*, London: I.B.Tauris, 2003, pp. 232–49 claimed that the 'biographical tradition about Muḥammad Ibn Tūmart is clearly hagiographical in character'.

9. In fact, in addition to the prominent role of the Berber tribes in the hierarchy of the Almohad Empire, the rise of the Almohads led to the creation of a local, Berber speaking literary and religious tradition based in the Sūs valley. The Berber speaking figure Sālim ibn Salama as-Sūsī (d. 1193), for example, translated Islamic jurisprudence into the Tashelhit Berber dialect. Cornell, *Realm of the saint*, p. 97.
10. Francesco Gabrieli, 'Le origini del movimento Almohad in una Fonte Storica d'Oriente', *Studia Arabica*, vol. 3, no. 1, January 1956, p. 3. Other accounts from outside North Africa include the somewhat disparaging mentions of the life of Ibn Tūmart in Ibn al-Athīr (d. 1233), *Al-Kāmil*, vol. 8, Beirut, 1978, p. 294. There is a passage about Ibn Tūmart's life in Ibn Khallikān (d. 1282) *Wafayāt al-a'ayān*, translated by Mac Gukin de Slane, Paris: Publications de l'Ecole des Langues Orientales, 1868, vol. 3, pp. 206–7, which also includes a reference to the account of the Wazir of Aleppo Ibn al Qifṭī (d. 1248). Another interesting and rare account, this time more approving of Ibn Tūmart but without 'hagiography' was written by Ḥasan ibn ʿAbdallāh al-ʿAbbāsī on the margins of a manuscript of Suyūṭī's *Tārīkh al-Khulafā'*, see Wasserstein, 'A Jonah theme', p. 246, note 2.
11. Patrick Geary, *The myth of nations: the medieval origins of Europe*, Princeton: Princeton University Press, 2003.
12. Madeleine Fletcher, 'Al-Andalus and North Africa in the Almohad ideology', in Salma Jayyusi (ed.) *The legacy of Muslim Spain*, Leiden, 1992, pp. 235–58.
13. Emile Fricaud, 'Les ṭālaba dans la société almohade (le temps d'Averroès)', *Al-Qanṭara*, vol. 18, 1997, pp. 331–87 first used the term de-Almohadization. Also see Mohammed Kably, *Société, pouvoir et réligion au Maroc à la fin du Moyen Age*, Paris: Maisonneuve et Larose, 1986, p. xxvi.
14. See Fricaud, 'Les ṭālaba dans la société almohade'; also Madeleine Fletcher, 'The Almohad Tawḥīd: theology which relies on logic', *Numen*, vol. 38, 1991, pp. 110–27. Considering how much time Ibn Rushd spent in North Africa, one could even contest the notion that he was solely influenced by the Andalusi context, but that is another topic.
15. Dominique Urvoy, 'La pensée de Ibn Tumart', *Bulletin des Etudes Orientales*, vol 27, 1974, pp. 19–44.
16. Maribel Fierro, 'Le Mahdī Ibn Tūmart et al-Andalus: l'élaboration de la légitimité almohade', in Mercedes García-Arenal (ed.) *Millénarisme et Mahdisme, REMM*, vols 91–4, 2000, pp. 107–24.
17. Instead of moving most of his forces to Iberia in 1148 to clean up a series of rebellions against the Almohads in al-Andalus, ʿAbd al Muʾmin instead diverted most of his army to Tunisia to expel the Normans. 'Since to ʿAbd al Muʾmin Spain was a diversion from the consolidation of Almohad rule in the Maghrib, he was content for the time being to hold onto the position his commanders had reached in 1148' (Jamil Abun-Nasr, *A history of the Maghrib in the Islamic period*, Cambridge: Cambridge University Press, 1987, p. 92).
18. Wasserstein, 'A Jonah theme', p. 246, note 2.
19. E. Lévi-Provençal (ed.) *Documents inédits d'histoire Almohade*, Paris, 1928. (Includes

the *Kitāb al Ansāb*, letters by Ibn Tūmart and 'Abd al Mu'min, and Ibn Tūmart's biography by al-Baydhaq).

20. 'Abd al-Waḥid al-Marrākushī, *Al-Mu'jib fi Talkhis Akhbār al-Maghrib*, Rabat, 1949. Also, R. P. A. Dozy, *The history of the Almohades*, 2nd edn, Leiden: E. J. Brill, 1881.
21. M. A. Makkī described what little is known about the life of al-Qaṭṭān and his father in the introduction to the text Ibn al-Qaṭṭān, *Naẓm al-Jumān*, Rabat, 1966, 39–40. As al-Qaṭṭān noted, 'Every level among these levels was ranked according to its number.' He also noted, 'those who did not memorize their passages were rebuked.' This indicated that rank was determined by learning as well as political and tribal considerations. Those who did not learn their verses should be 'whipped' until they were sufficiently aware of both the Qur'ān and Ibn Tūmart's doctrine. If anything, this later writer is even more explicit than al-Baydhaq about the need to maintain the Berber hierarchy and the Almohad system. Ibn al-Qaṭṭān was no mere agent of Andalusi historical manipulation. He makes Ibn Tūmart into a man more concerned with teaching proper doctrine than the possible reactions that may ensue from whipping his students. If anything he seemed keen to maintain the faltering original institutions of the Almohads. *Naẓm al-Jumān*, p. 24. Also see Emile Fricaud, 'La notice biographique d'Abū al-Ḥasan 'Alī Ibn al-Qaṭṭān', in María Luisa Ávila and Maribel Fierro (eds) *Biografías Almohades*, Madrid: CSIC, 2000, vol. 2, pp. 223–83.
22. Georges Marcy, 'Les phrases berbères des documents almohades', *Hespéris*, vol. 14, no. 1, 1932, pp. 61–78.
23. Surprisingly, Ibn 'Abī Zar', *Rawḍ al-Qirṭās*, edited by Huici Miranda, Valencia, 1964, was less anti-Ibn Tūmart than many have supposed. See, also, for example Ibn 'Abī Zar' and his description of Ibn Tūmart standing up to the Almoravid sultan.
24. Ibn 'Abī Zar', *Rawḍ al-Qirṭās*, p. 361. Perhaps the reason for this was the affinity felt towards the Almohads as a powerful Berber dynasty that, like the Marinids, attempted to hold onto Al-Andalus and domains outside North Africa. It has been argued that the Marinids reduced or persecuted or even de-Almohadized, some aspects of Almohad history. See Maya Shatzmiller, *L'historiographie mérinide: Ibn Khaldūn et ses contemporains*, Leiden: E. J. Brill, 1982. What explains, however, some of the fairly favourable portrayals of Ibn Tūmart in the *Rawḍ al-Qirṭās*?
25. Perhaps the Marinids saw the usefulness of maintaining the shrine of a powerful Berber spiritual figure and not completely alienating the Atlas tribes. Ibn Khaldūn, *Histoire des Berbères*, translated by de Slane, Paris, 1927, vol. 2, p. 260.
26. Ibn Khaldūn, in just one example, described the Hintāta, the tribe of his Berber patron in Tunis as having a special 'bravery and authority' (Ibn Khaldūn, *Histoire des Berbères*, vol. 2, p. 269).
27. In a poem modelled on classical Arabic poetry, Ibn Khaldūn praised Abu 'l-'Abbās, the Ḥafṣid ruler, as the 'one to whom people turn their faces, and you are the great hope of all.' Ibn Khaldūn, 'Autobiographie', *Le Livre des exemples*, translated by A. al-Chedaddi, Paris: Gallimard, 2002, p. 159. This Ḥafṣid ruler also became Ibn

Khaldūn's patron for the first version of the *Muqaddima* – a later version was dedicated to the Mamluk Sultan of Egypt, Barquq – and in his autobiography he writes: 'From my work I offer to your [Abu al-'Abbās'] grandeur precious pearls and stars that never set. I have created glory for your realm. ... You are able to see truth in all things, who could pretend to say anything false. ... God has accorded you a position higher than all others. ... You are the most equitable.'

28. Ibn Khaldūn, *The Muqaddimah*, translated by Franz Rosenthal, vol. 1, Princeton, 1958, p. 327.
29. Ibn Khaldūn, *Histoire des Berbères et des dynasties musulmanes de l'Afrique septentrionale*, translated by de Slane, Paris, 1925, vol 2, pp. 161–73.
30. Ibn Khaldūn explained the fringes of power with a poetic flourish. 'A dynasty is stronger at its centre than it is at its border regions. When it has reached its farthest expansion, it becomes too weak and incapable to go any farther. This may be compared to light rays that spread from their centers, or to circles that widen over the surface of the water when it is struck.' *Muqaddimah*, vol. 1, p. 327.
31. Ibn Khaldūn explained the failure of al-'Abbās as a lack of *'aṣabiyya*, group feeling, *esprit de corps*, tribal solidarity. The necessary role of tribal *'aṣabiyya* (a word that comes from the Arabic *'aṣab*: the stringy sinews that bind) in the rise of dynasties was a central theme of his masterwork, the *Muqaddimah*, his introduction to the history of the world. He explained that tribes 'can acquire royal authority only by making use of some religious colouring, such as prophethood, or sainthood'. Ibn Khaldūn, *The Muqaddimah*, vol. 1, p. 305.

Chapter 1: The Life of Ibn Tūmart and the Birth of the Almohad Movement

1. Rachid Bourouiba discussed the differences in the sources about the date of Ibn Tūmart's birth in, 'A propos de la date de naissance d'Ibn Tūmart', *Revue d'Histoire et de Civilisation du Maghreb*, January 1966, pp. 19–25. In fact, the entire chronology of Ibn Tūmart's life, especially his early journey to the East differs in the sources, see Rachid Bourouiba, 'Chronologie d'Ibn Tūmart', *Revue d'Histoire et de Civilisation du Maghreb*, July 1967, pp. 39–47. Also Rachid Bouroubia, *Ibn Tūmart*, Algiers, 1974. To avoid confusion, in this book I shall rely on the dates used in Miranda's celebrated *Historia política*, which provides a narrative account of the Mahdī's life using the most probable dates. For further discussions of the various versions of the biography of Ibn Tūmart, see Wasserstein, 'A Jonah theme', pp. 232–49.
2. Miranda, *Historia política*, vol. 1, p. 24.
3. See the earliest, and most extensive primary source for the life of Ibn Tūmart, 'Les memoires d'al-Baydhaq', in E. Lévi-Provençal, *Documents inédits d'histoire almohade*, p. 45. Other important primary sources include al-Marrākushī, *Al-Mu'jib*; al-Zarkashī, *Tārīkh al-Dawlatayn*, Tunis, 1966; Anonymous Chronicler, *Al-Ḥulal al-Mūshiyyah*, edited by Huici Miranda, Tetuan, 1951; Ibn 'Abī Zar', *Rawḍ al-Qirṭās*; Ibn al-Qaṭṭān, *Naẓm al-Jumān*; Ibn Khaldūn, *Histoire des Berbères*. Convenient English translations of excerpts from other, sometimes unpublished, Arabic sources can be found in H. T. Norris, *The Berbers in Arabic Literature*, London: Longman, 1982, especially Chapter 8.

A recent collection of articles in Anonymous, *Los Almohades*, provides insight into the careers of Ibn Tūmart and ʿAbd al-Muʾmin. For the perspective of Moroccan historians, see Ferhat, *Le Maghrib aux XIIème et xiiième siècles*; and Bū Laqṭīb al-Ḥusayn, *Jawāīḥ wa awbīat Maghrib ʿAhd al-Muwaḥḥidīn*, Rabat, 2002.

4. It is difficult to say how successful the Almoravids were in the Atlas and how tied they were to the Maṣmūda tribes. Vincent Lagardère in *Les Almoravides jusqu'au regne de Yûsuf b. Tâsfîn (1039–1106)*, Paris, 1989, p. 68, suggested that the Almoravids had only a superficial impact on many Atlas tribes.
5. For two different perspectives on the rise of the Almoravids and Almoravid doctrine, see Lagardère, *Les Almoravides*; and Jacinto Bosch Vilá, *Los Almorávides*, Granada, 1990.
6. For a recent study, in Arabic, of social life in the Almohad and Almoravid periods, see Jamāl Ṭāhā, *al-Ḥayāt al-ijtimāīyah bi al-Maghrib al Aqṣa fī al-Aṣr al-Islāmī: ʿaṣray al Murābiṭīn wa al-Muwaḥḥidīn*, Alexandria, 2004, Although they focus on a small town in the north of Morocco, far from Igīlīz, the fascinating articles in Nancy L. Benco (ed.) *Anatomy of a medieval Islamic town: Al-Basra, Morocco*, Oxford, 2004, details archaeological finds that shed light on daily life in a medieval Moroccan town. See especially the article by Hannah Dodd, 'Beyond Al-Basra: settlement systems of medieval Northern Morocco in archaeological and historical perspective'.
7. The early life of the Mahdī Ibn Tūmart presented here is recorded in Ibn al-Qaṭṭān, *Naẓm al-Jumān*, pp. 3–6; and al-Marrākushī, *al-Muʿjib*, pp. 186–9.
8. For a discussion of the possible location of Igīlīz and the importance of Iglī, a city near Igīlīz, see Allen Fromherz, 'The Almohad Mecca: locating Igli and the cave of Ibn Tūmart', *al-Qanṭara*, vol. 26, no. 1, 2005, pp. 175–90; and Miranda, *Historia política*, vol. 1, p. 24. In my article I claim to present the need for more research on the precise location of Igīlīz. I also point out the use of the phrase *Igli n Wargan* as the birthplace of Ibn Tūmart in Al-Marrākushī's *Muʿjib*, as a possible reason to believe that the location may refer to or be near the modern Moroccan village of Igli. As I stated in the article, however, I did not set out to make any definitive claims. French scholar Jean Pierre Van Staëvel convincingly claimed to describe a more precise location of Igīlīz in the Anti-Atlas in a more recent article on the subject. Jean Pierre Van Staëvel and Abdallah Fili, 'À propos de la localisation d'Īgīlīz-des-harga', *Al-Qanṭara*, vol. 27, no. 1, 2006, pp. 153–94.
9. The 'Argan' is a sturdy oil-nut producing tree abundant in the region. Jacques Berque observed the Hargha and their use of the Argan tree in his ethnography *Structures sociales du Haut-Atlas*, Paris, 1955. For an analysis of the current existence of historical place names, see David M. Hart, 'Persistence and changes in names on the North African landscape: Berber tribes in Ibn Khaldūn's genealogies and as they appear today', *The Journal of North African Studies*, vol. 5, no. 1, Spring 2000, pp. 121–46.
10. For a discussion of the fluidity and transformative power of tribal alliances among the High Atlas Berbers, see David M. Hart, 'Berber tribal alliance networks in pre-

colonial North Africa: the Algerian saff, the Moroccan liff and the chessboard model of Montagne', *Journal of North African Studies*, vol. 1, no. 2, 1996, pp. 192–205.

11. For further details see the *Kitāb al-Ansāb*, in Lévi-Provençal, *Documents inédits*, pp. 25–75. Note: all page numbers cited for *Documents inédits* refer to the French translation by Lévi-Provençal.

12. There are few sources on the early life of Ibn Tūmart. Thus, in addition to the limited material provided by Ibn al-Qaṭṭān and al-Marrākushī, this bare historical reconstruction of Ibn Tūmart's life in the village of Igīlīz is based on my own observations of the region of the Anti-Atlas, the work of the anthropologists Ernest Gellner, Jacques Berque and David M. Hart, the last of whom developed a historical ethnographic reproduction of tribal life in precolonial Morocco in his book *Estructuras tribales precoloniales en Marruecos berber, 1860–1933*, Granada, 1997. Also see David M. Hart, *Tribe and society in rural Morocco*, London: Frank Cass, 2000; and David M. Hart, *The Aīt ʿAtta of southern Morocco: daily life and recent history*, Cambridge: Middle East & North African Studies Press, 1984. Ernest Gellner also bases most of his Moroccan ethnographic research on the Aīt ʿAtta of the south of Morocco. See Ernest Gellner, *Saints of the Atlas*, Chicago: University of Chicago Press, 1969. A controversial, but rich and important study of the High Atlas was done in the 1920s by the French colonial anthropologist Robert Montagne, *Les Berbères et le Makhzen dans le sud du Maroc*, Paris: Felix Alcan, 1930. Montagne spoke of the Berbers as the basis of the Almohad Empire and claimed that those of the High Atlas lived in small egalitarian republics, pp. 56–65. However, Montagne was allegedly tainted by colonial generalizations about the Berbers as distinct and more European than the Arabs. For a critique of French colonial historiography, see Abdallah Laroui, *L'Histoire du Maghreb*, Casablanca: Wizarat al-thaqafah wa-al-ittisal, 2001. There is also work on 'political' anthropology from a Moroccan perspective in Mohamed Othman Benjelloun, *Projet national et identité au Maroc: essai d'anthropologie politique*, Paris: l'Harmattan, 2002. Although he focuses on the Marinids and later, David Powers, *Law, society, and culture in the Maghrib, 1300–1500*, Cambridge: Cambridge University Press, 2002, provides a framework for historical anthropology in the Maghrib. Maya Shatzmiller, *The Berbers and the Islamic state: the Marinid experience in pre-protectorate Morocco*, Princeton: Markus Wiener Publishing, 1999, also provided a general overview of the unique influence of the Berbers in medieval North African history. For Arabic manuscript sources on the Sūs valley where Ibn Tūmart was born see the conveniently compiled book by Umar Afā Tansīq, *Al-Ṣaḥrā wa-Sūs min Khilāla al-Wathāiq wa al Makhṭūṭāt*, Muḥammad V University, Rabat, 2001. An interesting document in its own right, Bryan Clarke's, *Berber village: the story of the Oxford University expedition to the High Atlas Mountains of Morocco*, London: Longmans, 1959, illustrated some of the basic features of Berber village life in the Atlas.

13. A general from the Umayyad period, 'had a bundle of arrows brought to his sons on his deathbed: they could not break it, though they could break each arrow separately'. This was a famous story in the Islamic tradition of the Middle East

expressing the concept of tribal solidarity. See Patricia Crone, *Medieval Islamic political thought*, Edinburgh: Edinburgh University Press, 2005, p. 51, footnote 3. See also Ibn Khaldūn, *The Muqaddimah*, vol. 1, pp. 247–64, in which he discussed *'aṣabiyya*, tribal solidarity, as the basis for understanding history in tribally influenced societies.

14. The relationship between human society, land and agricultural production has a bibliography, of which the foundational philosophical work is L. Febvre's *La Terre et l'évolution humaine*, Paris: La Renaissance du Livre, 1922. Jacque Berque and the anthropologists of the French-Moroccan school relied heavily on the Annales school of Lucien Febvre.
15. For more on the often collective nature of Moroccan agriculture, see Nicholas Michel, 'The individual and the collectivity in the agricultural economy of pre-colonial Morocco', in Nelly Hanna (ed.) *Money, land and trade: an economic history of the Muslim Mediterranean*, London: I.B.Tauris, 2002.
16. E. Lévi-Provençal, 'Pratiques agricoles et fêtes saisonnières des tribus Djebalah de la vallée moyenne de l'Ouargha', *Bulletin Archéologique*, 1918, pp. 194–200.
17. For a standard ethnography and anthropological analysis of High Atlas tribal life and the tribal economy of weekly markets, see Berque's masterful *Structures sociales*. See his first chapters on the rural economy. For a study of tribal communal law see his discussion beginning on p. 369.
18. For a discussion of tribal decision making in an anthropological and historical context, see C. Lindholm, 'Quandries of command in egalitarian societies: examples from Swat and Morocco', in J. Cole (ed.) *Comparing Muslim societies: knowledge and the state in a world civilization*, Ann Arbor: University of Michigan Press, 1992, pp. 63–94. According to Ernest Gellner in *Conditions of liberty, civil society and its rivals*, London: Hamish Hamilton, 1994, if tribes resisted kings they were beholden to the authority, even the tyranny, of their kinsmen.
19. Lévi-Provençal provides a brief discussion of the many versions of Ibn Tūmart's name in his *Documents inédits*, p. 31. Huici Miranda also mentions the citation in his edition of Anonymous Chronicler, *Al-Ḥulal al-Mūshiyyah*, p. 6. Lévi-Provençal claims that Ibn Tūmart was never a sharifian but provides no conclusive proof either way. On names, naming and the validity of Berber genealogies see Hart 'Persistence and changes'. Also, see Jacque Berque's discussion of names in the first chapters of *Structures sociales*.
20. Lévi-Provençal, *Documents inédits*, p. 45.
21. On the Idrīsīds, see Rachid Benblal, *Histoire des Idrīssides, 172–337 (788–948)*, Oran: Dar el Gharb, 2002.
22. Al-Marrākushī, *al-Mu'jib*, p. 178, claimed that Ibn Tūmart was 'from the line of the Prophet'.
23. Ibn Khaldūn, *The Muqaddimah*, vol. 1, p. 53.
24. Ibid, p. 54.
25. Ibid, p. 55.
26. Lévi-Provençal, *Documents inédits*, p. 45.

27. Georges Marçais, *La Berbérie musulmane et l'Orient au moyen âge*, Paris: Aubier, 1946. The Fatimids let the Hilālian Arabs loose on rebellious North African domains. For a discussion of the validity of this legend and a balanced portrait of the Arab Hilālian influence in North Africa, see Michael Brett, 'The way of the nomad', in Michael Brett, *Ibn Khaldūn and the medieval Maghrib*, Aldershot: Ashgate, 1999, pp. 251–69.
28. Lévi-Provençal, *Documents inédits*, p. 25.
29. Gellner, *Saints of the Atlas*, p. 38.
30. The Romance of the Banū Hilāl, a long, epic poem in the style of Arab praise poetry, details the exploits of this Arab tribal confederation in North Africa. Although most is fiction, it reveals the legendary struggle, but also ultimate reconciliation, between the native Berbers and the invading Arabs. One climactic moment of the text occurs when the Arab chieftain Dhiyāb slays the Zanāta Berber leader Al-Khalīfa al Zanātī (A. Guiga, *La Geste hilalienne*, translated by Tahar Guiga, Tunis: La Maison *Tunisienne* d'Edition, 1968, pp. 81–2). For more on the controversy surrounding the Arab Banū Hilāl and their supposed conflict with the Berbers see Marçais's mostly negative account of the Arabs in *La Berbérie musulmane*. For more recent discussions see Michael Brett and Elizabeth Fentress, *The Berbers*, Oxford: Blackwell, pp. 135–42; also H. T. Norris, *The Arab conquest of the Western Sahara*.
31. This mythical combination of Arab and Berber legitimacy in the person of Ibn Tūmart seems to be a main political objective of the anonymous Almohad manuscript, *Kitāb al Ansāb*, or *Book of Ancestry*, Lévi-Provençal, *Documents inédits*, p. 25.
32. As with most dates related to the life and death of Ibn Tūmart, the primary sources are in disagreement about the exact date of Ibn Tūmart's departure. Ibn al-Qaṭṭān gives the date as AH 514, and describes his meetings with scholars outside the Maghrib.
33. Ibn al-Qaṭṭān, *Naẓm al-Jamān*, p. 4, recorded that Ibn Tūmart visited Córdoba.
34. A discussion of Ibn Tūmart's doctrine is found in Chapter 3 of this book. The sources are not very exact about Ibn Tūmart's early adventures. Al-Marrākushī describes his early journeys in *al-Mu'jib*, pp. 178–9, as does Ibn al-Qaṭṭān, *Naẓm al-Jamān*, pp. 1–10. The al-Baydhaq manuscript in Lévi-Provençal, *Documents inédits*, the richest source for Ibn Tūmart's life, does not begin until after Ibn Tūmart returned from the East.
35. Christopher Melchert, *The Formation of the Sunni schools of law 9-10th centuries CE*, Leiden: E. J. Brill, 1997, pp. 156–70, described how it was very common for important Maliki scholars in North Africa and Andalusia to travel to the East. 'Abd al Azīz bin 'Abd Allāh, *Al-Rihlāt min al-Maghrib*, Rabat, 2001, described the almost unbroken history of journeys, *rihlāt*, of pilgrims and scholars from North Africa to the East. Further discussion of travels and travellers in the Muslim west can be found in Dale F. Eickelman and James Piscatori (eds) *Muslim travellers: pilgrimage, migration, and the religious imagination*, London: Routledge, 1990.
36. According to Maribel Fierro, however, the obligation to perform the *ḥājj* was not

always universal, or even encouraged. Abū Bakr ibn al-ʿArabī had to contradict scholars who said that the *ḥājj* was not a necessary pillar of Islam. See Maribel Fierro, 'La Religión', in Ramon M. Pidal, *Historia de España,* vol. 8, no. 2, pp. 435–546.

37. In some cases, the tales of travellers were too fantastic. Ibn Baṭṭūṭa, the most famous chronicler of a journey intended for the pilgrimage, was ridiculed for his fantastic and strange stories, so far removed from normal, provincial life. For more on Ibn Baṭṭūṭa, see Ross Dunn, *The Adventures of Ibn Baṭṭūṭa, a Muslim traveler of the fourteenth century*, Los Angeles: University of California Press, 2005.
38. Eickelman and Piscatori, *Muslim travellers.*
39. Ibn Khaldūn, *Taʿrīf ibn Khaldūn Rihlatahu Gharban wa Sharqan*, Cairo, 1901.
40. For a short discussion of the similarities between Muḥammad the prophet and Muḥammad Ibn Tūmart, see the opening pages of Le Tourneau, *The Almohad movement*. See also Miranda, *Historia política*, pp. 1–30.
41. Ibn ʿAbī Zarʿ, *Rawḍ al-Qirṭās*, p. 361.
42. See Ibn ʿIsḥāq, *Sīrat al-Nabawiyya*, compiled and edited by Ibn Hishām, 2 vols, Cairo, 1900, p. 35 for a description of the prophet's physical features as used in Martin Lings, *Muḥammad: his life based on the earliest sources*, Rochester, Vermont: Inner Traditions, 2006.
43. For the life of the Prophet Muḥammad, see Ibn ʿIsḥāq, *Sīrat al-Nabawiyya.*
44. Peter M. Holt, *The age of the Crusades: the Near East from the eleventh century to 1517*, London: Longman, 1986. On the development of the caliphate and its eventual crisis of legitimacy in the Islamic East, see Hugh Kennedy, *The Prophet and the age of the caliphates: the Islamic Near East from the sixth to the eleventh century*, 2nd edition, London: Longman, 2004. A good comparative study, including articles on the caliphate, is Isabel Alfonso, Hugh Kennedy and Julio Escalona (eds) *Building legitimacy: political discourses and forms of legitimacy in medieval societies*, Leiden: E. J. Brill, 2004.
45. On legitimacy and leadership in the early medieval period when the power of the caliphs was waning, see the study of the Buyids by Roy Mottahedeh, *Loyalty and leadership in an early Islamic society*, London: I.B.Tauris and Islamic Publications, Ltd, 2001. Also see Crone, *Medieval Islamic political thought*, in which there are several well-researched chapters on legitimacy and leadership.
46. The caliphate had lost much of its legitimacy. Indeed, a tradition of the prophet developed that the true caliphate would only last 30 years. Several in the so-called Ḥadīth party believed that 'God the real ruler of the community, was represented in the here and now by the Qurʾān and the *sunna* of His Prophet, not by the Caliph.' For more on the delegitimization of the caliph see Crone, *Medieval Islamic political thought*, p. 138.
47. Al-Marrākushī, *al-Muʿjib*, p. 128.
48. Ibid., pp. 128–9.
49. For a basic summary of al-Ghazālī, his life and works, see William Montgomery Watt, *The faith and practice of al-Ghazālī*, London: Allen & Unwin, 1953. One of al-Ghazālī's most important works was his treatise against the limitations of

Aristotelian thinking, *The incoherence of the philosophers.* See Abū Ḥamid Muḥammad al-Ghazālī, *The incoherence of the philosophers: English translation of Imām Ghazali's Tahafut al-Falasifa*, translated with parallel text by M. Marmura, Salt Lake City: Brigham Young University Press, 2000.

50. Watt, *The faith and practice of al-Ghazālī*, p. 14. He was also known to have special powers. He knew the secret names of God and could interpret the most difficult and opaque passages of the Qur'ān. He was the 'restorer of religion'. See Ignaz Goldziher (ed.) 'Introduction', in Ibn Tūmart, *Kitāb A'azz mā Yuṭlab* (*Le Livre de Ibn Toumert*), Algiers: P. Fontana, 1903, p. 15.
51. Huici Miranda, *Historia política,* vol. 1, pp. 29–32.
52. An article by Madeleine Fletcher disputes Miranda's judgement on this issue. However, she provides no conclusive proof, but merely a probable scenario. See Madeleine Fletcher, 'Ibn Tūmart's teachers: the relationship with al-Ghazālī', *Al-Qanṭara*, vol. 18, 1997, pp. 305–30. Mercedes García-Arenal, 'La pratica del percepto de al-amr bi-l-ma'ruf wa-l-nahy 'an al-munkar en la hagiografia magrebi', *al-Qanṭara*, vol. 13, no. 1, 1992, pp. 147–70, however, argued for a plausible connection between Ibn Tūmart and al-Ghazālī. Also, Goldziher, 'Introduction', provides a comprehensive analysis of the possible influence of al-Ghazālī on Ibn Tūmart. Apparently, the main influence on Ibn Tūmart would have been al-Ghazālī's focus on the *al-uṣūl:* original sources, the *ḥadīth*, *sunna* and the Qur'ān as opposed to the encrusted law books of the main legal schools. In Chapter 3 on Almohad doctrine, I provide futher discussion of these issues and influences.
53. Vincent Cornell, 'Understanding is the mother of ability: responsibility and action in the doctrine of Ibn Tūmart', *Studia Islamica*, no. 66, 1987, p. 77.
54. Using various sources Farouk Mitha, *Al-Gazali and the Ismailis: a debate on reason and authority in medieval Islam*, London: I.B.Tauris, 2002, demonstrated al-Ghazālī's differences with the Ismaili position.
55. Al-Marrākushī, *al-Mu'jib*, p. 129. Also, according to Ibn al-Qaṭṭān, *Naẓm al Jumān*, p. 17, Ibn Tūmart met al-Ghazālī and told him of the burning of his works.
56. Al-Marrākushī, *al-Mu'jib*, p. 129.
57. Ibn 'Abī Zar', *Rawḍ al al-Qirṭās*, p. 342. Similarly, Abī al-Zarkashī, *Tārīkh al-Dawlatayn*, p. 4, also provides this colourful conversation between the scholar and the reformer.
58. Michael Cook, *Commanding right and forbidding wrong*, Cambridge: Cambridge University Press, 2000, pp. 431, 441, 456.
59. However, al-Ghazālī also wrote works on listening to music, for example, which Ibn Tūmart may have rejected, for, as I shall show, he had a habit of destroying musical instruments. Perhaps the real focus of Ibn Tūmart's commanding right, however, were local festivals with pre-Islamic undertones. See al-Ghazālī, *On Listening to music*, Islamabad, 2002. María Viguera even describes alleged letters from al-Ghazālī and al-Tarṭūshī supporting the Almoravid amir. See María Viguera, 'Las cartas de al-Ghazālī y al-Tarṭushi al soberano almorávide Yūsuf b. Tāshufīn', *Al-Andalus*, vol. 42, 1977, pp. 341–74.

60. Crone, *Medieval Islamic political thought*, pp. 168–9.
61. Ibn Khaldūn, *Histoire des Berbères*, vol. 1, Algiers, p. 323.
62. Ibn Khaldūn ends his peripatetic autobiography with despair and sarcastic coolness as he notes the winds of fate and the whims of politics in Ibn Khaldūn, *Taʿrīf ibn Khaldūn*, p. 1.
63. Abū Bakr Muḥammad al-ʿArabī, *Shawāhid al-Jilla*, in Muḥammad Yaʿla (translator and editor) *Tres textos arabes sobre beréberes en el occidente islámico*, Madrid: Consejo Superior de Investigaciones Científicas, 1996 includes official Almoravid letters (*al-Rasāʾīl al-dīwāniyya*) to the ʿAbbāsid caliph al-Mustaẓahir, basically asking for the latter's blessing. See also E. Lévi-Provençal, 'Le titre souverain des almoravies et sa légitimation par le califat ʿAbbāside', *Arabica*, vol. 2, 1955, pp. 265–80. There is also a request in *Tres textos arabes* for al-Ghazālī to legitimize *jihād* against the Christians of Spain, showing yet another connection between the Almoravids and al-Ghazālī, even as Ibn Tūmart allegedly accused the Almoravids of burning the master's books. Al-Ghazālī seemed to be a source of legitimacy for both the Almoravids and the Almohads.
64. See Maribel Fierro's 'Introduction' to her translation of the *Ḥawādith waʾl bidaʿ* by Abī Bakr Ṭarṭushī, Madrid 1993. Al-Marrākushī, *al-Muʿjib*, p. 179, recorded that 'Ibn Tūmart went to Alexandria and went to the meeting room of Abī Bakr al-Ṭurṭushī ... and asked him the meaning of commanding right and forbidding wrong'.
65. Jonathan Berkey, *The formation of Islam: religion and society in the Near East, 600–1800*, Cambridge: Cambridge University Press, 2003, p. xii, defines the term *ijāza* as 'The authorization issued by an author or scholar to a pupil allowing the pupil to transmit a text on his authority'.
66. Al-Marrākushī, *al-Muʿjib*, p. 179. Lévi-Provençal, *Documents inédits*, pp. 75–8. Al-Baydhaq's biography of Ibn Tūmart begins with descriptions of the popularity of his sermons in Egypt.
67. Al-Ghazālī devotes a section of his *Munqidh min al Dalal* to discrediting the entire concept of the *Imām al Maʿṣūm*, the infallible imām: a concept that was at the core of Ibn Tūmart's claims. See the translation of the *Munqidh* in Watt, *The faith and practice of al-Ghazālī*.
68. Although the first section of al-Baydhaq is missing, it was perhaps no mistake that the intricate details of Ibn Tūmart's life only start emerging in the sources after he returns from the east and was well on his way to set up with his band of followers in the Sūs Valley. See Lévi-Provençal's introduction to Lévi-Provençal, *Documents inédits* and my study of the manuscript in Chapter 3 for a discussion of the al-Baydhaq manuscript in the Escorial Library.
69. The biography of Ibn Tūmart in Lévi-Provençal, *Documents inédits* starting on p. 75 shows a steady progress in the power of Ibn Tūmart's conviction as he commands right first against mere clerics, then against governors, and finally against the ruler of the Almoravids. Not once does al-Baydhaq allow for fear in the personality of the 'infallible' Mahdī. Of course, the reality of the situation may have been

different and Ibn Tūmart's itinerant lifestyle was at least partially the result of fleeing from the wrath of unappreciative rulers.

70. There were also several intellectual currents that had begun in North Africa as well. These will be discussed in Chapter 3. An introduction to the spiritual movements of the Almohad period are described by Maribel Fierro, 'Revolución y tradición: algunos aspectos del mundo del saber en época almohade', in María Luisa Ávila and Maribel Fierro (eds), *Estudios Onomástico-biográficos de al-Andalus*, vol. 10, Madrid-Granada, 2000, pp. 131–65.

71. The idea that God is the only true ruler of humanity is found in the theological origins of Islamic government. Ibn Tūmart made this clear in his letter to the Almohads when he proclaimed that just as 'God directs the stars', he also directs the Almohads, Lévi-Provençal, *Documents inédits*, pp. 4–5. As Patricia Crone, *Medieval Islamic political thought*, pp. 1–6 observed, 'God rules in the most literal sense of the word, appointing rulers, governors, judges, and deputies and ordering armies against insubordinate subjects.' Adam and Seth were both the original representatives of God on Earth but Cain broke the legitimate connection with God by killing Abel. (Adam was not the source of original sin in the Christian sense.) Only when the direct line to God is restored does true Muslim government by God through a true representative, a Mahdī or a prophet, exist. Ibn Tūmart basically claimed to restore the direct line to God that was cut by bad government, represented by the sin of Cain. Al-Ṭabarī (d. 923), discussed this theology of the origin of Muslim government in the first of the ten volumes of *Tārīkh al-Rasūl wa al-Mulūk*, ed. M.J. de Goeje et al., Leiden: E. J. Brill, 1879–1901. Al-Ṭabarī was from Tabaristan, Persia near the Caspian Sea. He wrote a famous *Tafsīr*, or commentary on the Qur'ān. He died a simple teacher in Baghdad.

72. This was similar to the Prophet Muḥammad whose life was a *sunna*, an example for all Muslims. Regarding the embellishment of the *sunna* of Ibn Tūmart, Maribel Fierro claims that the sources for Ibn Tūmart's biography should be revised, 'taking into account how the needs of the Almohad Caliphate, especially in the first stages, influenced the presentation of the founder's figure.' See Maribel Fierro, 'The Ghurabā' in al-Andalus', *Arabica*, vol. 47, 2000, note 46. Michael Brett makes a similar claim in his article 'The lamp of the Almohads: illumination as a political idea in twelfth-century Morocco', in Michael Brett, *Ibn Khaldūn and the medieval Maghrib*, Aldershot: Ashgate, 1999. The first stages of the caliphate were dominated by ʿAbd al-Muʾmin who was anxious to support his legitimacy. Brett argues that ʿAbd al-Muʾmin basically encouraged the historians to turn Ibn Tūmart into a type of John the Baptist figure for himself, the true saviour. There are, however, several problems with this thesis. First, there is no direct evidence that ʿAbd al-Muʾmin consciously manipulated the original sources as they exist today. Certainly, al-Marrākushī and al-Baydhaq would want to please their respective leaders, but that did not necessarily mean that they completely refabricated their observations. Second, far from being treated as a secondary John the Baptist character, Ibn Tūmart is described very clearly, even by later Almohad

sources like al-Marrākushī, as the *Mahdī al-Maʿṣūm*, the infallible Mahdī, al-Marrākushī, *al-Muʿjib*, p. 187. Ibn Tūmart discusses the relevance and importance of Miracles in his 'Azz mā Yuṭlab', *Le Livre de Ibn Toumert*, Algiers, 1903, p. 138. ʿAbd al-Mu'min was very much the successor, not the founding inspiration. It is not clear that he would even want the burden of miraculous expectation on his shoulders.

73. Lévi-Provençal, *Documents inédits*, p. 80.
74. Sūra, 3: 104.
75. Quoted in Cook, *Commanding right*, p. 33.
76. It is difficult to know why Ibn Tūmart was so generous to this possible non-believer. It is possible that those who accused him simply used the name Jew as a derogatory way of saying that he did not follow their own localized interpretation of Islam.
77. Lévi-Provençal, *Documents inédits*, pp. 75–6.
78. Lévi-Provençal, *Documents inédits*, p. 78; Ibn ʿAbī Zarʿ, *Rawḍ al-Qirṭās*, pp. 341–2.
79. Lévi-Provençal, *Documents inédits*, p. 79; Abū al-Ḥasan Muḥammad bin Alī Ibn al-Athīr, *Kāmil*, *Al-Kāmil fī al-Tārīkh*, edited by C. J. Tornberg, Uppsala, 1843–46, vol. 10, p. 401.
80. The Hammadids effectively ruled the region of Algeria at this time.
81. Ibn Tūmart was particularly vehement against alcohol: *al-ḥamra*. An entire chapter of Ibn Tūmart's book was devoted to reasons why alcohol was a significant sin; see Chapter 3 of this book.
82. Lévi-Provençal, *Documents inédits*, p. 80. Ibn Tūmart thus proclaims that he is a vehicle of God's will and the Prophet. It is worth quoting the entire anecdote. 'Arriving at the Bāb al Baḥr (the gate to the sea) he emptied out onto the ground the wine that was being sold there saying 'The believer eats dates and the unbeliever drinks wine.' The slaves of Sabʿ hit him and said to him 'Who made you morality police (*ḥisba*)?' He replied 'Allah and his Prophet!' The message is clear: believers eat the humble date, slaves and unbelievers drink wine and impertinently disobey Ibn Tūmart whose power and authority comes only from God and his Prophet. This scene is repeated in other sources including al-Marrākushī, *al-Muʿjib*, pp. 128–39.
83. Al-Saqatī, *Kitāb fī ādāb al-ḥisba*, edited by E. Lévi-Provençal and G. S. Colin, *Journal Asiatique*, 1931.
84. Ibn ʿAbdun, *Le traite d'Ibn ʿAbdun in Séville musulmane au début du XIIème siecle*, translated by E. Lévi-Provençal, Paris, 2001, pp. 42–3.
85. According to the great political thinker al-Mawardī (d. 1058) in *Al-Ahkām al-Sultāniyya*, the main reason of being for Islamic government was the institution of the *ḥisba* and the creation of the *muḥtasib*. The government failed if it did not properly enforce this duty. Al-Mawardī, *The ordinances of government*, a translation of *al-Ahkam al-sultaniyya w'al-wilayat al-diniyya* by Wafaa H. Wahba, Reading: Center for Muslim Contribution to Civilization, 1996.
86. Many of Ibn Tūmart's standards were probably picked up in the East, particularly

under the influence of al-Ghazālī's new, standardized system of law. Yet Ibn Tūmart never claimed to follow any particular school. Al-Ghazālī attempted desperately to save the concept of the caliph. Ibn Tūmart, however, did not even recognize the symbolic leader of Islam, the caliph, which the Turks in Baghdad controlled. For Ibn Tūmart, his authority came directly from God and the Prophet, Lévi-Provençal, *Documents inédits,* p. 80.

87. Lévi-Provençal, *Documents inédits,* pp. 100–1. He equates some Berber customs to practices in the pre-islamic period, the *Jāhiliyya.* Ibn Tūmart calls for the tribes to 'Put an end to the wrong path, to all pagan practices: among which are the pleasures of music, the lamentations at funerals.' Lévi-Provençal, *Documents inédits*, p. 14.
88. Lévi-Provençal, *Documents inédits*, p. 93.
89. Ibn Tūmart's attacks on musical celebrations may be explained by their particular importance to local spiritual practices among North African Berbers. This spiritual significance of dance and performance has been convincingly described and argued by Earle H. Waugh, *Memory, music and religion: Morocco's mystical chanters*, Raleigh, NC: SciTech Pub., 2005. For Ibn Tūmart, Musical devotion seems to distract from a focus on the foundations of Islam.
90. Lévi-Provençal, *Documents inédits*, p. 101.
91. The male citizens of Bougie who wore sandals, perfume and flamboyant tunics 'like women' disgusted Ibn Tūmart. On seeing them, he said 'Do not dress yourselves like women, for this is a forbidden act.' Lévi-Provençal, *Documents inédits*, p. 79.
92. In a letter to the Almohads, Ibn Tūmart commands his followers to 'invite those among the tribes who give them [the Almoravids] assistance to repent, to make penance, and return to the Qur'ān and the *sunna*, not to aid those who give God a bodily form'. Lévi-Provençal, *Documents inédits*, p. 3.
93. Al-Marrākushī, *al-Muʿjib*, pp. 179–83. This scene and the different accounts of sources from North Africa and the East are analysed in Wasserstein, 'A Jonah theme', pp. 232–49.
94. Ibn ʿAbī Zarʿ, *Rawḍ al-Qirṭās*, pp. 341–5, emphasized that Ibn Tūmart had no official permission to command right and forbid wrong while on the boat.
95. See Fierro, 'The Ghurabā in al-Andalus', pp. 230–60.
96. He even 'mounted a mule' at his death, Lévi-Provençal, *Documents inédits*, p. 131.
97. Lévi-Provençal, *Documents inédits*, pp. 95–6.
98. This is one of many references to the 'infallible' Ibn Tūmart, Lévi-Provençal, *Documents inédits*, p. 95.
99. Lévi-Provençal, *Documents inédits*, p. 97.
100. See discussions of al-Ghazālī's comparatively extreme views in Cook, *Commanding right*, pp. 427–68. Michael Cook also contends, p. 458, that it is impossible to know if Ibn Tūmart actually met al-Ghazālī.
101. As Cook (*Commanding right*, p. 389) suggests, Ibn Tūmart's moral reforms led to 'state formation'.

102. A *zāwiya* was a prayer hall and place for lodging often dedicated to a particular Muslim leader. These leaders were often, but not always, Sufī sheikhs.
103. Al-Baydhaq may simply be embellishing Ibn Tūmart's role in restoring and founding mosques. A proper archaeological survey of Ibn Tūmart route could clarify the issue.
104. Lévi-Provençal, *Documents inédits*, p. 89. 'The Imām returned to Mallala. When they saw him, the sons of al-Azīz said "Oh *faqīh*, we wish to build you a *zāwiya* for your use if you wish." The mosque was built near the house of ʿAbū Muḥammad who Ibn Tūmart renamed ʿAbd al-Wāḥid or "Servant of the One".' (Ibn Tūmart would often rename his loyal followers.) Students studied religion there and gathered around Ibn Tūmart as they recited the names of God. They thus became a small cadre of Ibn Tūmart's followers. Did Ibn Tūmart really found all the mosques and *zāwiyas* as al-Baydhaq claimed? Without a comprehensive archaeological survey of these obscure communities, it is not possible to say. Some mosques could have been built after the Almohad conquest.
105. Lévi-Provençal, *Documents inédits*, p. 95.
106. Was this extremism? Perhaps, but it may have been just as extreme for these communities to rely on religious jurists who knew little of the original sources of Islam and who relied almost exclusively on secondary legal manuals. This was one explanation for the appeal of Ibn Tūmart's message, despite his angry performances in the markets. 'Extremism' existed in the medieval tradition of *Ghulū*: see Crone, *Medieval Islamic political thought*, p. 80. These extremists used gnostic methods to undermine Islamic orthodoxy completely. Ibn Tūmart wished to refound true Islam under his leadership and guidance in the Berber context. He should not, therefore, be compared with the *Ghuluū*. Some scholars have also suggested a connection between Ibn Tūmart and extreme forms of *Khārijism*. However, these connections are, at best, tenuous. See A. Ben Hamadi, 'Y a-t-il une influence kharigite dans la pensée d'Ibn Tūmart', *Mélanges offerts a Mohamed Talbi*, Tunis: Université de *Tunis*, 1993.
107. Again, the example of the ostrich and the governor, Lévi-Provençal, *Documents inédits*, p. 96.
108. Al-Marrākushī, *al-Muʿjib*, p. 180, 'This was learned from the astrologers of the East.' See Ibn Khaldūn's discussion of sand writing and geomancy in Ibn Khaldūn, *The Muqaddimah*, vol. 3, pp. 156–227.
109. A part of the Zanāta confederation who dominated the region of modern-day Algeria, Tunisia and parts of east Morocco. The Kūmya were near Tāghrā, which, according to al-Bakrī, *Description de l'Afrique septentrionale*, translated by G. de Slane, Paris: G.-P. Maisonneuve et Larose, 1965, p. 80, was the name of a mountain near Nédroma.
110. For a discussion of ʿAbd al-Muʾmin's convenient genealogy, see Maribel Fierro, 'Las genealogías de ʿAbd al-Muʾmin, primer califa Almohade', *Al-Qanṭara*, vol. 24, 2003, pp. 77–107.
111. Lévi-Provençal, *Documents inédits*, p. 86.
112. Lévi-Provençal, *Documents inédits*, p. 88.

113. He also met some fellow travellers from Tīnmallal who spoke Berber while he was in Mallala. See Lévi-Provençal, *Documents inédits*, p. 88.
114. Lévi-Provençal, *Documents inédits*, pp. 107–8. The opening chapter of the Qur'ān says, 'Show us the straight way.' Sūra, I: 6.
115. There will be a methodological discussion of the primary sources for the life of Ibn Tūmart in general and this scene in particular later in the chapter.
116. In addition to al-Baydhaq, in Lévi-Provençal, *Documents inédits*, there is also a rich rendering in the work of the so-called Anonymous Chronicler, *Al-Ḥulal al-Mūshiyyah*, Arab text published after the new manuscripts by I. S. Allouche, Rabat, 1936, pp. 82–4. For this scene, the chronicler quoted an account by Ibn Bajir, which is the source for most quotations used in this scene.
117. Sūra, LXXII: 18.
118. Anonymous Chronicler, *Al-Ḥulal al-Mūshiyyah*, p. 82.
119. Ecclesiastes 10:6.
120. For a full discussion of illumination as it related to Ibn Tūmart's claims to power see Brett, *Ibn Khaldūn and the medieval Maghrib*.
121. Anonymous Chronicler, *Al-Ḥulal al-Mūshiyyah*, p. 83.
122. Anonymous Chronicler, *Al-Ḥulal al-Mūshiyyah*, p. 85. Built in the year AH 520/ AD 1126, 'because of the appearance of the Mahdī'.
123. Al-Marrākushī, *al-Mu'jib*, p. 179.
124. Cook, *Commanding right*, p. 100, discusses the very specific Ḥanbali school attitude towards chess, for example, and how it differs from other schools.
125. See Chapter 3 for more on the Almohad doctrine of the infallible Mahdī.
126. On the domination of the Maliki school and Ibn Tūmart's determination to destroy the influence of jurists and juridicial texts as opposed to the Qur'ān, see Goldziher, 'Introduction' and Chapter 3 in this book on Doctrine. Also Melchert, *The Formation of the Sunni schools*, pp. 156–77 for a discussion of early Maliki law.
127. On the originality of Ibn Tūmart's doctrine, see Goldziher, 'Introduction' and Chapter 3.
128. Al-Baydhaq described how 'Abd al Mu'min, inspired by Ibn Tūmart, purified the mosques of Marrakech after he conquered it in AD 1147, Lévi-Provençal, *Documents inédits*, p. 174.
129. The original historical sources have quite different versions of this historically pivotal meeting between Ibn Tūmart and the amir 'Alī bin Yūsuf, versions that vary according to each chronicler's own immediate political context. The different versions of this meeting in the historical sources and the implications of these differences will be discuseed at the end of this chapter.
130. Lévi-Provençal, *Documents inédits*, p. 111.
131. Ibid.
132 Lévi-Provençal, *Documents inédits*, p. 111. See Lévi-Provençal's note 1 and the quotation of the Qur'ān.
133. Excavations at Āghmāt Ūrīka, which is clearly located on the transition between foothills and the plains, not the mountains, are currently being led by Ronald

Messier of Vanderbilt University. The Almoravids wanted to use Marrakech to dominate the lucrative trans-Saharan trade routes. Al-Idrīsī made several references to these central Atlas trading centres. See Edrisi (al-Idrīsī), *Description de l'Afrique*, Arabic text, edited by Reinhart Dozy and de Goeje, Amsterdam: Oriental Press, 1969.

134. Lévi-Provençal, *Documents inédits*, p. 113.
135. In *Historia política*, p. 56, Huici Miranda outlines Ibn Tūmart's basic arguments against the Almoravid camp. He asked whether or not the sources or ways of theological knowledge were limited, and what were the bases of truth and falsehood. Ibn Tūmart established the authority of *al-uṣūl*, the basic sources, the Qur'ān, the *ḥadīth* and the *sunna*, over the *furū'*, derivations of the law the Almoravids commonly used in an often exclusive manner. *Al-uṣūl* and *al-furū'* are discussed later in Chapter 3.
136. Lévi-Provençal, *Documents inédits*, p. 113.
137. Lévi-Provençal, *Documents inédits*, p. 116.
138. This was a major thesis of Miranda's *Historia política*.
139. Lévi-Provençal, *Documents inédits*, p. 116.
140. Lévi-Provençal, *Documents inédits*, p. 117.
141. Lings, *Muḥammad*, pp. 50–1.
142. Sūra, XXVI: 214.
143. Berque, *Structures sociales*, pp. 369–84, describes the '*doit communal*'.
144. Lévi-Provençal, *Documents inédits*, pp. 59–62.
145. Lévi-Provençal, *Documents inédits*, pp. 60–1.
146. Ibn Tūmart went beyond the traditional role of Berber saint, a role that Gellner described in *Saints of the Atlas*.
147. Paul Dresch, *Tribes, government and history in Yemen*, Oxford: Oxford University Press, 1989, p. 329.
148. The broader implications of this manipulation of tribal identities will be explained in the second chapter.
149. See Chapter 2 for a more detailed discussion of segmentary relationships. Also, E. E. Evans-Pritchard, *Kinship and marriage among the Nuer*, Oxford: Clarendon Press, 1951.
150. Most sources, with the exception of al-Baydhaq, claim that Ibn Tūmart spoke in Tīnmallal and place the location of his sermon on the *ribāṭ* near Igīlīz. See Miranda, *Historia política*, p. 63. It is, of course, quite possible that Ibn Tūmart spoke both in Tīnmallal and Igīlīz.
151. This speech was recorded in several sources in different forms. I use Allouche's Arabic manuscript edition of the *Ḥulal al-Mūshiyyah*, which seems to include elements of all other sources. See al-Baydhaq's description of his speaking 'according to rank' in Lévi-Provençal, *Documents inédits*, pp. 117–18. Also, see Chapter 3 for futher discussion of the Mahdī declaration.
152. For a detailed discussion of the Almohad hierarchy and the issues of tribalism and the rise of the Almohads, see Chapter 2.

153. For a discussion of Almoravid taxation, see J. F. D. Hopkins, *Medieval Muslim government in Barbary until the sixth century of the hijra*, London: Luzac, 1958.
154. Detailed accounts of the battles exist in al-Baydhaq, the Anonymous Chronicler, *Al-Ḥulal al-Mūshiyyah*, and in Ibn ʿAbī Zarʿ. Al-Baydhaq will be used for most references as he was a contemporary participating in the campaigns. See Ibn ʿAbī Zarʿ, *Rawḍ al-Qirṭās*, pp. 353–4.
155. I discuss Ibn Tūmart's doctrine of *jihād* in Chapter 3.
156. Sūra, XXII: 39–40.
157. Lévi-Provençal, *Documents inédits*, p. 119.
158. Lévi-Provençal, *Documents inédits*, p. 120.
159. For the different commanders of the Almohad army and their colours, see Lévi-Provençal, *Documents inédits*, p. 121.
160. Lévi-Provençal, *Documents inédits*, p. 122.
161. Al-Baydhaq seems to avoid mentioning that it was a complete defeat. He does mention, however, that the army was weighed down by hundreds of elderly women. Lévi-Provençal, *Documents inédits*, p. 127.
162. Lévi-Provençal, *Documents inédits*, p. 120.
163. The *tamyīz* is also discussed in Chapter 3.
164. Lévi-Provençal, *Documents inédits*, p. 130.
165. For a study of this fortress and its strategic importance, see Henri Basset and Henri Terrasse, 'Sanctuaires et forteresses almohades', *Hespéris*, vol. 7, 1927, pp. 157–71.
166. All of which were futile without the support of the mountain tribes. Al-Baydhaq named and located the 20 fortresses. Lévi-Provençal, *Documents inédits*, pp. 220–3.
167. Lévi-Provençal, *Documents inédits*, p. 131.
168. Al-Marrākushī, *Muʿjib*, p. 148, in H. Miranda's translation. See also Ibn ʿAbī Zarʿ, *Rawḍ al-Qirṭās*, pp. 116–17. Lévi-Provençal thinks it is possibly an apocryphal addition: see note 131 in his al-Baydhaq translation Lévi-Provençal, *Documents inédits*. However, one should remember, it certainly would have been Ibn Tūmart's intention to go as far as Persia with his new vision of Islam.
169. See Le Tourneau, *The Almohad movement*, p. 41 and Miranda, *Historia política*, p. 84.
170. Lévi-Provençal, *Documents inédits*, p. 130.
171. Lévi-Provençal, *Documents inédits*, p. 132.
172. See the Escorial manuscript number 1919.
173. Ibn ʿAbī Zarʿ, *Rawḍ al-Qirṭās*, p. 358. Lévi-Provençal, *Documents inédits*, p. 132.
174. Lévi-Provençal, *Documents inédits*, p. 130.
175. Ibid.
176. Probably because of some confusion over the extent of his sickness, and his being hidden away in his house for up to three years, there are several different dates for his death. Ibn Khaldūn, perhaps calculating the time the Mahdī may have been left in the house, claimed the Mahdī died in AH 522, an early date for his death. Al-Marrākushī, *al-Muʿjib*, claimed that he died in AH 524; Ibn Zarʿ in *Rawḍ al-Qirṭās* said it was the 25 Ramadan AH 524. All the other significant sources and historians,

including Ibn Khallikān, give some day in AH 524, usually Ramadan, as the date. See note 1 on p. 134 in Lévi-Provençal, *Documents inédits*.

177. ʿAbd al-Muʾmin built this mosque which still survives today. See the cover page of this work.

178. See ʿAlī Merad, ʿAbd al-Muʾmin à la conquête de l'Afrique du Nord', *Annales de l'Institut d'Etudes Orientales de la Faculté des Lettres d'Alger*, vol. 15, 1957, pp. 122–31.

179. Abū al-Ḥusayn Muḥammad bin Ahmad Ibn Jubayr, *The travels of Ibn Jubayr*, translated by R. J. C. Broadhurst, London: Jonathan Cape, 1952, p. 45.

180. The chronicler al-Maqqari recorded this story. Goldziher, 'Introduction', p. 2 also refers to it.

181. The Almohad Empire at its height spread to the present border between Tunisia and Libya and encompassed all of Muslim Andalusia. A primary purpose of this book has been to focus on the rise of the Almohads from the birth of Ibn Tūmart to his death and to provide a critique of the available primary sources. A full narrative history of the Almohads after Ibn Tūmart and ʿAbd al Muʾmin can be found in Miranda, *Historia política* and Le Tourneau, *The Almohad movement*. Hugh Kennedy, *Muslim Spain and Portugal: a political history of al-Andalus*, London: Longman, 1996, also provides useful accounts of the early Almohad caliphs. Also, for the successors of ʿAbd al-Muʾmin, see my articles 'Abū Yaʿqūb Yūsuf b. ʿAbd al-Muʾmin' and 'Abū Yūsuf Yaʿqūb b. Yūsuf b. ʿAbd al-Muʾmin al-Manṣūr' in the *Encyclopaedia of Islam*, 3rd edn, n.d.

182. Anonymous Chronicler, *Al-Ḥulal al-Mūshiyyah*, 1951. See also *Al-Ḥulal al-Mūshiyya*, Cronique anonyme des dynasties Almoravide et Almohade, texte Arabe, edited by I. S. Allouche. Even as it claims to quote from earlier accounts, the text was completed in AH 783 or AD 1381, long after the encounter. Allouche describes the lack of information about the name of the author in his introduction.

183. Ibn Baṭṭūṭa, who was born among the Merinids, for example 'witnessed the tyranny of the agents and governors of the Almohad [Ḥafṣid]', successors of the Almohads in the area around Tunisia in AH 725/AD 1304. Ibn Baṭṭūṭa, *The travels of Ibn Baṭṭūṭa*, translated by H. A. R. Gibb, London: Routledge, 1929, p. 11.

184. An even less favourable view of Ibn Tūmart comes from ʿAlī ibn al-Athīr (d. 1233) from the East who probably would not have had as much direct information about the Almohads. An extract of Ibn Athīr's account of Ibn Tūmart is found in Ibn Tūmart, *Le Livre de Ibn Toumert*.

185. Al-Baydhaq, *Tārīkh al-Mūahidīn* in Lévi-Provençal, *Documents inédits*, pp. 75–224 in French, pp. 50–133 in Arabic text. It is interesting to note that al-Baydhaq was from the Ṣanhāja tribe, a rival to the Maṣmūda who later rallied around Ibn Tūmart in the Atlas. He may have been one of several branches of the Ṣanhāja much closer to the Maṣmūda and later allied with Ibn Tūmart.

186. Lévi-Provençal, *Documents inédits*, pp. 108–9. The veil is almost certainly the *lithām* of the Almoravids: a veil worn by the ruling Lamtūna tribe in the desert to keep sand out of the face.

187. Ibn Tūmart is probably referring here to the use of unclean manure and refuse in

the making and dying of fabrics. Apparently, these would have defiled the mosque of God.

188. Despite various fires and damage to its collection thoughout history, the Escorial library is a particularly rich repository of Almohad era manuscripts and books. Manuscript number 1919 is an unbound book containing the collection of letters, genealogical descriptions and the biography of Al-Baydhaq discovered by Lévi Provençal. There is a wide discrepancy in the type of paper and the quality of the writing leading me to believe that they were not originally a part of the same collection. Certain sentences are highlighted in red ink for emphasis including a command about the 'infidel Anthropomorphists'. For a good, but unfortunately incomplete (nothing past number 1800 manuscripts) catalogue of the Escorial Arabic collection see Hartwig Derenbourg, *Les manuscrits arabes de l'Escorial*, Paris, 1884.
189. Lévi-Provençal, *Documents inédits*, p. ix.
190. Le Tourneau, *The Almohad movement*, p. 10.
191. Commenting on the unique features of the manucript Lévi-Provençal stated, 'One need not have much exposure to the works of Maghribi historians to perceive at first glance that the work of al-Baydhaq is something completely different. It is not a chronicle in the ordinary sense, a relation of events following the classic Arab, historical model, but a veritable "mémoire": the account of a man who played an active role in the events which he described, and who appeared in every sense to be one of the Almohads "of the first hour" who passed their lives under the reign of the Mahdī and 'Abd al-Mu'min.' Lévi-Provençal, *Documents inédits*, p. ix.
192. Miranda, 'La leyenda y la historia', p. 339.
193. Miranda, *Historia política*, p. 11, thus, uses him least among the sources. He considers, with good reason, the *Rawḍ al Qirṭās* to be the least reliable source because of its apparent errors and its distance from the events described.
194. Ibn 'Abī Zar', *Rawḍ al-Qirṭās*, vol. 2.
195. Ibid., p. 346.
196. Miranda, *Historia política*, p. 11.
197. Al-Marrākushī, *Al-Mu'jib*, Arabic version ed. Reinhart Dozy, Amsterdam: Oriental Press, 1968, pp. 128–30.
198. Ibn Khaldūn's own autobiography explains the reasons behind his thinking better than any seminar or colloquium on Ibn Khaldūn. Ibn Khaldūn, *Ta'rīf bi Ibn Khaldūn*. Ibn Khaldūn mentioned here his use of the Tunis library to write the *Kitāb al-'Ibār*.
199. Ibn Khaldūn frequently used astrology in his autobiography, saying that astrologers had predicted the coming of Tamerlane. He also wrote an extensive exposition of the science of astrology in Ibn Khaldūn, *The Muqaddimah*, vol. 3 of the unabridged version translated by F. Rosenthal, Princeton: Bollingen Series, 1969.
200. Lévi-Provençal, *Documents inédits*, p. 110.
201. 'Alī bin al Ḥusayn al-Mas'ūdī (d. 345/956) (ed.) *Murūj al-Dhahab* (Meadows of Gold), translated into French by C. Barbier de Meynard and A. Pavet de Courteille, 9 vols,

Paris 1861–77, did provide some elements of interpretation but it achieved nothing close to the scale, depth and systematic reasoning of Ibn Khaldūn.

202. The issues of sources, meaning and truth in history have sparked significant debate throughout the previous century. Ibn Khaldūn asked, what can we know from the past? How do we judge the truthfulness of sources? Some of the most famous modern historians dealing with many of the same questions as Ibn Khaldūn include Marc Bloch, *The historian's craft*, translated by Peter Putnam, Manchester: Manchester University Press, 1976; Michel Foucault, *The archaeology of knowledge*, New York: Pantheon, 1982.

203. *Wa fī bāṭnhi naẓr* (This phrase could be translated as the 'hidden' meaning of history), see Arabic edition, *Muqaddimaht Ibn Khaldūn*, Tunis, 1991, p. 4.

204. In original, *lithalik 'aṣīl fī al-ḥikma*, p. 4.

205. Ibn Khaldūn, *The Muqaddimah*, vol. 1, p. 15.

206. 'Little effort is being made to get at the truth. The critical eye, as a rule, is not sharp. Errors and unfounded assumptions are closely allied and familiar elements in historical information. Blind trust in tradition is an inherited trait in human beings.' Ibid., p. 7.

207. Michael Brett, *The rise of the Fatimids*, Leiden, 2001.

208. That is not to say that one might not still be found.

209. For a contemporary critique of Ibn Khaldūn's methodology from a Morocccan perspective see 'Alī Oumlil, *L'histoire et son discours: essai sur la methodologie d'Ibn Khaldoun*, Rabat, 1982.

210. It should be said here that it is not my aim in this book to note and analyse every minute contradiction in the Almohad historical narratives. Huici Miranda and Lévi-Provençal have, by and large, done such work already. Rather than writing a detailed political history, which Huici Miranda has already accomplished, my aim is to answer the question surrounding the rise of the Almohad Empire. I examine the broader social context, the role of the tribes, and the role of Ibn Tūmart's largely untranslated ideology in the initial birth of the Almohad state: Huici Miranda, Le Tourneau and others did not provide convincing answers to these questions. Some work has been done to compare the contradictions between historical narratives over questions like the date of Ibn Tūmart's birth, or the names of his closest followers, but only as footnotes.

211. Cook, *Commanding right*, provides several examples of those who inappropriately associated with women (see especially pp. 10 and 68), as well as injunctions against inappropriate clothing worn by men and boys (pp. 63, 240). As mentioned previously, Ibn Tūmart denounced the men of Bougie for being 'like women', Lévi-Provençal, *Documents inédits*, p. 79.

212. See especially the reference to the veils of the Lamtūna men and the amir, Lévi-Provençal, *Documents inédits*, pp. 108–9. The veil is almost certainly the *lithām* of the Almoravids – a veil the ruling Lamtūna tribe wore in the desert to keep sand out of the face. Also, refer again to Ibn Tūmart's admonishment of the men of Bougie for wearing clothes like women, Lévi-Provençal, *Documents inédits*, p. 79.

213. Norris, *The Berbers in Arabic literature*, provides several sources on the power of Almoravid women. He describes an Almoravid princess who led the last battle against the Almohads at the gates of Marrakech. The Tuareg [probable descendants of the Almoravids] matriarch 'names' children during a secret naming ceremony two weeks before birth. Ethnographical descriptions of the matriarchal nature of the Tuareg descendants of the Lamtūna Almoravids can be found in Susan Rasmussen, 'Within the tent and at the crossroads: travel and gender identity among the Tuareg of Niger', *Ethos*, vol. 26, no. 2, 1998, pp. 153–82; also Susan Rasmussen and J. H. Keenan, 'Lack of prayer: ritual restrictions, social experience and the anthropology of migration among the Tuareg', *American Ethnologist*, vol. 18, no. 4, November 1991, pp. 751–69.

214. This was, of course, the Almohad perspective. Norris, *The Berbers in Arabic literature*. See his chapter on the Almoravids.

215. On twentieth-century Tuareg traditions, see Johannes Nicolaisen, *Ecology and culture of the pastoral Tuareg*, Copenhagen: National Museum of Copenhagen, 1963. On Tuareg literature and poetry, see Casajus, Dominique, *Gens de parole: langage, poesie et politique en pays Touareg*, Paris: La Découverte, 2000. A Tuareg story of nomadism is translated from the original *tamajaght* language in Hélène Claudot-Hawad (editor and translator) *Notre horizon de gamelles pour une gamelle d'horizons*, Paris, 2001. The current dispute between the polisario of the Western Sahara and Morocco is partially driven by different conceptions of gender that can be traced back to the advent of Islam in Africa and the invasion of Arab tribes. The women of the Western Sahara enjoyed more traditional rights to divorce than Moroccan women who were confined by the old Mudawana, a family code based on Islamic law. This code has recently been reformed. See Boubou Hama, *Recherches sur l'histoire des Touareg sahariens et soudanais*, Paris: Présence Africaine, 1967. For a recent study on Atlas Berber women see Margaret Courtney-Clarke, *Imazighen: the vanishing traditions of Berber Women*, New York: C. Potter, 1996.

216. Norris, *The Berbers in Arabic literature*, London, 1982, p. 173.

217. For a summary of Almoravid doctrine and claims, especially by the founder Yasīn, who, like Ibn Tūmart, commanded right and forbade wrong and assembled a group of Berber tribes see Chapter 3 in this book and Lagardère, *Les Almoravides*. Also, see Farias Moraes, 'The Almoravids: some questions concerning the character of the movement during the period of closest contact with the Western Sudan', *Bulletin de l'Institut Fondamental d'Afrique*, vol. 29, 1967, pp. 794–898.

218. For the meaning of these differences see Michael Brett and Elizabeth Fentress, *The Berbers*, and their discussion of the 'Ṣanhāja' of the desert, p. 102. Al-Bakrī, writing in 1068, immediately before the conquest of the Almoravids, describes their desert origins. See Al-Bakrī, *Description de l'Afrique septentrionale*. See also the contrasting descriptions of desert and mountain tribes in Edrisi, *Description de l'Afrique*. Although David Hart makes a strong argument against dividing the Berbers into broad ethnic categories, he does not consider the fact that Ibn Tūmart and the Almoravids, in certain circumstances, would have created their

own generalized categories. David M. Hart, 'Maṣmūda, Sanḥāja, Zanāta: a three ring circus', *Revue d'Histoire Maghribine*, vol. 9, nos 27–8, 1982, pp. 361–5.

219. Transhumant tribes are those that migrate between mountain pastures for grazing in the summer and low, valley pastures during the winter.

220. See Michael Brett and Elizabeth Fentress. *The Berbers*, Chapters 1–4. The Barghwata and the Hā Mīm were both powerful Berber heresies not long before the birth of Ibn Tūmart, see the first chapters of Norris, *The Berbers in Arabic literature*. For an account of the original conquest see, Al-Nuwaīri, 'Conquête de l'Afrique septentrionale', in Ibn Khaldūn, *Histoire des Berbères*, translated by De Slane, Algiers, vol. 4, 2001, p. 347. For a rather uncritical study of the early conquest, see A. D. Taha, *The Muslim conquest and settlement of North Africa and Spain*, London: Routledge, 1989.

221. It could be argued that this rivalry between Saharan customs and those of the Berber-Arabs of the mountain and coastal plains continues today over the question of western Saharan sovereignty. Norris, *The Arab conquest of the western Sahara*.

222. Lévi-Provençal, *Documents inédits*, p. 15. The issue of the embodied nature of God or *tajsim* will be discussed in Chapter 3. Even as Ibn Tūmart condemned the Almoravids as more worthy of *jihād* than the Christians, he also promised mercy to those who repented and joined the Almohads.

223. Cook, *Commanding right*, describes this personal duty in his introduction.

224. Ibn Tūmart's doctrine proclaimed that definition of piety as a return to the original sources of Islam, as opposed to the legalistic texts of Almoravids. Ibn Tūmart wrote a book laying out the details of his revolutionary vision. The untranslated Arabic text from a surviving Paris Library manuscript can be found in I. Goldziher (ed.) *Le livre de Mohammad Ibn Toumert*, Algiers: P. Fontana, 1903.

Chapter 2: The Rise of the Almohads: The Tribal Roots of Monotheism

1. For more on the Kitāb al-Ansāb as a primary source see Lévi-Provençal's introduction to his *Documents inédits*. It seems that the *Kitāb al-Ansāb* was written under the successors of the Mahdī. This seems to have influenced some of the names listed in the hierarchy although it is doubtful that the entire system was simply reconstructed. For a study of medieval tribal structure in the Maghrib see Laroussi Amri, *La tribu au Maghrib medieval: pour une sociologie des ruptures*, Tunis: Publications de l'Université de Tunis, 1997.
2. The *Kitāb al-Ansāb* stated categorically that genealogy did not determine who entered paradise or hell. The only factors were 'piety, good works, and the grace of God the Highest.' The book derides the pretences of the Quraysh, the Meccan tribe related to Muḥammad, who said, 'We will enter paradise solely because of our ancestors.' It mentioned Cain (Qābil) and Abel (Hābil). Although both the original 'kin' of humankind, one was sent to hell and the other was saved. There were also the disobedient sons of the patriarchs, the son of Noah who did not help build the Ark. None of these entered paradise. Their blood or genealogy guaran-

teed nothing when their actions went astray from the truth and word of God. This sentiment echoed Muḥammad the Prophet's famous last sermon, delivered on the Ninth Day of the month Dhul-Hijjah AH 10 in the 'Uranah valley of Mount Arafat' in Mecca. Muḥammad explicitly forbade any ethnic preference in matters of religion. 'All mankind is from Adam and Eve, an Arab has no superiority over a non-Arab nor a non-Arab has any superiority over an Arab; also a white has no superiority over a black nor a black has any superiority over a white – except by piety and good action.' Lévi-Provençal, *Documents inédits*, p. 25. If Lévi-Provençal was correct about this section of the *Kitāb al-Ansāb*, these may be the words of Ibn Tūmart. It was supposedly written in response to those who claimed that Ibn Tūmart did not descend from the Prophet Muḥammad.

3. To drive his point home, Ibn Tūmart used the example of the paternal uncle of the Prophet, Abū Ṭālib, who, though a great supporter of the Prophet Muḥammad, did not convert to Islam. In Ibn Tūmart's reading of the *ḥadīth*, the Prophet begged his uncle to pronounce his faith in Allah and the Prophet. Yet his relatives, most notoriously Abī Umaiya, asked him, 'Oh Abū Ṭālib, will you abandon the [ancestral] faith of ʿAbd al-Muṭṭalib?' Abū Ṭālib did not give up his ancestral religion. Although the surrogate father of Muḥammad, he was condemned to the fires of hell for not accepting the true religion. According to an al-Bukhārī *ḥadīth* cited by Ibn Tūmart Al-ʿAbbās ʿAbd al-Muṭṭalib said to the Prophet, 'For what have you done with your Uncle Abū Ṭālib? For he had protected you and defended you and done so much for you!' The Prophet reportedly said in reply, 'He is in the fire of hell. ... Without my intervention he would be at the very bottom of hell!' *Kitāb al-Ansāb* in Lévi-Provençal, *Documents inédits*, p. 29, al-Bukhārī, *Ṣaḥiḥ*, 81, chapter 51, p. 13.
4. The *Kitāb al-Ansāb* quotes the Qur'ān saying, 'Oh Mankind! We created you from a single pair of a male and a female, and made you into nations and tribes, that you may know each other. Truly, the most honoured of you in the sight of God is the most righteous of you' (Sūra, XLIX: 13). This quote was from one of the 'Medina' sūras: those sūras revealed to Muḥammad as he attempted to consolidate the Muslim community at Medina just as Ibn Tūmart was consolidating the Almohad community in Tīnmallal and Igīlīz. Later in the sūra, there is an explicit statement against the faith of the tribal, desert Arabs. 'The desert Arabs say, 'We believe'. Say, 'You have no faith; but you only say "We have submitted our wills to God." For not yet has faith entered your hearts' (Sūra, XLIX: 14).
5. Instinct manipulates identity in R. Byrne and A. Whiten, *Machiavellian intelligence: social expertise and the evolution of intellect in monkeys, apes and humans*, Oxford: Oxford University Press, 1988. The media shapes identity in Benedict Anderson, *Imagined Communities*, London: Verso, 2000.
6. D. Z. H. Baneth, 'What did Muḥammad mean when he called his religion 'Islam?', *Israel Oriental Studies*, vol. 1, 1971, pp. 183–90, interpreted the meaning of the term Islam at the time of Muḥammad as 'belonging to one only' or 'being the exclusive property of one [Allah]' Also, see Wheatley's attempt at a definition in Paul

Wheatley, *The places where men pray together*, Chicago: University of Chicago Press, 2000, p. 19.

7. On the reinvention and refashioning of lineage among the Bedu, see William Lancaster, *The Rwala Bedouin today*, Cambridge: Cambridge University Press, 1981, pp. 152–4. Lancaster was one of the few anthropologists actually to live the harsh life of the Bedu; he wrote that, 'despite the fact that inter-group relationships are conceived in genealogical terms, the genealogy is so fluid as to be relatively unimportant.'
8. As outlined by the *Kitāb al-Ansāb*. For a visual representation of the transformation from the tribal segmentary system to the Almohad hierarchy see Tables 1–4.
9. The first example of the use of genealogy to establish authority was Ibn Tūmart's own illustrious, but probably largely invented ancestry, cited to confirm the legitimacy of his leadership. One version of his genealogy put Ibn Tūmart in the line of the first sharifian rulers of the Maghrib, the Idrīssids. Other, Berber genealogies appealed to different loyalties. Muḥammad, son of ʿAbd Allah, son of Ūgallīd, son of Yāmṣal, son of Ḥamza, son of ʿIsā, son of ʿUbaid Allah, son of Idrīs, son of ʿAbd Allah, son of al-Ḥasan, son of Fātima, daughter of the Prophet Muḥammad: this was one version of Muḥammad Ibn Tūmart's name and genealogy. Another, longer, more Arab version of his name also traces his lineage to al-Ḥasan and the daughter of the Prophet. It was unlikely that this was Ibn Tūmart's original name, the name at his birth, but rather a name he acquired from his later fame. Although he was born into a respected Berber family, it seemed doubtful that Ibn Tūmart actually had both distinguished ancestries. The writer, or writers, of the *Kitāb al-Ansāb* did not seem to pick up on this irony. Lévi-Provençal believes that the first section of the *Kitāb al-Ansāb* was in fact a letter written by Ibn Tūmart and ʿAbd al Muʾmin in response to those who denied their sharifian origins, Lévi-Provençal, *Documents inédits*, p. 30. Different genealogies, both Berber and Arab, might seem to have harmed Ibn Tūmart's reputation to outsiders. Yet they would have also allowed for a convenient situation where Ibn Tūmart seemed to have possible connections to every significant group in the region. In this sense, Ibn Tūmart's genealogy was that of the universal tribe, both Berber and Arab, the Amghar and the Sharif. Despite his preaching against lineage, he did not abandon it as a tool for solidifying the support of the North African tribes. His successor, ʿAbd al Muʾmin would do the same. Indeed, one of Ibn Tūmart's first questions to ʿAbd al-Muʾmin was about his genealogy, whether or not his genealogy was suitable for a successor to the Mahdī. See Fierro, 'Las genealogías de ʿAbd al-Muʾmin, pp. 77–107; and al-Baydhaq in Lévi-Provençal, *Documents inédits*, p. 85.
10. For example, the *tamyīz* or 'ordering' of the tribes.
11. While Ibn Tūmart and his followers appealed to the popular and disenfranchised, they also manipulated the pre-existing tribal elite with another overarching hierarchy. Miranda, *Historia política*, p. 79.

12. See the section on the Almohad hierarchy later in this chapter. After the death of Ibn Tūmart even the caliph himself followed communal regulations, Berber tribal traditions, for the distribution of booty. Montagne, *Berbères et le Makhzen*, p. 65. See also Lévi-Provençal, *Documents inédits*, p. 171 where ʿAbd al Muʾmin is forced to kill the young Almoravid prince.
13. As will be discussed, this transformation was also the result of particular social and economic conditions, namely the growing domination and urbanization of the Almoravids that favoured the development of a more efficient and disciplined pyramid structure.
14. Evans-Pritchard, *Kinship and marriage among the Nuer.*
15. 'Each section of a tribe, from the smallest to the largest, has its sheikh or sheikhs. The tribal system, typical of segmentary structures everywhere, is a system of balanced opposition between tribes and tribal sections from the largest to the smallest divisions, and there cannot therefore be any single authority in a tribe. Authority is distributed at every point of the tribal structure and political leadership is limited to situations in which a tribe or a segment of it acts corporately. ... There cannot, obviously, be any absolute authority vested in a single sheikh of a tribe when the fundamental principle of tribal structures is opposition between its segments, and in such segmentary systems there is no state and no government as we understand these institutions' (E. E. Evans-Pritchard, *The Sanusi of Cyrenaica*, Oxford: Clarendon Press, 1949). The segmentary model has been the subject of a debate among anthropologists. Several, including Henry Munson Jr, have rejected the value of the model. Others, including the expert on Moroccan tribes, D. M. Hart, have defended the validity of segmentary systems in real, observed, circumstances. See D. M. Hart, 'Rejoiner to Henry Munson Jr, "On the irrelevance of the segmentary lineage model in the Moroccan Rif"', *American Anthropologist*, vol. 91, no. 3, 1989, pp. 765–9.
16. E. A. Gellner, *Muslim society*, Cambridge: Cambridge University Press, 1981, p. 37.
17. Abun-Nasr, *History of the Maghrib*, p. 11, illustrated a lasting contradiction at the heart of Maghribi society: the pull between both 'centrifugal and centripetal' forces in Maghribi history. Through a very rapid process of transformation, Ibn Tūmart, the Maṣmūda tribes and the Almohads as a body, managed to take a hold of the centripetal forces of expansion and abandon the forces of fragmentation. From isolated mountain hamlets and tribes they spun out an ever-expanding circle of discipline, alliance, and power.
18. Lévi-Provençal, *Documents inédits*, p. 3.
19. See my description of the Saksāwa later in the chapter.
20. His education in the East exposed him to revivalist ideas, especially those of al-Ghazālī, but even al-Ghazālī would have disapproved of Ibn Tūmart, both his method and his message. See Goldziher, 'Introduction'.
21. Edrisi, *Description de l'Afrique*, p. 74, observed that the mountaintop fortifications of the Maṣmūda were practically impregnable. It would take 'only four men' inside a fort on a strategic pass to control and defend an entire valley.

22. Indeed, it was the rigid, disciplined alliances of tribes like the Saksāwa that would form the backbone of the Almohad hierarchy.
23. The great Umayyad general who conquered North Africa. He died in AD 683.
24. Ibn Khaldūn, *Histoire des Berbères*, vol. 1, p. 321.
25. Lévi-Provençal, *Documents inédits*, pp. 26–31.
26. As discussed above, the most immediate example of this transformation of Berber society was his own tribe, the Hargha: he opened up membership of his tribe to those who were sufficiently loyal or important.
27. The rise of the Maṣmūda could not be explained simply by improved economic or environmental factors. The Maṣmūda tribes were not necessarily at an economically strong point in their history and simply needed a leader to bring them forward. Ibn Tūmart came to power just as the Maṣmūda were in disarray, isolated in their valleys, and burdened by taxes and the overriding power of the Almoravid state that had built its capital in nearby Marrakech only decades before. As will be discussed later, the economic situation did not seem to favour the Maṣmūda. It may have been precisely these unusually poor economic conditions that made the Atlas Berbers that much more willing to join Ibn Tūmart.
28. Other tribal contributions to the development of the Almohad state will be discussed in my description of each major tribal group.
29. Montagne, *Berbères et le Makhzen*, p. 221. This book discusses the *agrao* later when describing the Almohad council of fifty. The *agrao* will be discussed in more detail when the structure of the Almohad hierarchy is described. For now I will describe the *tamyīz*, or delineation; the formal means by which the tribes identified themselves and organized into confederations.
30. Dresch, *Tribes, government and history in Yemen*, pp. 97–106, described a similar 'gathering' of tribes in Yemen. These gatherings were used to resolve disputes. They often revolved around a ceremonial meal or sacrifice, rather like the Berber *āsmās*. He also described the role of the *muqawwil*, an arbitrator who was similar to the Berber *mizwār*.
31. Montagne, *Berbères et le Makhzen*, p. 63, called the *tamyīz* something like 'un ordre de bataille'.
32. Montagne, *Berbères et le Makhzen*, p. 63.
33. Lévi-Provençal, *Documents inédits*, p. 117. See my description of the *āsmās* of Ibn Tūmart in Fromherz, 'The Almohad Mecca'.
34. Similar ceremonies exist in the Arab tribal context of Yemen. Paul Dresch, *Tribes, government and history in Yemen*, p. 330, described how the al-Dawā'ir faction of the Banū ʿAlī near the border with South Yemen broke away from the Banū ʿAlī and joined the solidly pro-North Khārif in order to cement closer ties with the North Yemen government. 'Political influence, then, at a number of levels, made membership of Khārif desireable in the circumstances. The result was redefinition. The villages slaughtered bulls at Khārif's weekly market, and with the spilling of blood became part of the tribe.'

35. See Allen Fromherz, 'The Almohad Mecca' for a description of Ibn Tūmart's communal meal. Also, Lévi-Provençal, *Documents inédits*, p. 117.
36. Dale Eickelman, *The Middle East and Central Asia: an anthropological approach*, New Jersey: Prentice Hall, 2001, p. 130. Eickelman saw the prevalence of the communal meal as evidence that *qarāba*, 'closeness', was more important than blood ties.
37. See the scene of the ritual meal described in al-Baydhaq, Lévi-Provençal, *Documents inédits*, pp. 116–17.
38. Lévi-Provençal, *Documents inédits*, p. 137.
39. Montagne, *Berbères et le Makhzen*, p. 64.
40. Lévi-Provençal, *Documents inédits*, p. 126.
41. The Almohad general who was martyred when he led the Almohads in battle against Marrakech at al-Buḥayra.
42. This would be the blundered battle of Buḥayra in which the Almohad cause was almost lost because of a rash and unprepared attack on Marrakech.
43. Lévi-Provençal, *Documents inédits*, p. 54.
44. See Marcy, 'Les phrases berbères', pp. 61–78. A translation of the Berber phrases used in this dream is provided. Lévi-Provençal was unable to translate the Berber in his text so this article is a valuable resource for the many interesting Berber phrases transliterated into Arabic in Almohad texts. Berber seemed to be used in the text when it held a certain special meaning: Berber is used at the defining moments in the life of the Mahdī. The devil said to the Sheikh in Berber, '*ma-tētfārēt kikēs?*' Meaning 'Will you follow him?' He replies, '*i-yekka kkegh-t*', meaning 'I go where my brother goes.'
45. Miranda, *Historia política*, p. 79.
46. The anthropologist Robert Montagne, *Berbères et le Mahkzen*, did, however, provide a historical sketch of Almohad tribes. Also, see Robert Montagne, *The Berbers: their social and political organisation*, translated by David Seddon, London: Frank Cass, 1973 for a discussion of Berber tribal organization under the French protectorate. For an uncritical and basic description of the Berbers' particular institutions, see the work of another French colonial author, Georges Henri Bousquet, *Les Berbères: histoire et institutions*, Paris: Presses Universitaires de France, 1957.
47. The Hargha, Tīnmallal, Gadmīwa, Ganfīsa, Ūrīka, Hintāta and Hazargha were all relatively native to their respective regions, inhabiting separate valleys and mountains of the Atlas, all protected by a *qaṣr*, fortified village, and ruled by independent chieftains. After the Almohad revolution, however, other, outside tribes were moved into the army, for military purposes or perhaps to further consolidate the powers of the amir who could use the loyalty of newcomers against any hesitation by the native elite. These were Turkish Ghuzz, Muslim and even Christian Spaniard mercenaries. Rather like the social conflict between Arabs and their non-Arab clients after the birth of Islam, the struggle for power between the original Maṣmūda, who felt they were entitled to power, and outside newcomers would later result in a dangerous rift that threatened the future of the Almohads.

48. For his fascinating discussion of the mythical origins of the Berbers, see Ibn Khaldūn, *Histoire des Berbères*, vol. 1, pp. 116–55.
49. Marcy, 'Les phrases berbères'.
50. To see how different tribes were ranked and integrated into the Almohad hierarchy, see Tables 2.3–2.4.
51. Fromherz, 'The Almohad Mecca'.
52. Ibn al-Qaṭṭān, *Naẓm al-Jumān*, p. 37, claimed that the specific location of Ibn Tūmart's birth was called Nūmkarān, a place 'without water where the people drink water from wells.' Possibly this was an even smaller village on the mountainside near Igīlīz.
53. The main products of the Hargha were olive oil, Argan tree oil from the hillsides, dates, and oranges from the Sūs plain. For a description of Berber architecture and economy in the then remote Anti-Atlas, see André Adam, *La maison et le village dans quelques tribus d'Anti-Atlas*, Paris: Imprimerie Nationale, 1951.
54. Lévi-Provençal, *Documents inédits*, p. 55. This review according to well organized clans and subclans was also done to other tribes, but the Hargha seem to have been first in line.
55. Ibn Khaldūn, *The Muqaddimah*, pp. 100–1.
56. Miranda, *Historia política*, p. 69.
57. For a discussion of how ʿAbd al-Muʾmin may have allowed the manipulation of the *Kitāb al-Ansāb* to display his proper Berber and Arab credentials, see Fierro, 'Las genealogías', pp. 77–107.
58. ʿ*Akhā baynahu wa baynahum*ʾ, Lévi-Provençal, *Documents inédits*, p. 57.
59. Lévi-Provençal, *Documents inédits*, p. 58.
60. Ibid. The text says he remained imām throughout the reign of ʿAbd al-Muʾmin and into the reign of Abū Yaʾqūb.
61. This secret knowledge and magic would have been consistent with the Atlas tribal culture of the twelfth-century and today. Lévi-Provençal, *Documents inédits*, p. 59 footnote 4, provided an interesting note here about the Syriac. This was not the language known to linguists but 'a magic language – employed, *sans doute*, for political purposes – and used to allow the *rapport* between humans and genies and the past. In the eyes of the magicians, it was the first language of humanity.' See E. Doutté, *Magie et religion dans l'Afrique du Nord*, Algiers: Jourdain, 1909.
62. The number of Hargha factions was not as high as the Gadmīwa or Ganfīsa, it could have been a fairly small tribe in comparison. However, it is difficult to know exact numbers. More factions could simply mean more divisions within a tribe, not necessarily more tribesmen.
63. Lévi-Provençal, *Documents inédits*, p. 56.
64. Which sheikh is uncertain, presumably the *amghar* or chief, possibly of Ibn Tūmart's clan.
65. Possibly a self-identified Arab tribe as there was no Berber 'Aīt' or 'Īdā' attached to its name.

66. Note the combination of Muslim Arab names like Zakarīyā and purely Berber names like Īndāawazāl. Lévi-Provençal, *Documents inédits*, p. 56.
67. Hopkins, *Medieval Muslim government in Barbary*, p. 89.
68. Ibid.
69. Lévi-Provençal, *Documents inédits*, p. 61, footnote 1.
70. Lévi-Provençal, *Documents inédits*, p. 44.
71. 'A large tribe on the western side of the Anti-Atlas that today has elements dispersed to the south of Marrakech.' Lévi-Provençal, *Documents inédits*, p. 61, footnote 3.
72. 'A grand confederation that today has its centre in Sīrwā to the southeast of Marrakech. They consider as their own all the factions of the Jabal Kīk, of the Wādī Naffīs and of Tīfnaut.' Ibid, p. 62, footnote 1.
73. Ahl and Aīt were often used interchangeably. Again, suggesting the somewhat fluid distinction between 'tribe' and 'people' in the Atlas. The Tīfnaut is a region that corresponds to the high valley of the Wādī Sūs. One can still find there ten factions ethnically attached to the Ūzgīta confederation.
74. Lévi-Provençal called them 'les gens du sud'. Interestingly, this faction did not even have an ancestral name. It was just a generic '*qābila*', or 'tribe'.
75. Miranda, *Historia política*, pp. 74-5.
76. Ibn Khaldūn, *Histoire des Berbères*, vol. 2, p. 53. 'The tomb of the Mahdī still exits among them, as honoured, as revered as ever. The Qur'ān is recited day and night; men still come there. There is a corps of guardians, conserving the same organization and following the same ceremony as that followed during the time of the Almohad Empire, receiving pilgrims and devotees from afar who are introduced into the sanctuary with an order and solemnity that inspires profound respect.'
77. Although there was little indication of the numerical size of each tribal group, one might assume that the Hintāta were smaller than the Ahl Tīnmallal given their specialized status and geographic area.
78. According to Lévi-Provençal, the tribe may have dispersed or may now be called the Galgā'iya near the river of the same name, Lévi-Provençal, *Documents inédits*, p. 62, footnote 4.
79. These may have been interrelated with the Hargha, see Lévi-Provençal, *Documents inédits*, p. 62, footnote 5. Tables 2.2 and 2.3 illustrate the complex crossover and interrelationships between tribal factions and subgroups.
80. See Table 2.5. A collection of Berber Gadmīwa texts showing the importance of literacy and written accounts of ancestry in the Atlas Berber tribes was compiled recently by Harry Stroomer, *Textes berbères des Guedmioua et Goundafa: basés sur les documents de F. Corjon, J.-M. Franchi et J. Eugène*, Aix-en-Provence: Édisudā, 2001.
81. Lévi-Provençal, *Documents inédits*, p. 63. Lévi-Provençal described the Gadmīwa as a 'grand confederation that has not, it seems, changed its habitat. ... The two great sub-groupings or *leff* of this tribe remain the Īndgertīt and the Īnsfāṭen which correspond to the factions listed.'
82. Hopkins, *Medieval Muslim government in Barbary*, p. 95.

83. Ibid.
84. Īnad Gartīt means faction.
85. Lévi-Provençal, *Documents inédits*, p. 64.
86. Berque, *Structures sociales*, pp. 100–19, described the 'rapport' between plain and mountain among the Saksāwa of the Ganfīsa in the High Atlas.
87. The book also mentioned a possibly semi-independent tribe called the Ṣauda of the plains. Today they consider themselves a part of the Gadmīwa and are situated on one of the best escarpments of the Atlas. Lévi-Provençal, *Documents inédits*, p. 64, footnote 1. Table 2.5 represents the ready-made internal system of the Gadmīwa under the Almohads and demonstrates the typically complex relationship between different sections of the confederation. This same relational complexity could be found in other Almohad tribes.
88. Lévi-Provençal, *Documents inédits*, p. 55.
89. The Banu Masīfū were 'the first that were passed during the review'. Lévi-Provençal, *Documents inédits*, p. 63.
90. Ibn Khaldūn, *Histoire des Berbères*, Paris, 1925, vol. 2, p. 59.
91. Al-Bakrī, *Description de l'Afrique septentrionale*, p. 292.
92. Ibn Khaldūn, *Histoire des Berbères*, Algiers, vol. 2, p. 59.
93. Ibid.
94. Haddū may have been the ruling family of the Saksāwa. The Aīt D'alh'a still trace their ancestry to a certain Amer u Haddū, a heroic descendant of Haddū who ruled in the fourteenth century.
95. Ibn Khaldūn, *Histoire des Berbères*, Algiers, vol. 2, p. 60.
96. See Gellner, *Saints of the Atlas*, pp. 9–10. Haddū is not alone. As Berque described in *Structures sociales*, the use of books and the writing of ancestral history was widespread throughout the Atlas.
97. Berque, *Structures sociales*, see plates 13, 14 and 15 for illustrated examples of Saksāwa manuscripts. Perhaps the Aīt Atta of Gellner's study, *Saints of the Atlas*, were not as involved in writing. To say the least, one can not reasonably claim that urban centres had a monopoly over writing and literacy.
98. Berque, *Structures sociales*, p. 62. Some of these documents may even date from before the sixteenth century. However, Berque mentioned that it was almost impossible for him to read any of them because of their 'confusing script and paleness'. They were also jealously guarded. They may have listed the names and deeds of ancestors.
99. Lévi-Provençal, *Documents inédits*, p. 65, footnote 1.
100. Lévi-Provençal, *Documents inédits*, p. 65.
101. Berque, *Structures sociales*, p. 62.
102. Berque, in *Structures sociales*, p. 59, noted: 'One can not write history with nothing. But this "nothing" may itself be historical. This is the case for the Saksāwa'.
103. 'They fought the Alaouites with the same resistance as against the Marinids' (Berque, *Structures sociales*, pp. 59–60).
104. Berque, *Structures sociales*, p. 108, rightly asks 'Why this discordance between two

economies ... "[agricultural] labourage and pasturage" even as they were well founded on each other?'

105. Interestingly, the traveller Johannes Leo Africanus (*Description de l'Afrique*, translated by Charles Schefer, 1896, vol. 1, p. 222) only witnessed the Saksāwa in villages.
106. Berque, *Structures sociales*, p. 112.
107. Ibn Khaldūn, *Histoire des Berbères*, vol. 1, p. 174.
108. Hopkins, *Medieval Muslim government in Barbary*, p. 110.
109. Abun-Nasr noted, 'In the state which 'Abd al Mu'min founded the supremacy of the tribes which had constituted the Tīnmallal community was preserved. The original tribes formed the aristocracy of the empire, and during the whole of the Almohad period, and afterwards in the Āfṣid state, the name Almohad was used to refer specifically to them. The Almohads were the only group entitled to discuss and elaborate Ibn Tūmart's doctrine' (Abun-Nasr, *A history of the Maghrib*, p. 94).
110. The conference took place at the Casa de Velázquez in June 2001. María Jesús Viguera Molíns provides a brief summary of the political organization of the Almohads in her chapter 'Historia política', in R. Menéndez Pidal, *Historia de España*, Madrid: Edicion Espasa-Calpe, 1997, vol. 7, p. 79.
111. Hopkins, *Medieval Muslim government in Barbary*, pp. 85–111.
112. See Tables 2.1–2.5.
113. Lévi-Provençal, *Documents inédits*, p. 53. The full name of the book is *Kitāb al-Ansab fī Ma'rifat al-Aṣḥāb*, The Book of Ancestries in Order to Know the Companions.
114. See introduction to Ibn al-Qaṭṭān, *Naẓm al Jumān* by Dr al-Makki. For a detailed discussion of the Almohad *ṭullāb*, see Fricaud, 'Les ṭālaba dans la société almohade', 1997.
115. Ibn al-Qaṭṭān, *Naẓm al-Jumān*, p. 27.
116. See Table 2.3 for al-Qaṭṭān's version and the *Kitāb al-Ansāb* version. There are slight but important variations.
117. One can assume this punishment was not used for the upper ranks, Ibn al-Qaṭṭān, *Naẓm al-Jumān*, p. 24. As master, Ibn al-Qaṭṭān may have used the whip regularly with the students at the school that 'Abd al-Mu'min originally established in Marrakech.
118. As translated in a footnote by the editor al-Makki, p. 28, note 3.
119. Lévi-Provençal, *Documents inédits*, p. 41.
120. Lévi-Provençal claimed that the book was written in the first half of the thirteenth century. Lévi-Provençal, *Documents inédits*, p. viii.
121. In general, however, it is parallel in most respects with al-Qaṭṭān's description.
122. Hopkins, *Medieval Muslim government*, pp. 86–7, noted that this lack of detail was true for all the sources.
123. An *'arīf* was a teacher, monitor, or assistant, probably the latter in this case.
124. Referring to this group, Ibn al-Qaṭṭān said, 'The Mahdī had men who served him in his house, called *ahl al-dār*, from among his *aṣḥāb*, they formed his particular

entourage night and day.' Translated in Hopkins, *Medieval Muslim government in Barbary*, p. 87.

125. Ibid.

126. Levi Provençal speculated that this may be the very same Abū Bakr bin 'Alī al-Ṣanhājī al-Baydhaq who wrote the biography of Ibn Tūmart, the source of so much information on the Mahdī.

127. Roger Le Tourneau, 'Du mouvement almohade à la dynastie mu'minide: la révolte des frères d'Ibn Tūmart de 1153–1156', *Mélanges d'histoire et d'archéologie de l'Occident musulman*, vol. 2, 1957, pp. 111–16.

128. Lévi-Provençal, *Documents inédits*, p. 32.

129. Lévi-Provençal, *Documents inédits*, p. 33.

130. Abū Sa'īd Yakhluf ibn al-Ḥasan, Lévi-Provençal, *Documents inédits*, 48.

131. 'Abd al-Mu'min ibn 'Alī ibn 'Alwī ibn Ya'lā al-Kūmī Abū Muḥammad was the builder of the Almohad Empire. A great military leader and able administrator, 'Abd al-Mu'min led the Almohad movement for *tawḥīd*, absolute monotheistic unity, after the death of the Mahdī Ibn Tūmart in 524/1130. After defeating the Almoravid Empire at Marrakech, he established the administrative and military foundations of the Almohad state while securing a caliphal succession for his descendants, the Mu'minid dynasty. In a matter of decades, 'Abd al-Mu'min and his followers transformed the Almohads from a vigorous but vulnerable ideological movement in the small, Atlas mountain town of Tīnmallal to one of the largest and most successful Islamic empires in North African and Andalusian history. Effectively an outsider, 'Abd al-Mu'min's ancestry was different from the noble, Maṣmūda tribes who made up the core of the Almohad army and hierarchy. He was born into the Arabicized Berber tribe of the Kūmya of the Zanāta confederation in the province of modern Oran. Although he was not a member of the original Almohad tribes of the Moroccan Atlas, he was well suited for leadership and could use his status as an outsider to mediate inter-tribal jealousies. Only later, in the writings of the *Kitāb al-Ansāb*, a book found, like many Almohad sources, in a collection of manuscripts at the El-Escorial, did 'Abd al Mu'min claim an illustrious Arab and Berber ancestry that tied him to pre-Islamic prophets as well as to the Berber queen Kahina.

132. For more on Abū Ḥafṣ 'Umar al-Hintāti and his descendants who founded the Hafṣid dynasty in present-day Tunisia, see my forthcoming article in the *Encyclopaedia of Islam*, 3rd edn, a section of which is produced below: 'His original, Berber name was Faska u-Mzal Īntī. Ibn Tūmart changed his name to Abū Ḥafṣ: the same name as Muḥammad the Prophet's companion. Starting a family consistently loyal to the original al-Muwaḥid doctrine of Ibn Tūmart, his grandson, Abū Zakarīyā' b. 'Abd al-Wāḥid broke away from Ibn Tūmart's Mui'minid successors who altered elements of the original Almohad doctrine, and founded the Ḥafṣid Dynasty in the region of modern-day Tunisia. Abū Ḥafṣ was chief of the powerful Hintātā tribe of the Anti-Atlas whose warriors Abū Ḥafṣ commanded in battle against the ruling Almoravids. Realizing the need for a

unified core to unite the tribes of the Atlas, he was one of the few sheikhs allowed to command his own tribe into battle. It is doubtful that the seemingly unstoppable Almohad wave against the Almoravids would have arisen as quickly without the military support of the large and unified Hintātī tribe, or without the leadership and unshakeable loyalty of Abū Ḥafṣ.'

133. The *Kitāb al-Ansāb* was the only source not to call them the ten, thus possibly explaining the extra members. Rather, it called them the *Jamā'a*, the society or council.

134. Montagne, *Berbères et le Makhzen*, p. 221. See especially his chapter 'L'Organisation républicaine'. One should remember, of course, that the French were famously attempting to divide the Arabs and the Berbers of Maroc into two different constitutional systems. Political considerations would have certainly influenced the way Montagne paints the Berbers as republican and hence more 'French' than the Arabs. He dedicated his book to the French procounsul of Morocco, Le Maréchal Lyautey. Nevertheless, many of his basic anthropological observations were valid. Exploring the region before 1930, he observed rural Berber culture before the influx of extensive modern influence. The *Makhzen* was just penetrating the region.

135. Montagne, in *Berbères et le Makhzen*, p. 63, mentioned that many of the Almohads' practices were still being observed.

136. Dresch, *Tribes, government, and history*, pp. 88–9.

137. Ibn Tūmart, *Kitāb A'zz mā Yuṭlab*, p. 267.

138. Hopkins, *Medieval Muslim government in Barbary*, p. 91.

139. Fricauld, 'Les ṭālaba dans la société almohade', pp. 331–87.

140. Ibid., p. 345.

141. Ibid.

142. Anonymous Chronicler, *Al-Ḥulal al-Mūshiyyah*, pp. 179–80. It is interesting to note how the chronicler identified the *A'azz mā Yuṭlab* of Ibn Tūmart alongside the *Muwaṭṭa'* of Mālik ibn Anas, the Maliki school rule book that the Almoravids followed. The description continued: 'one day he would have them ride horses; another day shooting with bows. Then he would have them swimming in the pool of water that he dug outside his gardens: its perimeter measured about 700 yards. Then he had them rowing on small boats which he had there for them. They were educated in all those activities, receiving alternatively rewards and punishments, and all their expenses and maintenance were paid for by the Caliph as were their horses and weapons. When he had carried into effect what he had planned for them, he appointed them as governors of provinces and as senior officers in the place of Maṣmūḍa chiefs to whom he said: "The learned men come before you." The chiefs gave the manangement of affairs to the *ḥāfiẓ* but 'Abd al Mu'min had them remain beside the *ḥāfiẓ* to give them advice.'

143. Le Tourneau, *The Almohad movement*, described the gradual breaking away from the original ideals of the Almohad movement. The councils and the hierarchy still had a role in the Almohad state even after the rise of powerful caliphs like Ya'qūb al Manṣūr who ruled mainly from Seville.

144. Amor Ben Hamadi, 'Rutas transaharianas en el Maghrib oriental', in Anon, *Mauritania y Espana: una historia común*, Granada: Fundación El Legado Andalusí, 2003, pp. 37–75.
145. Ibn Khaldūn, *Muqaddimah*, vol. 2, p. 338.
146. J. Devisse, 'Approximatives, quantitatives, qualitatives: valeurs variables de l'étude des traversées sahariennes', in M. Garcia-Arenal and M. J. Viguera (eds) *Relaciones de la Península Ibérica con el Magreb, siglos XIII–XVI*, Actas del Coloquio, Madrid, 1987.
147. The trans-Saharan trade remains profitable, especially if traders manage to avoid detection from government authorities. This is still largely possible on the vast and largely disputed borders of Mauritania and the western Sahara.
148. Edrisi (al-Idrīsī), *Description de l'Afrique*, p. 31.
149. Hamadi, 'Rutas transaharianas', p. 61.
150. Edrisi (al-Idrīsī), *Description de l'Afrique*, pp. 69–70.
151. Ibid.
152. Al-Bakrī, *Description de l'Afrique septentrionale*, p. 291. Although still fairly rich, the Wādī Draā of today has suffered signficantly from drought and will often evaporate completely.
153. Marine fossils are especially abundant in the region. They still comprise one of Morocco's large cottage industry exports.
154. Al-Bakrī, *Description de l'Afrique septentrionale*, p. 291.
155. Al-Bakrī may have have meant the governor, or even Abū Bark bin 'Umar (d. 1072) who was leader of the Almoravids at the time.
156. That they had to close off one of their main cities and later build a strong fortress at an important pass indicated the need to prevent regular uprisings, possibly against trade taxation. On the many mountain pass fortresses of the Almoravids and Almohads see Lévi-Provençal, *Documents inédits*, pp. 222–3.
157. Al-Bakrī, *Description de l'Afrique septentrionale*, p. 292.
158. Ibid.
159. For the economic dynamic of combined settled agriculture with pastoral transhumance in a historical context, see David M. Hart, 'Four centuries of history on the hoof: the northwest passage of Berber sheep transferments across the Moroccan Atlas, 1550–1912', *Morocco: Journal of the Society for Moroccan Studies*, vol. 3, 1993, pp. 21–55.

Chapter 3. The Doctrine of Muḥammad Ibn Tūmart: Mahdī of the Almohads

1. Ibn al-Qaṭṭān records the year as AH 511. The sources differ on the exact date of the Mahdī's proclamation. According to Ibn al-Qaṭṭān, author of *Naẓīm al-Jamān*, p. 36, Ibn Tūmart said simply, 'I am Muḥammad Ibn 'Abd Allah Tūmart, and I am Mahdī of the end of time'.
2. For recent and relevant discussions of the history of the Mahdī doctrine and Ibn Tūmart see the special issue of *Revue des Mondes Musulmanes et de la Mediterranee* (1999, nos 91–4). Especially relevant to this book are Michael Brett, 'Le Mahdī dans

le Maghrib medieval: l'elaboration de la légitimité Almohade', pp. 93–106; Maribel Fierro, 'Le Mahdī Ibn Tūmart'; Tilman Nagel, 'Le mahdīsme d'Ibn Tūmart et d'Ibn Qasi: une analyse phenomenologique', pp. 125–36; and Mercedes Garcia-Arenal, 'Imām et Mahdī: Ibn Abī Mahalli', pp. 157–80, who is also publishing a forthcoming book on the Mahdī concept in history. She includes a chapter on Ibn Tūmart in this book. There is also the excellent colloquium collection *Mahdīsme: crise et changement dans l'histoire du Maroc*, Rabat, 1994.

3. Ibn Khaldūn provided a good explanation of this belief in the year AH 500 as the beginning of a new era in his Ibn Khaldūn, *The Muqaddimah*. As it is said in the Qur'ān XXII: 47 'One day according to your Lord is like a thousand years as you might comprehend.' Al-Ṭabarī added: 'It is well established in the two *Ṣaḥīḥ* [established *ḥadīth*] that the Prophet said, "Your term, compared with the term of those who have come before, is come the time between the afternoon prayer and the setting of the sun." From this *ḥadīth*, Muḥammad seemed to say that the Mahdī would appear on Earth some 500 years after the life of the Prophet.' See Ibn Khaldūn, 'Autobiographie', p. 683, for the full text. Miranda, *Historia política*, pp. 60-5, discusses Ibn Tūmart's speech and the legend of 500 years for the coming of the Mahdī.
4. There is some disagreement in the sources over whether Ibn Tūmart proclaimed himself Mahdī, as Ibn al-Qaṭṭān records, or was proclaimed by his followers. See a discussion of this issue in Miranda, *Historia política*, p. 63.
5. This was recorded by the *Saḥīḥ* of al-Bukhārī. See Al-Bukhārī, *Ṣaḥīḥ*, vol. 4, Book 56, no. 783 narrated by Ibn Umar: 'The Prophet used to deliver his sermons while standing beside a trunk of a date palm. When he had the pulpit made, he used it instead. The trunk started crying and the Prophet went to it, rubbing his hand over it (to stop its crying).'
6. Miranda, *Historia política*, p. 63. Anonymous Chronicler, *Al-Ḥulal al-Mūshiyyah*, p. 128 in Miranda's translation. The *Naẓm al-Jumān* by Ibn al-Qaṭṭān copied partially from the *Ḥulal al-Mūshiyya*.
7. Mercedes García-Arenal, 'Pouvoir sacré et mahdīsme: Aḥmad al-Manṣūr al Dhahalī', *al-Qanṭara*, vol. 17, no. 2, 1996, pp. 453–73, discussed a Mahdī figure appearing much later in Maghribi history. However, her observation about the relationship between the development of mahdīsm and the power of the *'ulamā* would apply to Ibn Tūmart's reaction against the domination of Almoravid doctrine by jurists who ignored the *al-uṣūl*, the roots of religion. 'The stratification of Islamic power is always relative and can be realized only through the figure of the Mahdī. Such sanctification of the sovereign is necessary when he is not legitimate enough for the *'ulamā*' (García-Arenal, 'Pouvoir sacré', p. 471).
8. A good historical background for Almohad doctrine and its context is found in Michael Brett's series of published articles, *Ibn Khaldūn and the medieval Maghrib*. Two articles in it are of particular interest, namely 'The realm of the imām: the Fatimids in the tenth century', and 'The lamp of the Almohads: illumination as a political idea in twelfth-century Morocco'.

9. On the relationship between the Shīʿites and the Almohads, see Maribel Fierro, 'The legal policies of the Almohads and Ibn Rushd's Bidāyat al-Mujtahid', *Journal of Islamic Studies*, Oxford, vol. 10, no. 3, 1999, pp. 226–48.
10. On the theory that Ibn Tūmart was possibly influenced by Khārijite doctrine, see Urvoy, 'La pensée d'Ibn Tūmart', p. 35.
11. Crone, *Medieval Islamic political thought*, pp. 21–2.
12. The Almoravids, however, did accept the theoretical authority of the eastern caliphs.
13. Crone, *Medieval Islamic political thought*, p. 31. The Umayyad ʿAbd al Raḥmān I and the Andalusians refused to recognize the caliph as early as 756.
14. This is pointed out by Mohamed Zniber, 'L'Itineraire psycho-intellectuel d'Ibn Toumert', in Abdelmajid Kaddouri (ed.), *Mahdisme: crise et changement dans l'histoire du Maroc*, Rabat, 1994, p. 16. See also Maribel Fierro, 'Mahdīsme et eschatologie dans al-Andalus', in Abdelmajid Kaddouri (ed.), *Mahdisme: crise et changement dans l'histoire du Maroc*, Rabat, 1994, pp. 47–69.
15. Crone, *Medieval Islamic political thought*, p. 75.
16. S. A. Arjomand, 'Messianism, millennialism, and revolution in early Islamic history', in A. Amanat and M. Bernhardsson (eds), *Imagining the end*, London, 2002, pp. 106–125.
17. Crone, *Medieval Islamic political thought*, p. 75.
18. For more on the early caliph who was named al-Mahdī, see Al-Ṭabarī, *The history of al-Ṭabarī: English selections*, vol. 29, translated by Hugh Kennedy, Albany: State University of New York Press, 1990.
19. Zniber, by contrast, believed there were only two, the ordinary and the inspired.
20. Cook, *Commanding right*, provides several examples of normal Muslims commanding right and forbidding wrong for no political gain.
21. Zniber, 'L'Itineraire psycho-intellectual d'Ibn Toumert', pp. 17–18.
22. Crone, *Medieval Islamic political thought*, p. 79. For a perspective on Mahdīsm among Shīʿites, see Abdulaziz Sachedina, *Islamic messianism: the idea of the Mahdī in Twelver Shīʿism*, Albany: State University of New York Press, 1981.
23. Although personally unwilling to be labelled the Mahdī, Ibn al-Ḥanafiyya had become an extraordinary type of Mahdī to many Shīʿites by the time he died. He allegedly went into hiding in a cave near Medina and would come back down from the cave proclaiming the end of time and the new era of justice.
24. Patricia Crone and Michael Cook, *Hagarism: the making of the Islamic world*, Cambridge: Cambridge University Press, 1977, p. 165.
25. See Chapter 1 for the life of Ibn Tūmart.
26. The Mahdī who would bring about the end of time was not mentioned by the two most reliable collections of the sayings of the Prophet *(ḥadīth)*. These two collections, written by al-Bukhārī and Muslim, were often called the 'true' or the 'sound' *ḥadīth*. Al-Ghazālī disputes the doctrine of the Mahdī in his work *al-Munqidh min al-Dalal*, Damascus: Fons Vitae, 1956; see Watt, *The faith and practice of al-Ghazālī*, pp. 19–85.

27. See Timothy Furnish, 'Eschatology as politics, eschatology as theory: modern Sunni Arab Mahdīsm in historical perspective', unpublished Ph.D. thesis, Ohio State University, 2001; and Muḥammad Bāqir Ṣadr, *The awaited saviour*, translated by M. Ansari, Albany: State University of New York Press, 1982.
28. Al-Marrākushī suggested that a main impetus behind Ibn Tūmart's journey back to the Maghrib was to enforce al-Ghazālī's views. See al-Marrākushī, *al-Muʿjib*, pp. 187–90. At the same time, Ibn Tūmart seemed to violate many of al-Ghazālī's views, especially by claiming to be the Mahdī of the entire Muslim community, a concept rejected by al-Ghazālī. Al-Ghazālī believed that there should be an imām for the Muslim community and that the imāmate existed for the unity of Muslims. He referred to the *ḥadīth* that 'The Imāms are of the Quraysh' to build on his elaborate argument for the imāmate. Ibn Tūmart referred to these ideas in his doctrine of the imāmate. Al-Ghazālī did not, however, believe that the imām should be an apocalyptic figure or Mahdī. Aware of political and tribal realities, Ibn Tūmart seemed to have shaped aspects al-Ghazālī's thought for the twelfth-century Berber context. A Mahdī promising salvation was much easier to follow than a temporary imām. See Goldziher, 'Introduction', pp. 1–20. Despite enticing similarities between the Mahdī doctrine of the Almohads and the Shīʿites, there is little direct evidence of influence by earlier, Shīʿite doctrine of the exceptional Mahdī in occultation.
29. See Sachedina, *Islamic messianism*.
30. Ibn Khaldūn provided a clear summary of the debate and the positions on both sides of the argument over the coming of a Mahdī in the Islamic community. He provides arguments used both by Sunni and Shīʿite Muslims. Although he seemed personally sceptical of the idea of the Mahdī, Ibn Khaldūn still provided the main arguments for the Mahdī in the *ḥadīth* literature. For an updated version see Ibn Khaldūn, *Le Livre des examples*, translated by A. Cheddadi, Paris: Gallimard, 2002, pp. 652–81. Most contemporary sources focus on the early classical period and do not treat the later emergence of Mahdī figures in any depth. See S. A. Arjomand, 'Islamic apocalypticism in the classic period', in Bernard McGinn (ed.) *The Encyclopedia of apocalypticism*, vol. 2, New York: Continuum Press, 1998; *Encyclopaedia of Islam*, 2nd edition, sv. *al-Mahdī*; and Wilferd Madelung, 'Some notes on non-Ismāʿīlī Shiism in the Maghrib', *Studia Islamica*, no. 44, 1976, pp. 87–97. Also Jan Olaf Blichfeldt, *Early Mahdism*, Leiden: E. J. Brill, 1985, is at best only an introduction to the subject. He speculates that the Mahdī concept can be explained by a specific incident, mainly the death of ʿUmar bin al-Khaṭṭāb but does not take into account the vast literature on the subject and the recurring rise of the Mahdī concept throughout the Muslim world. For a contemporary Muslim perspective on the Mahdī and his meaning, see Ṣadr, *The awaited saviour*.
31. Heinz Halm, *Shiism*, Edinburgh: Edinburgh University Press, 1991. Also see Heinz Halm, *The empire of the Mahdī: the rise of the Fatimids*, Leiden: E. J. Brill, 1996.
32. See Ibn Khaldūn's explanation of the book of *al-Jafr*: an alleged book of divination.

'Common people pretend that all the predictions related to the destiny of dynasties are found in a book where the names, genealogies, lengths of reigns, kings and their successors until the end of creation are written. ... They pretend that the Mahdī of the Almohads discovered it in the Orient. ... It was this that allowed him to found his state.' See A. Cheddadi's translation of the explanation by Ibn Khaldūn found in his version of the manuscripts. 'Chapitres de la version primitive de la Muqaddimah' (Ibn Khaldūn, *Le Livre des exemples*).

33. Goldziher, 'Introduction', pp. 15–19.
34. For a discussion of the possible connections with the Fatimids, see Brett's articles in *Ibn Khaldūn and the medieval Maghrib*, especially 'The lamp of the Almohads' and 'The realm of the imām'.
35. Brett and Fentress, *The Berbers*, p. 93. This probably explained the Almoravid claim that the Almohads were Khārijites: they also followed a Mahdī.
36. For a comprehensive study of the Fatimids and the fourth-century Islamic Mediterranean, see Brett, *The rise of the Fatimids*. Also, see Michael Brett, 'The Fatimid revolution and its aftermath in North Africa, in J. D. Fage (ed.) *Cambridge History of Africa*, Cambridge: Cambridge University Press, 1978 vol. 2, Chapter 8.
37. Biography by al-Baydhaq in Lévi-Provençal, *Documents inédits*, p. 125. The original Khārijites were famous for their radicalism and egalitarian philosophy. Even more radical than the Shīʿites they left the army after refusing the Caliph ʿAlī's decision to allow his authority to be subject to arbitration at the battle of Siffīn.
38. Madelung, 'Some notes'.
39. Lévi-Provençal, *Documents inédits*, p. 19.
40. Cf. Brett, 'The lamp of the Almohads'.
41. Halm, *The empire of the Mahdī*, p. 20.
42. For Ismāʿīlī secret doctrine about the time of gloom before the coming of the imām and Mahdī, see Michael Brett, 'The Mīm and the ʿAyn, and the making of Ismaʿilism', in Michael Brett, *Ibn Khaldūn and the medieval Maghrib*, Aldershot: Ashgate, 1999.
43. Al-Bakrī (d. 1069) discussed the Barghwata as 'heretics' and provided an Arabic translation of a portion of the Barghwata Berber Qurʾān: the Book of Job. See Al-Bakrī, *Description de l'Afrique septentrionale*, p. 209. Also Ibn Khaldūn described the Barghwata in *Histoire des Berbères*, vol. 1, p. 295.
44. H. T. Norris discussed the Barghwata and Arabic sources for the movement in *The Berbers in Arabic literature*. There does not seem to be an extant copy, in Berber, of the Barghwata Qurʾān.
45. Ibn Tūmart also rode on a mule or donkey. For an example, see Lévi-Provençal, *Documents inédits*, p. 117.
46. It was recorded that in AD 1058 he went on an expedition to the lands of the mountain, Maṣmuda tribes to reform their '*jāhiliyya* ways' and to encourage the tribes to give their nominal allegiance to the new Almoravid amir Abū Bakr b. ʿUmar. Several chronicles note that there was great resistance to ʿAbd Allah bin Yasīn. See references in Lagardère, *Les Almoravides*, p. 68.

47. Al-Bakrī, *Description de l'Afrique septentrionale*, pp. 313–14.
48. The Saadians who emerged from Zagora centuries after the Almohads also invoked the Mahdī claim. Ibn Khaldūn provided a stirring description of Siʿada of the Riab branch of the Muslim tribe around the early part of the fourteenth century. Siʿada was raised according to 'the most exalted practices and devotions'. After easily reforming his immediate relatives in the just ways of the *sunna*, his reputation and his inspiring presence attracted many followers and disciples, not only among his own tribe but also among neighbouring tribes. Persons of the highest merit were numbered among the followers who 'marched along the way that he had traced'. Ibn Khaldūn emphasized that Siʿada would not have succeeded in spreading his moral vision were it not for this tribal support. Ibn Khaldūn, *Histoire des Berbères*, vol. 1. Many of his closest followers were chiefs of tribal families and groupings who wished to hear his message. He reformed them all in the ways of the *sunna*, the acts and words of Muḥammad.
49. The Islamic East was also experiencing a revival of Mahdīsm. By the twelfth and thirteenth centuries books began to emerge on the coming of the mahdī, detailing his characteristics and his mission. See, for example, Muḥammad ibn Yūsuf Kanjī (d. 1259), *al-Bayān fī akhbār ṣaḥib al zamān*, Beirut: Riyad al-Rayyis lil-Kutub wa-al-Nashr, 2000. It should also be noted that the anthropology of present-day tribes, especially in the Middle and High Atlas, and the work of Ernest Gellner and David Hart, revealed an inherent tendency for tribes to rely on 'saints' or holy figures as impartial mediators in tribal disputes. This was often necessary as nomadic and settled tribes engaged in different herding and agricultural activities that crossed paths and resources. Constant warfare would have been unduly costly; thus, the need for the holy man who could mediate between tribes. See Gellner, *Saints of the Atlas*; Hart, *Tribe and society in rural Morocco*.
50. Zniber, 'L'Itineraire psycho-intellectual d'Ibn Toumert', p. 16.
51. Ibid.
52. Georges Gurvitch, *La vocation actuelle de la sociologie*, Paris: Presses universitaires de France, 1963, p. 466. A foundation text for the study of North African geography remains Jean Despois, *L'Afrique du Nord*, Paris: PUF, 1958.
53. Fletcher, 'Al-Andalus and North Africa', pp. 235–58.
54. Zniber, 'L'Itineraire psycho-intellectual d'Ibn Toumert', pp. 16–20.
55. Ibid.
56. Maribel Fierro discusses Ibn Tūmart's Mahdīsm in the Andalusian context in, 'Le Mahdī Ibn Tūmart'. Several articles in this useful collection deal with the rise of the Mahdī concept in general. An even more thorough examination of medieval biographical literature would probably reveal several other local Mahdī figures existing in the Maghrib and Andalusia in the time immediately before Ibn Tūmart's proclamation as Mahdī.
57. For a discussion of prophethood in pre-Islamic Arabia, see Robert Hoyland, *Arabia and the Arabs: from the Bronze Age to the coming of Islam*, London: Routledge, 2001, 139–67.

58. See Miranda's speculation about the year 500 in *Historia política*, pp. 60–5.
59. See my discussion of the economic context for the Almohad movement in Chapter 2.
60. Quoted in Fierro, 'The Ghurabā' in al-Andalus', pp. 231–60. For a further elaboration, see Tilman Nagel, *The history of Islamic theology: from Muḥammad to the present*, translated by Thomas Thornton, Princeton: Markus Wiener, 2000.
61. Fierro, 'The Ghurabā' in al-Andalus', pp. 231–60.
62. See references in Chapter 1.
63. The Almohads did not recognize even the symbolic authority of the caliphs. If anything, the entire Almohad project was to make Ibn Tūmart the new divinely installed messianic leader of the entire Muslim community, the new source of divine expectation. The caliphate was coming to an end. So, it was easily believed, was the world.
64. Crone explains this goal in the opening chapters of her *Medieval Islamic political thought*.
65. Erwin Rosenthal, *Political thought in medieval Islam*, Cambridge: Cambridge University Press, 1958, p. 39.
66. Hugh Kennedy, *The court of the caliphs*, London: Weidenfeld & Nicolson, 2004. Also, see Patricia Crone's depiction of the ideal Muslim society ruled by Allah at the beginning of creation, Crone, *Medieval Islamic political thought*, pp. 3–10.
67. See 'al-Mahdī' entry in *Encyclopaedia of Islam*, 2nd edition.
68. Ibid.
69. As Ibn Tūmart explained in the beginning of his book, there were certain reliable *ḥadīth* and unreliable *ḥadīth*. The 'reliable' accounts he used would be the *Ṣaḥīḥ* of al-Bukhārī, the collections of al-Tirmudhi even Mālik ibn Anas. Ibn Tūmart, *Kitāb A'azz mā Yuṭlab*, pp. 1–60.
70. On the book of *al-Jafr* see an early manuscript translation of Ibn Khaldūn, *Le livre des exemples*, pp. 1247–55.
71. Ibn Khaldūn, *The Muqaddimah*, vol. 2, p. 196.
72. The success of Ibn Tūmart's movement led to a shift in the legends surrounding Mahdīsm. Many false Mahdīs tried to mimic Ibn Tūmart's success, often making wild claims in order to do so. This was the sort of figure Ibn Khaldūn referred to in his rant against false Mahdīs. Ibn Tūmart's success created an entirely new set of legends about the Mahdī, reorienting the centre of the Islamic faith from the sumptuous caliphal palaces of Baghdad, and the grand mosques of Cordoba to the relatively remote hills of the Atlas and Sūs valley. Ibn 'Arabi, along with other widely respected scholars and mystics, said that the Mahdī would, like Ibn Tūmart, appear in the Maghrib. According to Ibn Khaldūn, some even claimed to know the specific location of this appearance at the fortress (*ribāṭ*) of Māssa, about 40 kilometres south of present-day Agadir. There are still remains of a fortress on the mouth of this river, which disappears into the sand before flowing into the Atlantic. Ibn Khaldūn, *The Muqaddimah*, vol. 2, p. 197.
73. Ibn Tūmart, *A'azz mā Yuṭlab*, pp. 235–45. He justified his demand for complete

loyalty in this section. Also, see Robert Brunschvig, 'Sur la doctrine du Mahdī Ibn Tūmart', *Arabica*, vol. 2, 1955, pp. 137–49.

74. Due to the requirement of strict obedience, Ibn Tūmart could not expect the mind of the Berbers to be immediately responsive to his preaching. The geographer al-'Idrīsī mentioned several of the divisive and 'non-Islamic' characteristics of the Atlas tribes. For example, 'in Tarūdant they follow the Maliki school of Islam ... in Tawyīyīn they follow the madhhab of Musa ibn Ja'fir.' Edrisi (al-Idrīsī), *Description de l'Afrique*, pp. 62–3 in the Arabic. This led to constant fighting and differences between the factions. Tarūdant, an important settlement, was famous for the production of a honey-based, alcoholic liquor that sold well in the Marrakech souk. The Barghwata still promulgated their heretical version of the Qur'ān written in Berber, it was described by the geographer al-Bakrī as the book of the devil himself. Al-Bakrī, *Description de l'Afrique septentrionale*, p. 269, contains excerpts from the Barghwata 'Book of Job'. He would not have expected all members of even the more loyal tribes willingly to give up their sovereignty to this man born into a not particularly distinguished tribe who used his eastern learning to preach to the Berbers. Faced with the challenging task of imposing a new way of life on the Atlas, Ibn Tūmart demanded complete obedience. Thus, 'If there is an issue, do not go forward without him. Do not raise your voice above his own.' Ibn Tūmart, *Kitāb A'azz mā Yuṭlab*, pp. 245–6, from the chapter entitled 'Imāma wa 'alāmat al Mahdī', which explained the Almohad concept of the infallible imām and Mahdī.

75. Describing the initial conflict between religious authority and tribal custom Ignaz Goldziher wrote, 'Muḥammad could not expect the mind of his people to be readily responsive to his preaching. He offered them the opposite of their established view on life, their ideals and ancestral traditions. Hence the great opposition that he encountered everywhere. The pagans opposed less the shattering of their idols than the pietistic disposition which they were to accept: that the whole of their life should be determined by thinking of God and His omnipotence which predestines and requites; that they should pray, fast, abstain from enjoyable indulgences, sacrifice money and property, all demanded from them in the name of God. In addition they were to consider barbaric many things which hitherto had been esteemed cardinal virtues, and were to recognize as their leader a man whose claim to this title seemed unusual and incomprehensible and radically different from the attributes upon which had been founded the glory of their ancestors.' Ignaz Goldziher, *Muslim Studies* (*Muhammedanische Studien*), vol. 1, *The classical age of Islam*, edited by S. M. Stern, translated from the German by C. R. Barber and S. M. Stern, London: Allen & Unwin, 1967, p. 14.

76. Ibn Tūmart, *Kitāb A'azz mā Yuṭlab*, p. 246.

77. Whereas Ibn Tūmart was considered infallible, there are several instances in the sayings of the prophet where he admits his fallibility, even in important matters of prayer. Al-Bukhārī, *Saḥiḥ*, vol. 1, Book 8, no. 394. Narrated by 'Abdullah: 'If there had been anything changed in the prayer, surely I would have informed you but I

am a human being like you and liable to forget like you. So if I forget remind me and if anyone of you is doubtful about his prayer, he should follow what he thinks to be correct and complete his prayer accordingly and finish it and do two prostrations (of Sahu).'

78. Ibn Tūmart, *Kitāb A'azz mā Yuṭlab*, p. 247.
79. Ibid., p. 250.
80. Ibid.
81. Ibid., p. 245.
82. Yet even as so much of the Almohad movement and doctrine was dependent on the person of the Mahdī, his death was something of an anticlimax. 'Abd al Mu'min and the Almohad commanders attempted to hide the Mahdī's death and sickness from his followers until victory over the Almoravids was in sight. The millennial promise never materialized, nor did the Mahdī become a crucified figure, his death or 'transformation' being brought about by God, not Almoravids. It is thus, in a way, surprising that the Paris manuscript used here and dated 1179 was still so evocative of the infallible imām and the command to obey his every word and action as the path towards knowledge, light and ultimately salvation. At the beginning, the focus on the person of the Mahdī was the Almohad movement's greatest strength. In the end, however, it was possibly the greatest weakness of the Almohad doctrine of Mahdīsm. The obedient followers of the Mahdī inevitably clashed with the new, more sophisticated, ruling elites who rejected the concept of the Mahdī. The later Almohad caliph Ma'mūn rejected the idea that Ibn Tūmart was the Mahdī, Le Tourneau, *The Almohad movement*, pp. 94, 97.
83. Ibn Tūmart, *Kitāb A'azz mā Yuṭlab*, p. 254.
84. Ibid.
85. 'Muḥammad [Ibn Tūmart], son of 'Abd Allah, son of Ūgallīd, son of Yāmṣal, son of Hamza, son of 'Isā, son of 'Ubaid Allah, son of Idrīs, son of 'Abd Allah, son of Ḥasan, son of Fātima, daughter of the Prophet of God – may God's blessings be upon him – this is an exact genealogy.' Lévi-Provençal, *Documents inédits*, p. 21. The alleged descent of the Mahdī Ibn Tūmart from the Prophet Muḥammad, a requirement for being Mahdī, was addressed in another book, the *Kitāb al-Ansāb* (the Book of Ancestry) probably written some time after his death. With a claim based on certain 'respected sources' that trace his descent through Idrīs, founder of the first Islamic Moroccan dynasty, to Muḥammad, Ibn Tūmart fulfilled the requirement of being a descendant of Muḥammad.
86. Al-Marrākushī, *Al-Mu'jib*, pp. 128–30.
87. Ibn Tūmart, *Kitāb A'azz mā Yuṭlab*, untranslated Arabic text, in Goldziher, *Le livre de Ibn Toumert*.
88. See Chapter 2 for a discussion of the role of the *ḥāfiẓ* in the Almohad hierarchy. Also, Hopkins, *Medieval Muslim government in Barbary*.
89. The opposite of *tawḥīd* is *shirk* – the admission of anything by word or deed that anything or anybody could share the nature of God. As mentioned, this was the main sin of the Almoravids who took the Qur'ān so literally that they limited

God's nature. The doctrine of *tawḥīd* is a difficult and controversial topic among Muslim scholars today and has been since the beginnings of Muslim theology. I only represent Ibn Tūmart's version of *tawḥīd* here. The doctrine of *tawḥīd* became particularly important to Muslim theology in the East after the writings of Ibn Taymiyya who died in prison in Damascus in 1328. See Ibn Taymiyya, *al-ʿAqidah al wasitiyya: the principles of Islamic faith*, Chicago: University of Chicago Press, 1992. *Tawḥīd* remains a popular and controversial topic, especially as certain globalized movements have arisen to 'standardize' Islamic thought and theology. See Muḥammad Abd al-Wahhab, *The Book of Tawheed*, translated by Samah Strauch, Riyadh: International Islamic Publishing House, 1998.

90. Abū Bakr ibn Ṭufayl (d. 1185), *The history of Hayy ibn Yaqẓān*, translated by Simon Ockley, London: Darf Publishers, 1986.
91. On this concept of 'in-born monotheism' in Almohad doctrine, see discussion below and notes 47–48.
92. The last stage of the archetypal mystic journey towards unification with God, *tawḥīd* was an important Sufī concept. For Sufīs *tawḥīd* was more than the verbal confession of God's unity. It meant the negation of self and unification with God even as the self maintained its separate essence, like a drop of fresh water in the ocean. According to Margaret Smith, an expert on Sufī thought, Ruwaym al-Baghdadī, an early mystic, said that *tawḥīd* was 'the effacement of human nature and keeping separate that which is Divine' (Margaret Smith, *Rābiʿa the mystic and her fellow saints in Islam*, Cambridge: Cambridge University Press, 1984, p. 79).
93. There was a major reason why some philosophers like al-Fārābi (d. 950) believed that the most profound theological and philosophical speculations should be reserved for a ruling, philosophical elite. See Abū Nasr al-Fārābi, *Falsafat Aflāṭūn*, edited by F. Rosenthal and R. Walzer, London: Plato Arabus, 1943.
94. Ibn Tūmart, *Kitāb Aʿazz mā Yuṭlab*, p. 241.
95. Lévi-Provençal, *Documents inédits*, p. 7.
96. Ibid.
97. For the complete *ḥadīth*, see Book 33, Number 6428 of the Ṣaḥīḥ Muslim, *The Book of Destiny*: 'Abū Huraira reported from Allah's Messenger (may peace be upon him) many *ḥadīth* and one amongst them is that he is reported to have said: An infant is born according to his (true) nature. It is his parents who make him a Jew, a Christian, just as a she-camel gives birth to its young ones. Do you find any deficiency in their limbs? You cut their ears (i.e. after birth). They (the Companions of the Holy Prophet) said: What is your opinion about him who dies in infancy? Thereupon Allah's Apostle (may peace be upon him) said: It is Allah alone who knows best what they would be doing.' Abū Ḥusayn Muslim was a student of al-Bukhārī and died in AD 873. This is one of 4000 out of 30,000 of his *ḥadīth* that were deemed especially sound. For searchable text see http://www.usc.edu/dept/MSA/fundamentals/hadithsunnah/muslim
98. Ibn Khaldūn, *The Muqaddimah*, vol. 1, pp. 253–4.
99. Camilla Adang, 'Islam as the inborn religion of manhood: the concept of *Fiṭra* in

the words of Ibn Ḥazm', *Al-Qanṭara*, vol. 21, no. 2, 2000, pp. 391–411, explained the view of Ibn Ḥazm of Cordoba (d. 456/1064) that 'literally everyone is born as a Muslim including polytheists and other unbelievers ... they will be considered believers until they come of age.' It was likely that Ibn Tūmart interacted with members of Ibn Ḥazm's Zāhirī school although the scholar himself would have been dead by the time of Ibn Tūmart's alleged visit to Cordoba. The Almoravids were not born anthropomorphists; they were simply led astray by their supposed paganism. Crucially, this belief in the inherent true belief of man, not only in monotheism but also in the Almohad version of monotheism, kept the door of conversion open.

100. Also, see Lagardère, *Les Almoraivdes*, p. 68, for a description of Ibn al-Yasīn's failed attempt to win over the Maṣmūda.
101. Ibn Tūmart, *Kitāb A'azz mā Yuṭlab*, p. 258.
102. Lévi-Provençal, *Documents inédits*, p. 6.
103. Ibn Tūmart, *Kitāb A'azz mā Yuṭlab*, p. 256.
104. Ibid., p. 291.
105. Maribel Fierro, 'The Qadi as ruler', *Saber religioso y poder político en el Islam: Actas del Simposio Internacional (Granada, 15-18 Octobre 1991)*, Madrid: Agencia Espanola de Cooperacion Internacional, 1994, pp. 71–116, discussed the 'rulership of the Qadi', the Islamic judge. E. Rosenthal, a traditional scholar of Islamic historiography, observed that 'Islam ... is ideally a theocracy, and the Caliphate is its earthly political form. The *sharīʿa* rules supreme. Once the authority of the *sharīʿa* is impaired, the *mulk* or power-state comes into being. In it, secular laws compete with, and often submerge, the rule of the *sharīʿa*', Rosenthal, *Political thought in medieval Islam*, p. 117.
106. Chapter 1, and Miranda, *Historia política*, p. 56.
107. Ibn Tūmart insisted that the Berbers learn the Qur'ān and sound *ḥadīth* and even memorize parts of his own doctrine. The Almoravid jurists, by contrast, were content to control the ultimate interpretation and implementation of Islam in society.
108. A prime example of this unapologetic preference for *al-furūʿ* was the work of *al-muḥadīth al-fāṣul bayn al-rāwā wa al-wāʿā* by Abū Muḥammad al-Ramahurmuzi who claimed that Mālik ibn Anas himself, the founder of the Maliki school, declared that it was better to study *fiqh* and *raʾy*, law and legal opinion, than the *ḥadīth*, the sayings of the Prophet. He even claimed it was better to study *fiqh* than to know the Qurʾān by heart. See Goldizher, *Le Livre de Ibn Toumert*, p. 105.
109. Ibn Rushd, *Faṣl al Maqāl*, edited and translated in parallel text by Charles Butterworth, Salt Lake City: Brigham Young University Press, 2001, p. 12. It was really a matter of where one put the full stop. 'But no one knows its hidden meanings except God, and those who are firmly grounded in knowledge. Say ...' compared with 'But no one knows its hidden meanings except God. And those who are firmly grounded in knowledge say, "We".' The different punctuation gives two very different meanings.

110. Mālik ibn Anas (715–96), writer of *al-Muwaṭṭa*, 'The approved', was one of the most respected scholars of Islamic law, *fiqh*. He spent most of his life in Medina. Unlike the Almoravid jurists who were beholden to politics, he was not easily swayed and even issued fatwas against the powerful caliph al-Mansur. He was flogged by the orders of al-Mansur but the caliph later recanted.
111. For a discussion of this spread, see Golziher, 'Introduction'. For a critique of the standard view of the rise of jurists in Islamic law, see M. M. Azami, *On Schacht's origins of Muḥammadan jurisprudence*, London: Graham & Trotman, 1986. For the standard, see Joseph Schacht, *An introduction to Islamic law*, Oxford: Oxford University Press, 1982. In his analysis of Almohad jurisprudence Schacht, *An introduction to Islamic law*, pp. 64–5, said: 'Ibn Tūmart, the founder of the religious and political movements of the Almohads in North Africa, held that religious law should be based on the Qur'ān, the *sunna*, and the *ijmā'*. ... At the same time he was strongly opposed to the system of positive law (*al-furū'*) as it had [to] be worked out in the Mālkī school and was exclusively studied under the Almoravids of North Africa in his time. In particular, he repudiated the authority of the mujtahids, the great masters of the established schools, against whom he asserted his own authority as "infallible imām".'
112. A Maliki *mudawana*, a collection of juridical decisions, commentary and formulae, continues to be the standard law book in present-day Morocco, Kingdom of Morocco, *Mudawana al-'Aḥwāl al-Shakhṣiyya*, Rabat, 2000–2001. It is also still a source of great controversy, especially with regard to women's rights.
113. There were also political reasons to keep the jurists under the control of the government. As Melchert, *The formation of the Sunni schools*, pp. 156–64, explains, the ruler selected the jurists of the Maghrib and al-Andalus, unlike in the East where scholars rose in their own ranks through merit. This made the Maliki jurists especially vulnerable to political manipulation.
114. Melchert, *The formation of the Sunni schools*, p. 163, describes these commentaries, including the famous lawbook by Ṣaḥnūn (d. AD 854). 'A traditionalist might deprecate *al-Mudawwanah*, Ṣaḥnūn's magnum opus, as including the merest speculation.' By 'traditionalist' Melchert means those who base their doctrine on *al-uṣūl*, including the sound 'traditions' or the *ḥadīth* of Muḥammad.
115. Quoted in Goldziher, 'Introduction', p. 25. See pp. 25–8 for further description of the Maliki dependence on *al-furū'*. Also, Cornell, 'Understanding is the mother of ability', p. 93.
116. Melchert, *The formation of the Sunni schools*, pp. 160–4.
117. Al-Marrākushī, *Al-Mu'jib*, p. 123.
118. Ibn Tūmart, *Kitāb A'azz mā Yuṭlab*, p. 18.
119. Ibid., p. 11.
120. Ibn Khaldūn disputes this, *The Muqaddimah*, vol. 1, p. 53.
121. Ibid., p. 96.
122. Ibid.

123. 'Divine laws affecting men are all for their good and envisage their interests. That is attested by religious law. Bad laws, on the other hand, all result from stupidity and from Satan.' Ibn Khaldūn, *The Muqaddimah*, p. 112.
124. Lévi-Provençal, *Documents inédits*, p. 7.
125. Ibn Khaldūn, *The Muqaddimah*, p. 96.
126. See description of the political nature of Almoravid jurists who were appointed by rulers in Melchert, *The formation of the Sunni schools*, p. 162. 'The form of chieftaincy in the Andalusian school [later adopted by the Almoravids] was intimately connected with state power, and commonly devolved on several jurisprudents at once. In the classical schools of Iraq, by contrast, chieftaincy was determined by prowess in debate and teaching, never by official appointment.' It was no wonder that Ibn Tūmart was skilled at silencing the Almoravid jurists if they were simply political appointees.
127. Ibn Tūmart, *Le livre de Ibn Toumert*, p. 41. It was printed in untranslated Arabic text by the Algerian government, which was keen to understand the historical background of France's colonial possessions in North Africa. The manuscript published in this edition is from the Bibliothèque nationale de Paris and dates back to AH 579. Luciani described it as being in an 'excellent' state with few lacunas. The fact that the manuscript dates back to AD 1182–83 indicates the possibility that some of the text could have been altered for the purpose of supporting the reign of ʿAbū Yaqʿūb Yūsuf (AD 1163–1184) who was then in power but who was still a strong believer in the Mahdī doctrine despite his famous taste for philosophy (See entry for ʿAbū Yaʾqūb Yūsuf in the *Encyclopaedia of Islam*). It would be impossible to know how exactly the text could have been changed. With a whole section of the Almohad hierarchy, the *ḥāfiẓ*, dedicated to memorizing the original doctrine of Ibn Tūmart while he was still alive, it seems unlikely that too much was significantly altered.
128. The actual title is not The Book of Ibn Tūmart, this is the common use of the name picked up from Luciani's edition, *Le Livre de Ibn Toumert*. The Arabic title is *Aʿazzmā Yuṭlab*.
129. See, for example, Erwin Rosenthal (ed.) *Averroes' commentary on Plato's Republic*, Cambridge: Cambridge University Press, 1956, in which Averroes compares the Almohad system and doctrine to philosophy behind the Republic of Plato. Averroes was widely known and translated in European scholastic circles.
130. Italics added. Ibn Tūmart, *Kitāb Aʿazz mā Yuṭlab*, p. 2.
131. Guidance, *huda* in Arabic, has the same grammatical root as Mahdī.
132. Ibn Tūmart, *Kitāb Aʿazz mā Yuṭlab*, p. 2.
133. Ibid., pp. 18–25.
134. Ibid., p. 48.
135. There is not enough room in this book to go into the vast details about the science of *ḥadīth* and its many forms. John Burton, *An introduction to the hadith*, Edinburgh: Edinburgh University Press, 1994, provides a good summary of the main arguments and issues.

136. Lévi-Provençal, *Documents inédits*, see the letters of Ibn Tūmart at the beginning of the book.
137. Ibn Tūmart, *Kitāb A'azz mā Yuṭlab*, p. 63.
138. Ibid.
139. He even cites Mālik ibn Anas (d. AH 197) in justifying his method of prayer, Ibn Tūmart, *Kitāb A'azz mā Yuṭlab*, p. 68. This was not to say that he supported the school of Malikism practised by the Almoravids. Mālik ibn Anas was simply an authoritative source, a reliable source of *ḥadīth*. The entire Mālik ibn Anas, *Al-Muwaṭṭa*, is available on the University of Southern California website http://www.usc.edu/dept/MSA/fundamentals/hadithsunnah/muwatta/mmtintro.html
140. Ibn Tūmart, *Kitāb A'azz mā Yuṭlab*, p. 71.
141. Ibid., p. 170.
142. For the often desperate conditions of the Jews and Jewish Berber tribes under Almohad rule, see H. Z. Hirschberg, *Toldot ha-Yehudim be-Afrikah ha-Tsefonit* (A history of the Jews in North Africa), Leiden: E. J. Brill, 1974.
143. Ibn Tūmart, *Kitāb A'azz mā Yuṭlab*, p. 171.
144. The details of this debate and its relevance to Ibn Tūmart's doctrine can be found in Goldziher, 'Introduction'. Also, for futher discussion of the dispute between the Ash'ari and the philosophers, see Nagel, *The history of Islamic theology*.
145. Ibn Tūmart, *Kitāb A'azz mā Yuṭlab*, p. 222.
146. Ibid., p. 222.
147. Ibid., p. 221.
148. Ibid., p. 229.
149. I use here Madeline Fletcher's brief translation in *Medieval Iberia* of the *'aqīda* text found in Ibn Tūmart, *Kitāb A'azz mā Yuṭlab*, p. 229. A Latin translation of the *'aqīda* was completed by Mark of Toledo in 1213, see G. Gajda and M. d'Alverny, 'Marc de Tolede, traducteur d'Ibn Tūmart', *al-Andalus*, vol. 16, 1951, pp. 1–56. He also translated hymns of praise and *murshidas*. For *Murshidas* see Ibn Tūmart, *Kitāb A'azz mā Yuṭlab*, pp. 241 and 243.
150. Ibn Tūmart, *Kitāb A'azz mā Yuṭlab*, p. 230.
151. Ibid.
152. Ibid., p. 231.
153. Ibid., p. 232.
154. Ibid., p. 233.
155. Ibid., pp. 233–4.
156. Ibid., p. 235. The *'aqīda* finishes with a discussion of the nature of miracles.
157. See Olivia Remie Constable (ed.) *Medieval Iberia: readings from Christian, Muslim and Jewish sources (Middle Ages series)*, Philadelphia: University of Pennsylvania Press, 1996, pp. 190–7, for Madeleine Fletcher's translation of the *'aqīda*.
158. Constable, *Medieval Iberia*, p. 190.
159. Ibn Tūmart, *Kitāb A'azz mā Yuṭlab*, p. 2.
160. Lévi-Provençal, *Documents inédits*, p. 7.
161. Ibn Tūmart, *Kitāb A'azz mā Yuṭlab*, p. 230.

162. Ibn Khaldūn, *The Muqaddimah*, vol. 1, pp. 89–94.
163. The doctrine of the infallible Imām and Mahdī is discussed on p. 223.
164. Ibn Tūmart, *Kitāb A'azz mā Yuṭlab*, p. 257.
165. Ibid., p. 260.
166. Ibid., p. 261.
167. Ibid., p. 261.
168. *Tajsīm*, or anthropomorphism, is discussed earlier in this chapter.
169. Ibn Tūmart, *Kitāb A'azz mā Yuṭlab*, p. 261. The Magians were the Zoroastrians of Persia.
170. Ibid.
171. Ibid., p. 266.
172. Ibid., p. 269.
173. Ibid., pp. 363–75.
174. Ibid., p. 337.
175. Ibid., p. 381.

Chapter 4. The Rise of the Almohads in Context

1. See A. Bel, 'Contribution à l'étude des dirhems de l'époque almohade', *Hespéris*, vol. 16, nos 1–3, 1933, pp. 1–69. So famous was the Almohad square coin in the lucrative western Mediterranean that several European false square dirham coins have been discovered in Marseille, Pisa and possibly Arles, Bel, 'Contribution à l'étude', p. 6. Several commercial treaties were sealed using Almohad square coins. In his hierarchy of the Almohads, al-Baydhaq mentioned the *sakkātūn*, those who struck the coins. This function was given only to those from the most esteemed 'Almohad tribes', the Tīnmallal, the Hintāta and the Ganfīsa, Lévi-Provençal, *Documents inédits*, p. 71.
2. Examples of millennial 'Mahdī' type movements that do not necessarily lead to the rise of monotheism can be found in Peter Worsley's account of Melanesian Cargo cults. These millennial cults, centred on a messianic figure, and calling for the end of time, arose in largely tribal people in response to political and economic challenges. Peter Worsley, *The trumpet shall sound: a study of cargo cults in Melanesia*, London: Paladin, 1970.
3. Max Weber, *The theory of social and economic organization*, edited and translated by A. M. Henderson and Talcott Parsons, New York: Free Press, 1947, pp. 358–9. Weber continues, saying that these powers, 'are not accessible to the ordinary person, but are regarded as of divine origin or as exemplary and on the basis of them the individual concerned is treated as a leader.'
4. Gellner, *Muslim society*, p. 38.
5. See the critical introduction to the collection of essays in Akbar S. Ahmed and David M. Hart (eds), *Islam in tribal societies: from the Atlas to the Indus*, London: Routledge & Kegan Paul, 1984.
6. Abun-Nasr, *History of the Maghrib*, p. 13.

7. Paul Pascon, *Le Haouz de Marrakech*, 2 vols, Rabat: Éditions marocaines et internationales, 1977.
8. Jacques Berque, 'Qu'est-ce qu'une "tribu" nord-africaine', in *Eventail de l'histoire vivante, hommage à Lucien Febvre offert [à l'occasion de son 75e anniversaire] par l'amitié d'historiens, linguistes, géographes, économistes, sociologues, ethnologues*, vol. 1, Paris: A. Colin, 1953, p. 271.
9. Lancaster, *The Rwala Bedouin today*, p. 24.
10. Ibn Khaldūn, *The Muqaddimah*, vol. 1, p. 267, from his chapter 'How lineages become confused'. Ibn Khaldūn started the chapter by saying, 'It is clear that a person of a certain descent may become attached to people of another descent, either because he feels well-disposed toward them, or because there exists an alliance or client-master relationship, or yet because he had to flee from his own people because of some crime committed. Such a person comes to be known as having the same descent as those (to which he has attached himself).'
11. The Arabic phrase *Bani Adam*, meaning essentially, tribe of Adam and Eve, remains today a common way of referring to people in general. The entire brotherhood of man could be encompassed in the genealogy. Those who were ejected from a tribe or who claimed no tribal identity also merely called themselves Bani Adam, descendants of Adam, and were accorded respect (Lancaster, *Rwala Bedouin*, p. 24). Similar observations were made about the imagined genealogy of early Arabs by Fred Donner, *The early Islamic conquests*, Princeton: Princeton University Press, 1981. Donner saw genealogies as becoming weaker and easier to manipulate further down the gene tree. In fact, it was at the roots of the genealogical tree that the lofty heights of religious feeling and solidarity were born. Islam was a new, imagined, community, the spiritual community of God the Creator: the ultimate founder.
12. Evans-Pritchard, *The Sanusi of Cyrenacia*, quoted in Abun-Nasr, *History of the Maghrib in the Islamic period*, p. 12.
13. Al-Idrīsī provided several apt descriptions of the difficulty of communications and transportation in the high Atlas during this period. See Edrisi (al-Idrīsī), *Description de l'Afrique*. Even today, transport along the narrow roads can be treacherous.
14. Miranda, *Historia política*, p. 100.
15. Hart, 'Berber tribal alliance networks in pre-colonial North Africa'.
16. Le Tourneau, the French historian of the medieval Maghrib, emphasized Ibn Tūmart's reliance on forceful conversion and military action against the tribes. From Le Tourneau's account it seemed that Ibn Tūmart's victory was more the result of military tactics as the deft manipulation of tribal structures and religious ideology (Le Tourneau, *The Almohad movement*, p. 38).
17. Abun-Nasr, author of *A history of the Maghrib in the Islamic period*, suggested that Ibn Tūmart simply gained alliances with old chiefs and leaders, maintaining much of the structure of Almohad tribal society under a thin hierarchical umbrella: 'Ibn Tūmart had great appeal to the Maṣmūda, but he could create unity amongst

them only through adopting the tribal form of organization' (Abun-Nasr, *A history of the Maghrib*, p. 89). See Chapter 3 for further discussions of the specific aspects of Ibn Tūmart's religious ideology. Among the more recent authoritative sources is Maribel Fierro, 'La religión', in R. Menéndez Pidal and J. M. Jover (eds), *Historia de España*, vol. 7, *La España cristiana* de *los siglos VIII al XI*, Madrid: Espasa-Calpe, 1997, pp. 479–86.

18. Peter Worsley, *The trumpet shall sound*, p. 290.
19. Ibid.
20. In Le Tourneau's view, by contrast, it was the personality and infallible power of the Mahdī alone that explained this transformation. 'One may therefore conclude that at the beginning the Almohad movement received its impetus from the spiritual evolution of a single man and his unswerving will to accomplish the mission he had undertaken' (Le Tourneau, *The Almohad movement*, p. 11).
21. Montagne, *Berberes et le Makhzen*.
22. Quoted in Gellner, *Muslim society*, p. 46.
23. Worsley, *The trumpet shall sound*, pp. 1–20.

Conclusions

1. Ibn Tūmart, *Kitāb Aʿazz mā Yuṭlab*, p. 241.
2. Mercedes García-Arenal, *Messianism and puritanical reform*, pp. 193–216.
3. As any traveller in the region can instantly recognize, the Almohad Empire left a common heritage in the lands of North Africa from Morocco to Tunisia, a cultural, architectural and social heritage that is markedly different from the rest of the Near Eastern world. The idea of Maghrebi unity still has a modern appeal even if it seems a virtual political impossibility. The proxy war between Algeria and Morocco in the Western Sahara and various nationalistic border disputes have basically guaranteed the failure of Maghrebi unity at the political level, at least for the forseeable future.
4. Ibn Tūmart, Kitāb Aʿazz mā Yuṭlab, pp. 145–55.

References

'Abd al Azīz bin 'Abd Allāh, *Al-Rihlāt min al-Maghrib*, Rabat, 2001.

Abun-Nasr, Jamil, *A history of the Maghrib in the Islamic period*, Cambridge: Cambridge University Press, 1987.

Adam, André, *La maison et le village dans quelques tribus d'Anti-Atlas*, Paris: Imprimerie Nationale, 1951.

Adang, Camilla, 'Islam as the inborn religion of manhood: the concept of *Fiṭra* in the words of Ibn Ḥazm', *Al-Qanṭara*, vol. 21, no. 2, 2000, pp. 391–411.

Ahmed, Akbar S. and David M. Hart (eds), *Islam in tribal societies: from the Atlas to the Indus*, London: Routledge & Kegan Paul, 1984.

Al-'Arabī, Abū Bakr Muḥammad, *Shawāhid al-Jilla*, in Muḥammad Ya'la (translator and editor) *Tres textos arabes sobre beréberes en el occidente islámico*, Madrid: Consejo Superior de Investigaciones Científicas, 1996.

Al-Bakrī (Abū al-Bakrī), *Description de l'Afrique septentrionale*, translated by G. de Slane, Paris: G.-P. Maisonneuve et Larose, 1965.

Al-Bukhārī, *Ṣaḥīḥ*, University of Southern California online searchable *ḥadīth* project, translated by Muhsin Khan, http://cwis.usc.edu/dept/MSA/fundamentals/hadithsunnah/bukhari/.

Al-Fārābi, Abū Nasr, *Falsafat Aflāṭūn*, edited by F. Rosenthal and R. Walzer, London: Plato Arabus, 1943.

Alfonso, Isabel, Hugh Kennedy and Julio Escalona (eds) *Building legitimacy: political discourses and forms of legitimacy in medieval societies*, Leiden: E. J. Brill, 2004.

Al-Ghazālī, Abū Ḥamid Muḥammad, *Munqidh min al-Dalal*, Damascus: Fons Vitae, 1956

Al-Ghazālī, Abū Ḥamid Muḥammad, *The incoherence of the philosophers: English translation of Imām Ghazali's Tahafut al-Falasifa*, translated with parallel text by M. Marmura, Salt Lake City: Brigham Young University Press, 2000.

Al-Ghazālī, Abū Ḥamid Muḥammad, *On listening to music*, Islamabad, 2002.

Al-Ḥusayn, Bū Laqṭīb, *Jawāīḥ wa awbīat Maghrib 'Ahd al-Muwaḥḥidīn*, Rabat, 2002.

al-Marrākushī, 'Abd al-Waḥid, *Al-Mu'jib fi Talkhis Akhbār al-Maghrib*, Rabat, 1949.

al-Marrākushī, 'Abd al-Waḥid, *Al-Mu'jib fi Talkhis Akhbār al-Maghrib*, Arabic version edited by Reinhart Dozy, Amsterdam: Oriental Press, 1968.

Al-Mas'ūdī, 'Alī bin al Ḥusayn (ed.) *Murūj al-Dhahab* (Meadows of Gold), translated into French by C. Barbier de Meynard and A. Pavet de Courteille, 9 vols, Paris 1861–77.

Al-Mawardī, *The ordinances of government*, a translation of *al-Ahkam al-sultaniyya w'al-wilayat al-diniyya* by Wafaa H. Wahba, Reading: Center for Muslim Contribution to Civilization, 1996.

Al-Nuwaīri, 'Conquête de l'Afrique septentrionale', in Ibn Khaldūn, *Histoire des Berbères*, translated by De Slane, Algiers, vol. 4, 2001.

Al-Saqatī, *Kitāb fī ādāb al-ḥisba*, edited by E. Lévi-Provençal and G. S. Colin, *Journal Asiatique*, 1931.

Al-Ṭabarī, Abū Jafr Muḥammad ibn Jarir, *Tārīkh al-Rasūl wa al-Mulūk*, vols 1–10, edited by M. J. de Goeje et al., Leiden: E. J. Brill, 1879–1901.

Al-Ṭabarī, Abū Jafr Muḥammad ibn Jarir, *The history of al-Ṭabarī: English selections*, vol. 29, translated by Hugh Kennedy, Albany: State University of New York Press, 1990.

Al-Wahhab, Muḥammad Abd, *The Book of Tawheed*, translated by Samah Strauch, Ryadh: International Islamic Publishing House, 1998.

Al-Zarkashī, Abī 'Abd Allah Muḥammad bin Ibraḥīm al-Ma'rūf, *Tārīkh al-Dawlatayn*, Tunis, 1966.

Amri, Laroussi, *La tribu au Maghrib medieval: pour une sociologie des Ruptures*, Tunis: Publications de l'Université de Tunis, 1997.

Anderson, Benedict, *Imagined communities*, London: Verso, 2000.

Anon, *Le Maghrib aux XIIème et XIIIème siècles: les siècles de la foi*, Casablanca, 1993.

Anonymous Chronicler, *Al-Ḥulal al-Mūshiyyah*, Cronique anonyme des dynasties Almoravide et Almohade, texte Arabe, edited by I. S. Allouche, Rabat, 1936

Anonymous Chronicler, *Al-Ḥulal al-Mūshiyyah*, edited by Huici Miranda, Tetuan, 1951.

Arjomand, S. A., 'Islamic apocalypticism in the classic period', in Bernard McGinn (ed.) *The Encyclopedia of apocalypticism*, vol. 2, New York: Continuum Press, 1998.

Arjomand, S. A., 'Messianism, millennialism, and revolution in early Islamic history', in A. Amanat and M. Bernhardsson (eds), *Imagining the end*, London: I.B.Tauris, 2002, pp. 106–25.

Azami, M. M., *On Schacht's origins of Muḥammadan jurisprudence*, London: Graham & Trotman, 1986.

Baneth, D. Z. H., 'What did Muḥammad mean when he called his religion 'Islam?', *Israel Oriental Studies*, vol. 1, 1971, pp. 183–90.

Basset, Henri and Henri Terrasse, 'Sanctuaires et forteresses almohades', *Hespéris*, vol. 7, 1927, pp. 157–71.

Bel, A., 'Contribution à l'étude des dirhems de l'époque almohade', *Hespéris*, vol. 16, nos 1–3, 1933, pp. 1–69.

Benblal, Rachid, *Histoire des Idrīssides, 172–337 (788–948)*, Oran: Dar el Gharb, 2002.
Benjelloun, Mohamed Othman, *Projet national et identité au Maroc: essai d'anthropologie politique*, Paris: l'Harmattan, 2002.
Berkey, Jonathan, *The formation of Islam: religion and society in the Near East, 600–1800*, Cambridge: Cambridge University Press, 2003.
Berque, Jacques, 'Qu'est-ce qu'une "tribu" nord-africaine', in *Eventail de l'histoire vivante, hommage à Lucien Febvre offert [à l'occasion de son 75e anniversaire] par l'amitié d'historiens, linguistes, géographes, économistes, sociologues, ethnologues*, vol. 1, Paris: A. Colin, 1953.
Berque, Jacques, *Structures sociales du Haut-Atlas*, Paris, 1955.
Blichfeldt, Jan-Olaf, *Early Mahdism*, Leiden: E. J. Brill, 1985.
Bloch, Marc, *The historian's craft*, translated by Peter Putnam, Manchester: Manchester University Press, 1976.
Bourouiba, Rachid, 'A propos de la date de naissance d'Ibn Tūmart', *Revue d'Histoire et de Civilisation du Maghreb*, January 1966, pp. 19–25.
Bourouiba, Rachid, 'Chronologie d'Ibn Tūmart', *Revue d'Histoire et de Civilisation du Maghreb*, July 1967, pp. 39–47.
Bouroubia, Rachid, *Ibn Tūmart*, Algiers, 1974.
Bousquet, Georges Henri, *Les Berbères: histoire et institutions*, Paris: Presses Universitaires de France, 1957.
Brett, Michael, 'The Fatimid revolution and its aftermath in North Africa', in J. D. Fage (ed.) *Cambridge History of Africa*, Cambridge: Cambridge University Press, vol. 2, 1978, Chapter 8.
Brett, Michael, *Ibn Khaldūn and the medieval Maghrib*, Aldershot: Ashgate, 1999.
Brett, Michael, 'The way of the nomad', in Michael Brett, *Ibn Khaldūn and the medieval Maghrib*, Aldershot: Ashgate, 1999, pp. 251–69.
Brett, Michael, 'The lamp of the Almohads: illumination as a political idea in twelfth-century Morocco', in Michael Brett, *Ibn Khaldūn and the medieval Maghrib*, Aldershot: Ashgate, 1999.
Brett, Michael, 'The Mīm and the ʿAyn, and the making of Ismaʿilism', in Michael Brett, *Ibn Khaldūn and the medieval Maghrib*, Aldershot: Ashgate, 1999.
Brett, Michael, 'The realm of the imām', in Michael Brett, *Ibn Khaldūn and the medieval Maghrib*, Aldershot: Ashgate, 1999.
Brett, Michael, *The rise of the Fatimids*, Leiden: E. J. Brill, 2001.
Brett, Michael, 'Le Mahdī dans le Maghrib medieval: l'elaboration de la légitimité Almohade', *Revue des Mondes Musulmanes et de la Mediterranee*, nos 91–4, 1999, pp. 93–106.
Brett, Michael and Elizabeth Fentress, *The Berbers*, Oxford: Blackwell, 1996.
Brunschvig, Robert, 'Sur la doctrine du Mahdī Ibn Tūmart', *Arabica*, vol. 2, 1955, pp. 137–49.

Byrne, Richard and Andrew Whiten, *Machiavellian intelligence: social expertise and the evolution of intellect in monkeys, apes and humans*, Oxford: Oxford University Press, 1988.

Burton, John, *An introduction to the hadith*, Edinburgh: Edinburgh University Press, 1994.

Casajus, Dominique, *Gens de parole: langage, poesie et politique en pays Touareg*, Paris: La Découverte, 2000.

Clarke, Bryan, *Berber village: the story of the Oxford University expedition to the High Atlas Mountains of Morocco*, London: Longmans, 1959.

Claudot-Hawad, Hélène (editor and translator), *Notre horizon de gamelles pour une gamelle d'horizons*, Paris, 2001.

Constable, Olivia Remie (ed.) *Medieval Iberia: readings from Christian, Muslim and Jewish sources (Middle Ages series)*, Philadelphia: University of Pennsylvania Press, 1996.

Cook, Michael, *Commanding right and forbidding wrong in Islamic thought*, Cambridge: Cambridge University Press, 2000.

Cornell, Vincent J., 'Understanding is the mother of ability: responsibility and action in the doctrine of Ibn Tūmart', *Studia Islamica*, no. 66, 1987, pp. 71–103.

Cornell, Vincent J., *Realm of the saint: power and authority in Moroccan Sufism*, Austin: University of Texas Press, 1998.

Courtney-Clarke, Margaret, *Imazighen: the vanishing traditions of Berber women*, New York: C. Potter, 1996.

Cressier, Patrice, Maribel Fierro and Luis Molina (eds) *Los Almohades: problemas y perspectivas*, 2 vols, Madrid: Consejo Superior de Investigaciones Científicas, 2006.

Crone, Patricia, *Meccan trade and the rise of Islam*, Princeton: Princeton University Press, 1987.

Crone, Patricia, *Medieval Islamic political thought*, Edinburgh: Edinburgh University Press, 2005.

Crone, Patricia and Michael Cook, *Hagarism: the making of the Islamic world*, Cambridge: Cambridge University Press, 1977.

Derenbourg, Hartwig, *Les manuscrits arabes de l'Escorial*, Paris, 1884.

Despois, Jean, *L'Afrique du Nord*, Paris: PUF, 1958.

Devisse, J., 'Approximatives, quantitatives, qualitatives: valeurs variables de l'étude des traversées sahariennes', in M. Garcia-Arenal and M. J. Viguera (eds) *Relaciones de la Península Ibérica con el Magreb, siglos XIII–XVI*, Actas del Coloquio, Madrid, 1987.

Dodd, Hannah, 'Beyond Al-Basra: settlement systems of medieval northern Morocco in archaeological and historical perspective', in Nancy L. Benco (ed.) *Anatomy of a medieval Islamic town: Al-Basra, Morocco*, Oxford, 2004.

Donner, Fred, *The early Islamic conquests*, Princeton: Princeton University Press, 1981.

Doutté, E., *Magie et religion dans l'Afrique du Nord*, Algiers: Jourdain, 1909.

Dozy, R. P. A. (ed.) *The history of the Almohades*, 2nd edn, Leiden: E. J. Brill, 1881.

Dresch, Paul, *Tribes, government and history in Yemen*, Oxford: Oxford University Press, 1989.

Dunn, Ross, *The Adventures of Ibn Baṭṭūṭa, a Muslim traveler of the fourteenth century*, Los Angeles: University of California Press, 2005.

Edrisi (al-Idrīsī), *Description de l'Afrique*, Arabic text, edited by Reinhart Dozy and de Goeje, Amsterdam: Oriental Press, 1969.

Eickelman, Dale F., *The Middle East and Central Asia: an anthropological approach*, New Jersey: Prentice Hall, 2001.

Eickelman, Dale F. and James Piscatori (eds) *Muslim travellers: pilgrimage, migration, and the religious imagination*, London: Routledge, 1990.

Evans-Pritchard, E. E., *The Sanusi of Cyrenaica*, Oxford: Clarendon Press, 1949.

Evans-Pritchard, E. E., *Kinship and marriage among the Nuer*, Oxford: Clarendon Press, 1951.

Febvre, Lucien, *La Terre et l'évolution humaine*, Paris: La Renaissance du Livre, 1922.

Ferhat, Halima, *Le Maghrib aux XIIème et XIIIème siècles: les siècles de la foi*, Casablanca, 1993.

Fierro, Maribel, 'Introduction', Abī Bakr Ṭurṭushī, *Ḥawādith wa'l bida'*, translated by Maribel Fierro, Madrid 1993.

Fierro, Maribel, 'Mahdīsme et eschatologie dans al-Andalus', in Abdelmajid Kaddouri (ed.), *Mahdisme: crise et changement dans l'histoire du Maroc*, Rabat, 1994, pp. 47–69.

Fierro, Maribel, 'The Qadi as ruler', *Saber religioso y poder político en el Islam: Actas del Simposio Internacional (Granada, 15-18 Octobre 1991)*, Madrid: Agencia Espanola de Cooperacion Internacional, 1994, pp. 71–116.

Fierro, Maribel, 'La Religión', in Ramón Menéndez Pidal, *Historia de España*, vol. 8, no. 2, Madrid, 1996, pp. 435–546.

Fierro, Maribel, 'La religión', in R. Menéndez Pidal and J. M. Jover (eds), *Historia de España*, vol. 7, *La España cristiana* de *los siglos VIII al XI*, Madrid: Espasa-Calpe, 1997, pp. 479–86.

Fierro, Maribel, 'Le Mahdī Ibn Tūmart', *Revue des Mondes Musulmanes et de la Mediterranee*, nos 91–4, 1999.

Fierro Maribel, 'The legal policies of the Almohads and Ibn Rushd's Bidāyat al-Mujtahid', *Journal of Islamic Studies*, Oxford, vol. 10, no. 3, 1999, pp. 226–48.

Fierro, Maribel, 'Le Mahdī Ibn Tūmart et al-Andalus: l'élaboration de la légitimité almohade', in M. García-Arenal (ed.) *Millénarisme et mahdisme, REMM*, vols 91–4, 2000, pp. 107–24.

Fierro, Maribel, 'Revolución y tradición: algunos aspectos del mundo del saber en época almohade', in María Luisa Ávila and Maribel Fierro (eds), *Estudios Onomástico-biográficos de al-Andalus*, vol. 10, Madrid-Granada, 2000, pp. 131–65.

Fierro, Maribel, 'The Ghurabāʾ in al-Andalus', *Arabica*, vol. 47, 2000.

Fierro, Maribel, 'Las genealogías de ʿAbd al-Muʾmin, primer califa Almohade', *Al-Qanṭara*, vol. 24, 2003, pp. 77–107.

Fletcher, Madeleine, 'The Almohad Tawḥīd: theology which relies on logic', *Numen*, vol. 38, 1991, pp. 110–27.

Fletcher, Madeleine, 'Al-Andalus and North Africa in the Almohad ideology', in Salma Jayyusi (ed.) *The legacy of Muslim Spain*, Leiden: E. J. Brill, 1992, pp. 235–58.

Fletcher, Madeleine, 'Ibn Tūmart's teachers: the relationship with al-Ghazālī', *Al-Qanṭara*, vol. 18, 1997, pp. 305–30.

Foucault, Michel, *The archaeology of knowledge*, New York: Pantheon, 1982.

Fricaud, Emile, 'Les ṭālaba dans la société almohade (le temps d'Averroès)', *al-Qanṭara*, vol. 18, no. 2, 1997, pp. 331–87.

Fricaud, Emile, 'La notice biographique d'Abū al-Ḥasan ʿAlī Ibn al-Qaṭṭān', in María Luisa Ávila and Maribel Fierro (eds) *Biografías Almohades*, Madrid: CSIC, 2000, vol. 2, pp. 223–83.

Fromherz, Allen, 'The Almohad Mecca: locating Igli and the cave of Ibn Tūmart', *al-Qanṭara*, vol. 26, no. 1, 2005, pp. 175–90.

Fromherz, Allen, 'North Africa and the twelfth-century Renaissance: Christian Europe and the Almohad Islamic Empire', *Islam and Christian-Muslim Relations*, vol. 20, no. 1, January 2009, 43–59.

Furnish, Timothy, 'Eschatology as politics, eschatology as theory: modern Sunni Arab Mahdism in historical perspective', unpublished Ph.D. thesis, Ohio State University, 2001.

Gabrieli, Francesco, 'Le origini del movimento almohade in una fonte storica d'Oriente', *Studia Arabica*, vol. 3, no. 1, January 1956, pp. 1–7.

Gajda, G. and M. d'Alverny, 'Marc de Tolede, traducteur d'Ibn Tūmart', *al-Andalus*, vol. 16, 1951, pp. 1–56.

García-Arenal, Mercedes, 'La pratica del percepto de al-amr bi-l-maʿruf wa-l-nahy ʿan al-munkar en la hagiografia magrebi', *al-Qanṭara*, vol. 13, no. 1, 1992, pp. 147–70.

Garcia-Arenal, Mercedes, 'Pouvoir sacré et mahdīsme: Aḥmad al-Manṣūr al Dhahalī', *al-Qanṭara*, vol. 17, no. 2, 1996, pp. 453–73.

Garcia-Arenal, Mercedes, 'Imām et Mahdī: Ibn Abī Mahalli', *Revue des Mondes Musulmanes et de la Mediterranee*, nos 91–4, 1999, pp. 157–80.

García-Arenal, Mercedes, *Messianism and puritanical reform: Mahdis of the Muslim west*, translated by Martin Beagles, Leiden: E. J. Brill, 2006.

Geary, Patrick, *The myth of nations: the medieval origins of Europe*, Princeton: Princeton University Press, 2003.

Gellner, Ernest, *Saints of the Atlas*, Chicago: University of Chicago Press, 1969.

Gellner, Ernest, *Muslim society*, Cambridge: Cambridge University Press, 1981.

Gellner, Ernest, *Conditions of liberty, civil society and its rivals*, London: Hamish Hamilton, 1994.

Goldziher, Ignaz (ed.) 'Introduction', in Ibn Tūmart, *Kitāb A'azz mā Yuṭlab* (*Le Livre de Ibn Toumert*) edited by Luciani, Algiers: P. Fontana, 1903.

Goldziher, I. (ed.) *Le livre de Mohammad Ibn Toumert*, Algiers: P. Fontana, 1903.

Goldziher, Ignaz, *Muslim Studies (Muhammedanische Studien)*, vol. 1, *The classical age of Islam*, edited by S. M. Stern, translated from the German by C. R. Barber and S. M. Stern, London: Allen & Unwin, 1967.

Guiga, A., *La Geste hilalienne*, translated by Tahar Guiga, Tunis: La Maison *Tunisienne* d'Edition, 1968.

Gurvitch, Georges, *La vocation actuelle de la sociologie*, Paris: Presses universitaires de France, 1963.

Halm, Heinz, *Shiism*, Edinburgh: Edinburgh University Press, 1991.

Halm, Heinz, *The empire of the Mahdi: the rise of the Fatimids*, translated by M. Bonner, Leiden: E. J. Brill, 1996.

Hama, Boubou, *Recherches sur l'histoire des Touareg sahariens et soudanais*, Paris: Présence Africaine, 1967.

Hamadi, Ben A., 'Y a-t-il une influence kharigite dans la pensée d'Ibn Tūmart, *Mélanges offerts a Mohamed Talbi*, Tunis: Université de Tunis, 1993.

Hamadi, Amor Ben, 'Rutas transaharianas en el Maghrib oriental', in Anon, *Mauritania y Espana: una historia común*, Seville, 2003, pp. 37–75.

Hart, David M., 'Maṣmūda, Sanhạja, Zanāta: a three ring circus', *Revue d'Histoire Maghribine*, vol. 9, nos 27–8, 1982, pp. 361–5.

Hart, David M., *The Aīt 'Atta of southern Morocco: daily life and recent history*, Cambridge: Middle East & North African Studies Press, 1984.

Hart, David M., 'Rejoiner to Henry Munson Jr, "On the irrelevance of the segmentary lineage model in the Moroccan Rif"', *American Anthropologist*, vol. 91, no. 3, 1989, pp. 765–9.

Hart, David M., 'Four centuries of history on the hoof: the northwest passage of Berber sheep transferments across the Moroccan Atlas, 1550–1912', *Morocco: Journal of the Society for Moroccan Studies*, vol. 3, 1993, pp. 21–55.

Hart, David, 'Berber tribal alliance networks in pre-colonial North Africa: the Algerian saff, the Moroccan liff and the chessboard model of Montagne', *Journal of North African Studies*, vol. 1, no. 2, 1996, pp. 192–205.

Hart, David M., 'The Moroccan liff and the chessboard model of Robert Montagne', *Journal of North African Studies*, vol. 1, no. 2, 1996, pp. 192–205.

Hart, David M., *Estructuras tribales precoloniales en Marruecos berber, 1860–1933*, Granada, 1997.

Hart, David M., *Tribe and society in rural Morocco*, London: Frank Cass, 2000.

Hart, David M., 'Persistence and changes in names on the North African landscape: Berber tribes in Ibn Khaldūn's genealogies and as they appear today', *The Journal of North African Studies*, vol. 5, no. 1, Spring 2000, pp. 121–46.

Hirschberg, H. Z., *Toldot ha-Yehudim be-Afrikah ha-Tsefonit* (A history of the Jews in North Africa), Leiden: E. J. Brill, 1974.

Holt, Peter M., *The age of the Crusades: the Near East from the eleventh century to 1517*, London: Longman, 1986.

Hopkins, J. F. D. *Medieval Muslim government in Barbary until the sixth century of the hijra*, London: Luzac, 1958.

Hoyland, Robert, *Arabia and the Arabs: from the Bronze Age to the coming of Islam*, London: Routledge, 2001.

Ibn 'Abdūn, *Le traite d'Ibn 'Abdun in Séville musulmane au debut du XIIème siecle*, translated by E. Lévi-Provençal, Paris, 2001.

Ibn 'Abī Zar', *Rawḍ al-Qirṭās*, edited and translated into Spanish by Huici Miranda, Valencia, 1964.

Ibn al-Athīr, Abū al-Ḥasan Muḥammad bin Alī, *Al-Kāmil fī al-Tārīkh*, edited by C. J. Tornberg, Uppsala, 1843–46.

Ibn al-Qaṭṭān, Abū Muhammad Ḥasan, *Naẓm al-Jumān*, edited by Muḥammad 'Alī Makkī, Rabat, 1966.

Ibn Baṭṭūṭa, *The travels of Ibn Baṭṭūṭa*, translated by H. A. R. Gibb, London: Routledge, 1929.

Ibn 'Isḥāq, *Sīrat al-Nabawiyya*, compiled and edited by Ibn Hishām, 2 vols, Cairo, 1900.

Ibn Jubayr, Abū al-Ḥusayn Muḥammad bin Ahmad, *The travels of Ibn Jubayr*, translated by R. J. C. Broadhurst, London: Jonathan Cape, 1952.

Ibn Khaldūn, *Ta'rīf ibn Khaldūn Rihlatahu Gharban wa Sharqan*, Cairo, 1901.

Ibn Khaldūn, *Histoire des Berbères*, translated by de Slane, Paris, 1927, 2 vols.

Ibn Khaldūn, *The Muqaddimah*, translated by Franz Rosenthal, 3 vols, Princeton, 1958 and unabridged version, Princeton: Bollinger Series, 1969.

Ibn Khaldūn, 'Abd al-Rahman, *Muqaddimah ibn Khaldūn*, Sous, Tunisia, 1991 (Arabic version). My primary source for pagination is the translation by Franz Rosenthal (ed.) Princeton: N. J. Dawood, 1989.

Ibn Khaldūn, *Histoire des Berbères* (*Kitāb al-'Ibār*), 3 volumes, Algiers, 2001.

Ibn Khaldūn, *Le Livre des exemples*, translated by A. al-Chedaddi, Paris: Gallimard, 2002.

Ibn Khaldūn, 'Autobiographie', *Le Livre des exemples*, translated by A. al-Chedaddi, Paris: Gallimard, 2002.

Ibn Khallikān, *Wafayāt al-a'ayān*, 4 vols, translated by Mac Gukin de Slane, Paris: Publications de l'Ecole des Langues Orientales, 1842–71.

Ibn Rushd, *Faṣl al Maqāl*, edited and translated in parallel text by Charles Butterworth, Salt Lake City: Brigham Young University Press, 2001.

Ibn Taymiyya, *al-'Aqidah al wasitiyya: the principles of Islamic faith*, Chicago: University of Chicago Press, 1992.

Ibn Ṭufayl, Abū Bakr, *The history of Hayy ibn Yaqẓān*, translated by Simon Ockley, London: Darf Publishers, 1986.

Ibn Tūmart, *Kitāb A'azz mā Yuṭlab*, (*Le livre de Ibn Toumert*), edited by I. Goldziher, Algiers, 1903.

Kably, Mohammed, *Société, pouvoir et religion au Maroc a la fin du Moyen Age*, Paris: Maisonneuve et Larose, 1986.

Kanjī, Muḥammad ibn Yūsuf, *al-Bayān fī akhbār ṣaḥib al zamān*, Beirut: Riyad al-Rayyis lil-Kutub wa-al-Nashr, 2000.

Kennedy, Hugh, *Muslim Spain and Portugal: a political history of al-Andalus*, London: Longman, 1996.

Kennedy, Hugh, *The Prophet and the age of the caliphates: the Islamic Near East from the sixth to the eleventh century*, 2nd edition, London: Longman, 2004.

Kennedy, Hugh, *The court of the caliphs*, London: Weidenfeld & Nicolson, 2004.

Kingdom of Morocco, *Mudawana al-'Aḥwāl al-Shakhṣiyya*, Rabat, 2000–2001.

Lagardère, Vincent, *Les Almoravides jusqu'au regne de Yûsuf b. Tâsfîn (1039–1106)*, Paris, 1989.

Lancaster, William, *The Rwala Bedouin today*, Cambridge: Cambridge University Press, 1981.

Laroui, Abdallah, *L'Histoire du Maghreb*, Casablanca: Wizarat al-thaqafah wa-al-ittisal, 2001.

Leo Africanus, Johannes, *Description de l'Afrique*, translated by Charles Schefer, 1896, vol. 1.

Le Tourneau, Roger, 'Du mouvement almohade à la dynastie mu'minide: la révolte des frères d'Ibn Tūmart de 1153–1156', *Mélanges d'histoire et d'archéologie de l'Occident musulman*, vol. 2, 1957, pp. 111–16.

Le Tourneau, Roger, *The Almohad movement in North Africa in the twelfth and thirteenth centuries*, translated from French, Princeton: Princeton University Press, 1969.

Lévi-Provençal, E., 'Pratiques agricoles et fêtes saisonnières des tribus Djebalah de la vallée moyenne de l'Ouargha', *Bulletin Archéologique*, 1918, pp. 194–200.

Lévi-Provençal, E. (ed.) *Documents inédits d'histoire almohade*, Paris, 1928. (Includes the *Kitāb al Ansāb*, letters by Ibn Tūmart and 'Abd al Mu'min and Ibn Tūmart's biography by al-Baydhaq).

Lévi-Provençal, E., 'Le titre souverain des almoravies et sa légitimation par le califat 'Abbāside', *Arabica*, vol. 2, 1955, pp. 265–80.

Lindholm, C., 'Quandries of command in egalitarian societies: examples from Swat and Morocco', in J. Cole (ed.) *Comparing Muslim societies: knowledge and the state in a world civilization*, Ann Arbor: University of Michigan Press, 1992, pp. 63–94.

Lings, Martin, *Muḥammad: his life based on the earliest sources*, Rochester, Vermont: Inner Traditions, 2006

Madelung, Wilferd, 'Some notes on non-Ismāʿīlī Shiism in the Maghrib', *Studia Islamica*, no. 44, 1976, pp. 87–97.

Mālik ibn Anas, *Al-Muwaṭṭa*, vols 1 and 2, Cairo, 1951. Also available in the MSA–University of Southern California database: http://cwis.usc.edu/dept/MSA/reference/searchhadith.html

Marçais, Georges, *La Berbérie musulmane et l'Orient au moyen âge*, Paris: Aubier, 1946.

Marcy, Georges, 'Les phrases berbères des documents almohades', *Hespéris*, vol. 14, no. 1, 1932, pp. 61–78.

Melchert, Christopher, *The formation of the Sunni schools of law 9–10th centuries* CE, Leiden: E. J. Brill, 1997.

Merad, ʿAlī, ʿAbd al-Muʾmin à la conquête de l'Afrique du Nord', *Annales de l'Institut d'Etudes Orientales de la Faculté des Lettres d'Alger*, vol. 15, 1957, pp. 122–31.

Michel, Nicholas, 'The individual and the collectivity in the agricultural economy of pre-colonial Morocco', in Nelly Hanna (ed.) *Money, land and trade: an economic history of the Muslim Mediterranean*, London: I.B.Tauris, 2002.

Miranda, Huici, *Historia política del imperio Almohade*, 2 vols, Tetuan, 1957.

Miranda, Huici, 'La leyenda y la historia en los origenes del Imperio Almohade, *al-Andalus*, vol. 14, no. 2, 1949, pp. 339–76.

Mitha, Farouk, *Al-Gazali and the Ismailis: a debate on reason and authority in medieval Islam*, London, 2002

Montagne, Robert, *Les Berbères et le Mahkzen dans le sud du Maroc*, Paris: Felix Alcan, 1930.

Montagne, Robert, *The Berbers: their social and political organisation*, translated by David Seddon, London: Frank Cass, 1973.

Moraes, Farias, 'The Almoravids: some questions concerning the character of the movement during the period of closest contact with the Western Sudan', *Bulletin de l'Institut Fondamental d'Afrique*, vol. 29, 1967, pp. 794–898.

Mottahedeh, Roy, *Loyalty and leadership in an early Islamic society*, London: I.B.Tauris and Islamic Publications, Ltd, 2001.

Muslim, Abū Ḥusayn, 'Ṣaḥīḥ', *The Book of Destiny*. See the searchable text translated by A. Siddiqui, http://www.usc.edu/dept/MSA/fundamentals/hadithsunnah/muslim

Nagel, Tilman, 'Le mahdīsme d'Ibn Tūmart et d'Ibn Qasi: une analyse phenomenologique', *Revue des Mondes Musulmanes et de la Mediterranee*, nos 91–4, 1999, pp. 125–36.

Nagel, Tilman, *The history of Islamic theology: from Muḥammad to the present*, translated by Thomas Thornton, Princeton: Markus Wiener, 2000.

Nicolaisen, Johannes, *Ecology and culture of the pastoral Tuareg*, Copenhagen: National Museum of Copenhagen, 1963.

Norris, H. T., *The Berbers in Arabic literature*, London: Longman, 1982.

Norris, H. T., *The Arab conquest of the Western Sahara*, London: Longman, 1986.

Oumlil, 'Ali, *L'histoire et son discours: essai sur la methodologie d'Ibn Khaldoun*, Rabat, 1982.

Pascon, Paul, *Le Haouz de Marrakech*, 2 vols, Rabat: Éditions marocaines et internationales, 1977.

Powers, David, *Law, society, and culture in the Maghrib, 1300–1500*, Cambridge: Cambridge University Press, 2002.

Rasmussen, Susan, 'Within the tent and at the crossroads: travel and gender identity among the Tuareg of Niger', *Ethos*, vol. 26, no. 2, 1998, pp. 153–82.

Rasmussen, Susan and J. H. Keenan, 'Lack of prayer: ritual restrictions, social experience and the anthropology of migration among the Tuareg', *American Ethnologist*, vol. 18, no. 4, November 1991, pp. 751–69

Rosenthal, Erwin, *Averroes' commentary on Plato's Republic*, Cambridge: Cambridge University Press, 1956.

Rosenthal, Erwin, *Political thought in medieval Islam*, Cambridge: Cambridge University Press, 1958.

Sachedina, Abdulaziz, *Islamic messianism: the idea of the Mahdī in Twelver Shī'ism*, Albany: State University of New York Press, 1981.

Ṣadr, Muḥammad Bāqir, *The awaited saviour*, translated by M. Ansari, Albany: State University of New York Press, 1982.

Schacht, Joseph, *An introduction to Islamic law*, Oxford: Oxford University Press, 1982.

Shatzmiller, Maya, *L'historiographie mérinide: Ibn Khaldūn et ses contemporains*, Leiden: E. J. Brill, 1982.

Shatzmiller, Maya, *The Berbers and the Islamic state: the Marinid experience in pre-protectorate Morocco*, Princeton: Markus Wiener Publishing, 1999.

Smith, Margaret, *Rābi'a the mystic and her fellow saints in Islam*, Cambridge: Cambridge University Press, 1984.

Stroomer, Harry, *Textes berbères des Guedmioua et Goundafa: basés sur les documents de F. Corjon, J.-M. Franchi et J. Eugène*, Aix-en-Provence: Édisud, 2001.

Taha, A. D., *The Muslim conquest and settlement of North Africa and Spain*, London: Routledge, 1989.

Ṭāhā, Jamāl, *al-Ḥayāt al-ijtimāīyah bi al-Maghrib al Aqṣa fī al-Aṣr al-Islāmī: ʿaṣray al Murābṭīn wa al-Muwaḥḥidīn*, Alexandria, 2004.

Umar Afā Tansīq, *Al-Ṣaḥrā wa-Sūs min Khilāla al-Wathāiq wa al Makhṭūṭāt*, Muḥammad V University, Rabat, 2001.

Urvoy, Dominique, 'La pensée d'Ibn Tumart', *Bulletin d'Etudes Orientales*, vol. 27, 1974, pp. 19–44.

Van Staëvel, Jean Pierre and Abdallah Fili, 'À propos de la localisation d'Īgīlīz-des-harga', *Al-Qanṭara*, vol. 27, no. 1, 2006, pp. 153–94.

Viguera Molíns, María Jesús, 'Las cartas de al-Ghazālī y al-Tarṭushi al soberano almorávide Yūsuf b. Tāshufīn', *Al-Andalus*, vol. 42, 1977, pp. 341–74.

Viguera Molíns, María Jesús, 'Historia política', in R. Menéndez Pidal, *Historia de España*, Madrid: Edicion Espasa-Calpe, 1997, vol. 7.

Vilá, Jacinto Bosch, *Los Almorávides*, Granada, 1990.

Wasserstein, David J., 'A Jonah theme in the biography of Ibn Tūmart', in Farhad Daftary and Josef Meri (eds) *Culture and memory in medieval Islam: essays in honour of Wilfred Madelung*, London: I.B.Tauris, 2003, pp. 232–49.

Watt, William Montgomery, *The faith and practice of al-Ghazālī*, London: Allen & Unwin, 1953.

Waugh, Earle H., *Memory, music and religion: Morocco's mystical chanters*, Raleigh, NC: SciTech Pub., 2005.

Weber, Max, *The story of social and economic organization*, edited and translated by A. M. Henderson and Talcott Parsons, New York: Free Press, 1947.

Wheatley, Paul, *The places where men pray together*, Chicago: University of Chicago Press, 2000

Worsley, Peter, *The trumpet shall sound: a study of cargo cults in Melanesia*, London: Paladin, 1970.

Zniber, Mohamed, 'L'Itineraire psycho-intellectual d'Ibn Toumert', in Abdelmajid Kaddouri (ed.), *Mahdisme: crise et changement dans l'histoire du Maroc*, Rabat, 1994, pp. 15–29.

Index